Evaluating Multiple Narratives

Junko Habu • Clare Fawcett • John M. Matsunaga
Editors

Evaluating Multiple Narratives

Beyond Nationalist, Colonialist, Imperialist Archaeologies

 Springer

Junko Habu
Department of Anthropology
University of California at Berkeley
Berkeley, CA

Clare Fawcett
Department of Sociology
 and Anthropology
St. Francis Xavier University
Antigonish, Nova Scotia
Canada

John M. Matsunaga
Department of Anthropology
University of California at Berkeley
Berkeley, CA

Library of Congress Control Number: 2007930709

ISBN-13: 978-0-387-71824-8   e-ISBN-13: 978-0-387-71825-5

Printed on acid-free paper.

9 8 7 6 5 4 3 2 1

springer.com

To Bruce Trigger, for his inspiration, dedication, and patience as both teacher and scholar

Acknowledgments

This volume was the result of the hard work and dedication of many people. We would like to take this opportunity to acknowledge them. All of the papers in this volume were initially presented in 2004 as part of a symposium entitled "Beyond Nationalist, Colonialist, Imperialist Archaeologies: Evaluating Multiple Narratives" at the 69th Annual Meeting of the Society for American Archaeology (SAA) in Montreal. We thank those who participated in this symposium and agreed to contribute their papers to this volume. We would also like to thank three scholars, Nadia Abu El-Haj, Dante Angelo, and Nenad Tasić, who presented papers at the symposium but were unable to contribute to this volume.

Teresa Krauss and Katie Chabalko of Springer provided sage editorial advice and we thank them for their patience and assistance. We would also like to thank two anonymous reviewers, who gave us invaluable comments and suggestions on the contents of this book.

Numerous other individuals, who provided assistance and support of various kinds, made this volume possible: Eric Atkinson, Mike Bisson, Patricia Fawcett, Marc Fawcett-Atkinson, Koji and Makiko Habu, Mark Hall, Katherine Howlett Hayes, Akiko and Mariko Idei, Tom and Sue Matsunaga, and Tanya Smith. We thank all of them for providing the help and support we needed to complete this work. In particular, Dr. Mark Hall helped us copyedit Chapter 11. John Matsunaga would like to thank the Department of Anthropology at the University of California, Berkeley for providing funding in the form of a Lowie Olsen grant for travel to the SAA meetings in Montreal. Clare Fawcett thanks her colleagues at St. Francis Xavier University for providing a stimulating academic environment for archaeological and anthropological research and teaching. Junko Habu thanks her colleagues at UC Berkeley for stimulating conversations about multivocality and the sociopolitics of archaeology.

While we were editing this volume, we received the sad news that Professor Bruce Trigger had passed away on December 1, 2006. We would like to express our sincere condolences to his family. Bruce's daughter, Dr. Rosalyn Trigger, helped us finalize his manuscript. We thank her for her assistance.

As former Ph.D. students at McGill University in Montreal, both Clare Fawcett and Junko Habu benefited greatly from Bruce Trigger's guidance. His work inspired us to initiate the symposium and this book project. Over the years, as graduate students and then as colleagues, we learned a great deal about being scholars, teachers, and archaeologists from his dedication to archaeology, his commitment to social justice, his gift for open and innovative thought, and his enthusiasm, fairness, and humanity. For these reasons, we dedicate this book to his memory.

Junko Habu
Clare Fawcett
John M. Matsunaga

Table of Contents

Contributors

Sonya Atalay, Department of Anthropology, Indiana University, Bloomington, IN 47405-7100

Michael L. Blakey, Institute for Historical Biology, Department of Anthropology, College of William and Mary, Williamsburg, VA 23187

Robert Chapman, University of Reading, Department of Archaeology, Reading, RG6 6AH, UK

Clare Fawcett, Department of Sociology-Anthropology, St. Francis Xavier University, Antigonish, Nova Scotia, B2G 2W5 Canada

Junko Habu, Department of Anthropology, University of California, Berkeley, CA 94720-3710

Ian Hodder, Department of Cultural and Social Anthropology, Stanford University, Stanford, CA 94305-2145

Matthew H. Johnson, Archaeology, School of Humanities, University of Southampton, Southampton SO17 1BF UK

Rosemary A. Joyce, Department of Anthropology, University of California, Berkeley, CA 94720-3710

Minkoo Kim, Department of Anthropology, Chonnam National University, Gwangju 500-757 Korea

David Kojan, Department of Anthropology, San Francisco State University, San Francisco, CA 94132-4155

John M. Matsunaga, Department of Anthropology, University of California, Berkeley, CA 94720-3710

Neil Asher Silberman, Ename Center for Public Archaeology and Heritage Presentation, Oudenaarde, Belgium

Bruce G. Trigger, Department of Anthropology, McGill University, Montreal, Quebec, H3A 2T7 Canada

Patrick F. Wallace, National Museum of Ireland, Dublin 2, Ireland

Alison Wylie, Departments of Philosophy and Anthropology,
    University of Washington, Seattle, WA 98195

Chapter 1
Introduction: Evaluating Multiple Narratives: Beyond Nationalist, Colonialist, Imperialist Archaeologies

Clare Fawcett, Junko Habu, and John M. Matsunaga

Goal and Scope of this Volume

The goal of this volume is to use archaeological case studies from around the world to evaluate the implications of providing alternative interpretations of the past. Our volume is based on papers that were originally presented at a 2004 SAA (Society for American Archaeology) session in Montreal entitled "Beyond Nationalist, Colonialist, Imperialist Archaeologies: Evaluating Multiple Narratives." Our work builds on the twin pillars of Bruce Trigger's (1984) work on alternative archaeologies and Ian Hodder's discussion of archaeological practice in the context of globalization (1999).

In 1984, Bruce Trigger published an article that strongly influenced subsequent discussions about the sociopolitical contexts of archaeological research. Using Wallerstein's (1974) world-systems theory, Trigger's paper, "Alternative Archaeologies: Nationalist, Colonialist, Imperialist," suggested that "the nature of archaeological research is shaped, to a significant degree, by the roles that particular nation-states play, economically, politically, and culturally, as interdependent parts of the modern world-system" (Trigger 1984:356). Thus, depending on the position of countries in the world system, there are many archaeologies, including nationalist, colonialist, and imperialist ones, and these different archaeologies provide alternative interpretations of the past.

Trigger (1984) started his paper with a discussion of nationalist archaeology, the primary function of which is to bolster the pride and morale of nations or ethnic groups aspiring to nationhood. Examples of nationalistic archaeological traditions cited by Trigger include those in Denmark, Israel, Egypt, Iran, Mexico, China, and Germany. The second category, colonialist archaeology, refers to archaeology practiced by colonizers in a colonized country. Examples show that colonial archaeologists often emphasized the primitiveness or lack of accomplishments of the ancestors of colonized people to justify discriminatory behavior as well as colonization itself. The United States, New Zealand, and parts of sub-Saharan Africa are examples of countries and regions that experienced periods of colonialist archaeology. Third, Trigger pointed out that states with worldwide political, economic, and cultural power have produced imperialist archaeological traditions.

1

J. Habu, C. Fawcett, and J. M. Matsunaga (eds.), *Evaluating Multiple Narratives: Beyond Nationalist, Colonialist, Imperialist Archaeologies.*
© Springer 2008

He included in this category the archaeological traditions of the United Kingdom, the Soviet Union, and the United States after the advent of processual archaeology. Archaeologists working within an imperialist tradition take for granted the superiority and universal applicability of their theoretical and methodological approaches. They also exert a strong influence on research around the world through their writings, the international nature of their research projects, and the key role they play in training archaeologists from various parts of the world.

Trigger's (1984) article is significant because it outlined the mutually constitutive relationship between archaeological interpretations and their sociopolitical contexts. He suggested that interpretations are never objective, but that they are always partly a product of their social, political, and historical contexts (see also Trigger 1980). Trigger did not, however, reject the necessity of striving for objectivity in archaeological interpretation, even if that objectivity always remained elusive. He believed that archaeologists needed to move toward objectivity by carefully analyzing archaeological findings as well as by constantly keeping in mind the socio-political context of research and interpretation (Trigger 1984:368–369). This position of moderate relativism was further elaborated in his later work (e.g., Trigger 1989, 1995, 1998, 2003, 2006; see also Wylie 2006).

Trigger's (1984) work, along with other publications that appeared in the early to mid-1980s (Gero et al. 1983; Leone 1981; Meltzer 1983; Patterson 1986; Wilk 1985), resulted in debates about the social and political implications of archaeological practice. One of the central issues in these debates is the role that politics and ethics play in the evaluation of archaeological interpretations (e.g., Fotiadis 1994; Kohl 1993; Lampeter Archaeological Workshop 1997; Shanks & Tilley 1987; Wylie 1992, 1993). Another important theme that has emerged is the analysis of the complex power relations within which individuals and groups create identities based on the archaeological past (e.g., Bond & Gilliam 1994; Dietler 1994; Gathercole & Lowenthal 1990; Kohl & Fawcett 1995; Layton 1989a,b; Leone et al. 1995; Meskell 1998, 2002; Schmidt & Patterson 1995; Swidler et al. 1997).

Ian Hodder (1999, see also 1997, 2000, 2004a,b) extends Trigger's (1984) discussion of the social contexts of archaeology by contextualizing current archaeological thought within the globalizing processes of the late twentieth century. According to Hodder, globalization has facilitated communication between individuals and isolated groups around the world through computer technology, mass communications, and global travel. This ease of communication has led to two contradictory patterns. On the one hand, globalization creates a homogenization of global culture and identity as archaeological sites and remains are interpreted as part of a pan-human heritage. On the other hand, globalization also results in the fragmentation of global culture, as small groups of people and individuals appropriate local heritage sites as symbols of their individual or local identities.

Hodder (1999) argues that archaeologists have the moral and ethical responsibility to facilitate the participation of many groups and individuals when interpreting a site. In this way, sites will be relevant to people from a variety of academic and non-academic backgrounds and multiple complementary and/or contradictory interpretations will be available. Hodder calls this process multivocality. It is generally presented as a way of empowering underrepresented groups to present their understandings and interpretations of the archaeological past. He states that the goal of multivocality is to allow multiple interpretations of the archaeological past. Some of these interpretations are academic, others are non-academic; some interpretations are the work of professional archaeologists, others are the work of non-archaeologists or amateurs interested in the site.

Although the recent discussion of multivocality was inspired largely by Hodder's (1999, 2004a,b) work, interest in promoting alternative interpretations in archaeology has deeper roots. One of the sources of multivocality was postmodernist and poststructuralist thought introduced into archaeology during the early 1980s. The postmodern challenge to scientific objectivity, based on an emphasis on the subjective nature of knowledge, and criticism of all forms of grand theorizing, opened up the possibility of multiple interpretations in archaeology (e.g., Jameson 1984; Lyotard 1984). In addition to this, the poststructuralist perspective that texts are not objective end products, but should be understood as having multiple meanings derived from different readers, led some archaeologists to question the objectivity of archaeological interpretations (e.g. Bapty & Yates 1990; Shanks & Tilley 1987; Tilley 1990, 1993; for a more recent example see Joyce 2002). Influences of both postmodernist and poststructuralist thought can be found in Hodder's discussion of multivocality as well as in his other writings (see Hodder 1982, 1986, 1993, 1999).

Another influence on the development of multivocality was the growth of social movements supporting the recognition of the rights of socially marginalized groups. Representative of these movements in the United States are the Civil Rights Movement and the Women's Rights Movement. These movements demanded economic and sociopolitical changes that would give more power to underrepresented ethnic and social groups, including African-Americans, Native Americans and women. Similar social movements developed in many other parts of the world. Parallel to these social movements was the decline of formal colonial structures that resulted in pressure on previous colonial powers, such as Britain, to allow other voices to be heard. While these influences made their way into the academy through the development of feminism, Marxism, postcolonialism, and multiculturalism during the late 1960s and 1970s, they became prevalent in archaeology only during and after the 1980s (see e.g., Conkey & Gero 1997; Conkey & Spector 1984; Gathercole & Lowenthal 1990; Gero & Conkey 1991; Gero et al. 1983; Layton 1989a,b; Leone, Potter, & Shackel 1987; Leone et al. 1995). These changes have led to legislation and professional codes of ethics that request archaeologists to give greater consideration to the opinions, interpretations and feelings of various stakeholders who are interested in the archaeological past, including descendant communities of indigenous peoples. This has translated into changes in how the ownership of the past is conceived and in how and by whom the past is represented. Examples of these legislation and ethics codes include NAGPRA (the Native American Graves Protection and Repatriation Act) functioning in the United States since 1990, and the Code of Ethics of professional associations like the Australian Archaeological Association (2007).

The authors in this volume share with Trigger and Hodder an understanding of the tension between the inherently subjective nature of archaeological interpretation and the constraining influence of the archaeological record. They also share an interest in the relevance of archaeological studies in contemporary societies. Furthermore, many of the authors are concerned about the effects of globalization on archaeological interpretation and heritage management.

The papers in this volume were written by scholars who work in various parts of the world, including areas where the political use of the past is particularly controversial. Unified by the common theoretical interests described above, each contributor to this volume examines an archaeological case study, usually of a specific site or set of sites, in a country or a region where two or more alternative interpretations of the past have been made. Alternative interpretations may have occurred within the context of different archaeological traditions (e.g., Anglo-American vs. Indigenous). They may represent different political and spatial scales (e.g., local, national, international or global). Alternatively, they may have been produced for different audiences (e.g., the general public, amateurs, groups with a specific interest in the site, tourist operators, or academic specialists). The broad range of topical and geographical interests covered here is best represented by the list of contributors. In addition, three eminent archaeological theoreticians, Ian Hodder, Bruce Trigger, and Alison Wylie, provide comments on these chapters.

Given these contexts, this volume seeks to contribute to several key aspects of contemporary archaeological discourse that relate to providing alternative interpretations. First, this book concerns the theory and methodology of multivocality. Second, papers in this book move the discussion of the sociopolitics of archaeology forward by providing concrete case studies from around the world. Special attention is paid to the dynamic and historically unique nature of the relationship between archaeology, nationalism, and peoples' identity. Third, many papers in this volume reflect a growing interest in the impact of global political, economic, and cultural forces on archaeological interpretation and heritage management. This includes tourism, commercialism, and the spread of information through the media and recently the Internet.

Evaluations of Multivocality

Evaluations of the theory and methodology of multivocality are an important dimension of this book. Because the concept of multivocality in archaeology developed originally in Britain and the United States, theoretical discussions of multivocality have been limited primarily to Anglo-American archaeology. Furthermore, to date explicit multivocal approaches can be found almost exclusively in situations where underrepresented groups in Anglo-American countries were involved in developing archaeological interpretations, or when Anglo-American archaeologists conducted research projects in non-Anglo-American countries.

Given the spirit of the concept, we believe that the advantages and limitations of the theory and method of multivocality should be discussed in relation to a variety of cultural and historical settings. In particular, given the political, economic, and cultural hegemony of the United States and Britain on the world scene, multivocality could be used to break down the power imbalance between Anglo-American and non-Anglo-American academic traditions. Thus, in our call for contributions for this volume, we raised the following three questions: (1) Is the concept of multivocality inseparable from the theory of contemporary Anglo-American archaeology, especially that of postprocessual archaeology? (2) In terms of archaeological practice, is the concept of multivocality relevant to local residents and non-Anglo-American archaeologists working in various parts of the world? (3) In the context described above, can the close examination of alternative interpretations contribute to a deeper understanding of the subjectivity/objectivity of archaeological interpretations?

With respect to the first question, chapters by several authors demonstrate that, while multivocality may have been *theorized* exclusively by Anglo-American postprocessual archaeologists, elements of multivocal approaches have been *practiced* in various forms in archaeological traditions around the world. For example, in discussing the existence of multiple interpretations of the past at Tiwanaku, Bolivia, David Kojan (Chapter 6) argues that the multiplicity exists regardless of how archaeologists feel about it, but that archaeologists can affect the manner in which the existence of the multiplicity is acknowledged. Sonya Atalay (Chapter 3) suggests from a perspective of Indigenous archaeology that Ojibwe concepts of multivocality can be useful in decolonizing archaeological practice. Rosemary Joyce (Chapter 5), in her analysis of Honduran archaeology, expands the discussion of multivocality by pointing out that academic studies of the history and sociopolitics of archaeology must be broad enough to encompass a variety of interpretative frameworks. By doing this, we avoid the assumption that concern with multivocality arose only within Anglo-American theoretical debates. Junko Habu and Clare Fawcett (Chapter 7) report a case study from Japan, in which local archaeologists independently developed strategies to encourage multiple interpretations of a Jomon period site and worked closely with local residents.

Regarding the second question, case studies in this volume demonstrate that multivocality has been, or can be, an effective tool to enhance the voices of underrepresented groups in both Anglo-American and non-Anglo-American archaeological settings. Michael Blakey (Chapter 2) provides a powerful case study in which the concept of multivocality has been critical in developing a research design for the study of the African Burial Ground in New York. Matthew Johnson (Chapter 4) argues that multivocality could be used to challenge the concept of Britishness, an ideology that has been closely tied to British imperialism and colonialism. Contrasting the definition of the state in North American and European archaeology with the definition used in Spanish archaeology, Robert Chapman (Chapter 10) suggests that the reexamination of the "alternative" state may challenge the dominant mode of thought in Anglo-American archaeology.

In his commentary, Ian Hodder (Chapter 13) argues that placing the local and global in opposition to each other ignores complex alliances and interaction between stakeholders at many levels. Multivocality, he says, is cosmopolitan, involving a "complex blending of the global and the particular in ways that do not replicate Western perspectives and which do not construct the local as a product of the global" (p. 198).

Several authors warn us that, if not introduced judiciously, promoting alternative interpretations might result in the opposite effect from the original democratizing goal of multivocality. Neil Silberman (Chapter 9) argues that multiple narratives communicated through new techniques, such as online interactivity, virtual reality, and theme park design, do not necessarily challenge dominant interpretive narratives; rather these dominant narratives may become even more deeply entrenched. Minkoo Kim (Chapter 8) introduces a case study in which alternative interpretations that are supported by non-archaeologists are used to bolster the dominant, nationalist ideology rather than to enhance the views of the underrepresented non-nationalist perspective.

Finally, many authors confront the issues that arise between multivocality and the subjectivity of archaeological interpretation. They take seriously the problems and dangers associated with hyperrelativism as discussed by Trigger (1989). Trigger (Chapter 12) further suggests that the process of evaluating multiple narratives shares with the method of multiple working hypotheses the outcome of narrowing down the range of viable interpretations of specific sets of archaeological data. As Wylie (Chapter 14) points out, multivocality does not necessarily lead to hyperrelativism. While many contributors see the virtues of multivocal engagement and the benefits such engagement can bring, all remain committed to the importance of archaeologically grounded interpretations. The various ways the authors in this volume address the relationship between multivocality and subjectivity provide important examples of how archaeologists can engage with other voices while maintaining interpretive rigor.

Archaeology, Nationalism, and Identities

Intersecting with the question of the validity and implications of multivocality within archaeology are the questions of the dynamic relationship between archaeological practice, political agendas, and the construction of people's identities. While these issues have been extensively discussed in previous publications, most authors of these texts either did not directly engage with recent discussions of multivocality (e.g., Kohl & Fawcett 1995), or had restricted areal/topical coverage (e.g., Meskell 1998 with a focus on the eastern Mediterranean and Middle East; Zimmerman et al. 2003 with a focus on ethical and legal responsibility of archaeologists in the Americas).

Chapters in this volume clearly indicate that nationalism, colonialism, and imperialism are key factors in understanding the broad features of the relationship between archaeology and identity. Minkoo Kim and David Kojan confirm Bruce Trigger's statement that nationalist archaeology continues to be a key type of archaeology in our classification. Pat Wallace (Chapter 11) outlines the sociopolitical contexts of Irish archaeology that, until recently, discouraged medieval and Viking period studies. What is striking here is that Ireland, despite its unique history, shares with other countries the tendency to dismiss later migrants as inauthentic components of national history (see e.g., the Danish case discussed by Kristiansen 1990). The reverse phenomenon is found in Matthew Johnson's case study, which describes historical archaeology in Britain as having closer ties to British national identity than does the country's prehistoric archaeological research.

In addition, the particular goals and interests of various stakeholders, including archaeologists, local residents and others, may differ between archaeological projects. For example, the Japanese case study presented by Habu and Fawcett describes how local residents, and ultimately the prefectural government, chose to preserve an archaeological site rather than build a baseball stadium. This decision resulted from a combination of social, political, economic, and historical factors unique to the independently developed academic tradition of Japanese archaeology and to the region of Japan where the site is located. Kojan's work also outlines the multiple meanings given to a Bolivian archaeological site by stakeholders using the site for their own political purposes. By examining individual case studies that describe the regional and historical settings and perspectives of stakeholders involved with specific archaeological projects, papers in this volume reveal the historically contingent nature of archaeological interpretations and the value of archaeological sites in particular local settings.

Tourism, the Media, and Globalization

In addition to the two dimensions of multivocality discussed above, issues related to archaeological tourism and the media coverage of archaeological findings have emerged as important themes in this volume. Archaeology and tourism are closely linked. Archaeology, like modern forms of tourism, arose during the nineteenth and twentieth centuries in tandem with industrialization, colonialism, and the Euro-American search for national identity (Chambers 2000; Trigger 2006). Throughout the twentieth century and into the twenty-first century, tourism has increased in importance as a global industry and as a cultural space. Tourism is now an important source of transnational migration, as well as a booming economic engine in many parts of the developed and developing worlds (for discussions about the relationship between tourism and archaeology, see e.g., Handler & Gable 1997; Silverman 2002).

Many contributions in this volume argue that archaeological tourism is an element in the construction of individual, local, regional, and national identities. They also indicate that authenticity is a central theme of archaeological tourism (see also Fife 2004). While many tourists seek "real" or "authentic" connections with the past, archaeologists, and curators recognize the partial, contextual, and constructed nature of their work and knowledge. Wallace's discussion of heritage tourism in Dublin, Ireland, Joyce's references to the relationship between government conceptions of the multicultural Honduran state, tourism, and the archaeological past, and Kim's analysis of "the oldest rice" in the sociopolitical context of South Korea demonstrate this point.

Chapters in this volume also reveal that archaeologists have a symbiotic relationship with the media, and, since the early 1990s, the Internet. Whether they like it or not, various forms of media and the Internet are powerful tools to disseminate information about their work to the public (see e.g., Wolle & Tringham 2000). For example, Habu and Fawcett describe how the long history of archaeological reporting by newspapers, and television has nurtured local citizens' enthusiasm for archaeological research in Japan. Kojan's analysis of indigenous politician Evo Morales's 2006 "spiritual" inauguration as Bolivia's president at the site of Tiwanaku shows how media presentations made Tiwanaku "...a stage for a contemporary dispute over politics, economic power and social authority, and a crucible in which these power struggles are tested" (p. 74). Kim uses a case study of the South Korean Sorori site to show how the Internet can provide small groups of non-specialists with opportunities to present interpretations of archaeological remains that contradict those of professional scholars and academics.

As Silberman's chapter demonstrates, archaeological knowledge disseminated through the media or by tourist operators has gained value as a product in many parts of the world. This commercialization of archaeological knowledge and remains influences interpretation. Silberman argues that many archaeological theme parks and museums in the United States and Europe seem to provide multiple views and interpretations of the past while actually supporting the dominant narrative of the "heritage tourism" industry based on commercial activities.

Many of the papers in this volume address the influence of cultural forces, like tourism and various forms of the media, on archaeological interpretation. These forms of communication are powerful tools for archaeologists who want to present their ideas to larger non-academic audiences. They are also important avenues through which people from outside the formal structure of archaeological research can suggest and evaluate interpretations. The analysis of both archaeological tourism and the reporting of archaeological information through traditional and new media demonstrates the shifting nature of archaeological interpretation.

Summary

In summary, the papers in this volume provide concrete examples for evaluating the implications of engaging with multiple interpretations of the past. The various theoretical and methodological approaches adopted by individual authors encourage reflection on issues that are central to current debates on archaeological theory and practice. Furthermore, the wide diversity of topics and geographical areas covered by these authors help to clarify the dynamic nature of the relationship between archaeology, sociopolitical conditions, and people's identities in various regional and historical settings. Finally, the papers in this volume encourage the recognition and appreciation of under-theorized examples of multivocality in non-Anglo-American contexts.

As Bruce Trigger states in his discussion, classifications of archaeologies have proliferated since his initial distinction between nationalist, colonialist, and imperialist archaeologies. This proliferation encourages us not only to acknowledge the inherently subjective nature of archaeological interpretations, but also to make archaeology a socially engaged discipline. Articles in this volume reflect the enthusiasm of individual authors to explore these issues in relation to their own research in different parts of the world. If this volume allows a greater diversity of interpretation to be considered globally, we will have done our job.

Acknowledgments We thank Mark Hall and Tanya Smith for their valuable comments on earlier drafts of this chapter. Responsibility for all the errors and interpretations in this chapter, of course, is ours.

References

Australian Archaeological Association (2007). Code of ethics. South Fremantle, WA, Australia (February 14, 2007); http://www.australianarchaeologicalassociation.com.au/ethics

Bapty, I., & Yates, T. (Eds.). (1990). *Archaeology After Structuralism: Poststructuralism and the Practice of Archaeology*. London: Routledge.

Bond, G., & Gilliam, A. (Eds.). (1994). *Social Construction of the Past: Representation as Power*. London: Routledge.

Conkey, M., & Gero, J. (1997). Programme to practice: Gender and feminism in archaeology. *Annual Review of Anthropology*, 26, 411–437.

Conkey, M., & Spector, J. (1984). Archaeology and the study of gender. In M. Schiffer (Ed.), *Advances in Archaeological Method and Theory, Volume 7* (pp. 1–38). New York: Academic Press.

Chambers, E. (2000). *Native Tours: The Anthropology of Tourism and Travel*. Prospect Heights, Ill.: Waveland Press.

Dietler, M. (1994). "Our ancestors the Gauls": Archaeology, ethnic nationalism, and the manipulations of Celtic identity in modern Europe. *American Anthropologist*, 96(3), 584–605.

Fife, W. (2004). Penetrating types: Conflating modernist and postmodernist tourism on the Great Northern Peninsula of Newfoundland. *Journal of American Folklore*, 117, 147–167.

Fotiadis, M. (1994). What is archaeology's 'mitigated objectivism' mitigated by? Comments on Wylie. *American Antiquity*, 59, 545–555.

Gathercole, P., & Lowenthal, D. (Eds.). (1990). *The Politics of the Past*. London: Unwin Hyman.

Gero, J., & Conkey, M. (Eds.). (1991). *Engendering Archaeology: Women and Prehistory*. Oxford: Blackwell.

Gero, J., Lacy, D., & Blakey, M. (Eds.). (1983). *The Socio-Politics of Archaeology*. Amherst: University of Massachusetts, Department of Anthropology, Research Report No. 23.

Handler, R., & Gable, E. (1997). *The New History in an Old Museum: Creating the Past at Colonial Williamsburg*. Durham, NC: Duke University Press.

Hodder, I. (1982). Theoretical archaeology: a reactionary view. In I. Hodder (Ed.), *Symbolic and Structural Archaeology* (pp. 1–16). Cambridge: Cambridge University Press.

Hodder, I. (1986). *Reading the Past: Current Approaches to Interpretation in Archaeology.* Cambridge: Cambridge University Press.

Hodder, I. (1993). The narrative and rhetoric of material culture sequences. *World Archaeology,* 25(2), 268–282.

Hodder, I., (1997). "Always momentarily, fluid, flexible:" Towards a reflexive excavation methodology. *Antiquity,* 71, 691–700.

Hodder, I. (1999). *Archaeological Process: An Introduction.* Oxford: Blackwell.

Hodder, I. (2004a). Dialogical archaeology and its implications. In I. Hodder, *Archaeology Beyond Dialogue* (pp. 1–7). Salt Lake City: University of Utah Press.

Hodder, I. (2004b). Who to listen to? Integrating many voices in an archaeological project. In I. Hodder, *Archaeology Beyond Dialogue* (pp. 23–28). Salt Lake City: University of Utah Press.

Hodder, I. (Ed.). (2000). *Towards Reflexive Method in Archaeology: The Example at Çatalhöyük.* Cambridge: McDonald Institute for Archaeological Research and British Institute of Archaeology at Ankara, Monograph 289.

Jameson, F. (1984). Postmodernism, or the cultural logic of late capitalism. *New Left Review,* 146, 52–92.

Joyce, R. (2002). *The Languages of Archaeology: Dialogue, Narrative, and Writing.* Oxford: Blackwell Publishers.

Kohl, P. (1993). Limits to a postprocessual archaeology (or, the dangers of a new scholasticism). In N. Yoffee & A. Sherratt (Eds.), *Archaeological Theory: Who Sets the Agenda?* (pp. 13–19). Cambridge: Cambridge University Press.

Kohl, P., & Fawcett, C. (Eds.). (1995). *Nationalism, Politics and the Practice of Archaeology.* Cambridge: Cambridge University Press.

Kristiansen, K. (1990). National archaeology in the age of European integration. *Antiquity,* 64, 825–828.

Lampeter Archaeological Workshop. (1997). Relativism, objectivity and the politics of the past. *Archaeological Dialogues,* 4(2), 164–198.

Layton, R. (Ed.). (1989a). *Conflict in the Archaeology of Living Traditions.* London: Unwin Hyman.

Layton, R. (Ed.). (1989b). *Who Needs the Past? Indigenous Values and Archaeology.* London: Unwin Hyman.

Leone, M. (1981). Archaeology's relationship to the present and the past. In R. Gould & M. Schiffer (Eds.), *Modern Material Culture: The Archaeology of Us* (pp. 5–14). New York: Academic Press.

Leone, M., Mullins, P. R., Creveling, M. C., Hurst, L., Jackson-Nash, B., Jones, L. D., Kaiser, H. J., Logan, G. C., & Warner, M. S. (1995). Can an African-American historical archaeology be an alternative voice? In I. Hodder, M. Shanks, A. Alexandri, V. Buchli, J. Carman, J. Last, & G. Lucas (Eds.), *Interpreting Archaeology: Finding Meaning in the Past* (pp. 110–124). London: Routledge.

Leone, M., Potter, P., & Shackel, P. (1987). Toward a critical archaeology. *Current Anthropology,* 28(3), 283–302.

Lyotard, J-F. (1984). *The Postmodern Condition: A Report on Knowledge.* Translated by G. Bennington & B. Massumi. Minneapolis: University of Minnesota Press.

Meltzer, D. (1983). Antiquity of man and the development of American archaeology. In M. Schiffer (Ed.), *Advances in Archaeological Method and Theory, Volume 6* (pp. 1–51). New York: Academic Press.

Meskell, L. (2002). The intersections of identity and politics in archaeology. *Annual Review of Anthropology,* 31, 279–301.

Meskell, L. (Ed.). (1998). *Archaeology Under Fire: Nationalism, Politics, and Heritage in the Eastern Mediterranean and the Middle East.* London: Routledge.

Patterson, T. (1986). The last sixty years: Towards a social history of Americanist archaeology in the United States. *American Anthropologist,* 88, 7–26.

Schmidt, P., & Patterson, T. (Eds.). (1995). *Making Alternative Histories: The Practice of Archaeology and History in Non-Western Settings.* Santa Fe: School of American Research Press.

Shanks, M., & Tilley, C. (1987). *Reconstructing Archaeology.* Cambridge: Cambridge University Press.

Silverman, H. (2002). Touring ancient times: The present and presented past in contempoarary Peru. *American Anthropologist,* 104(3), 881–902.

Swidler, N., Dongoske, K., Anyon, R., & Downer, A. (Eds.). (1997). *Native Americans and Archaeologists: Stepping Stones to Common Ground.* Walnut Creek: Altamira Press.

Tilley, C. (Ed.). (1990). *Reading Material Culture: Structuralism, Hermeneutics and Post-Structuralism.* Oxford: Blackwell.

Tilley, C. (Ed.). (1993). *Interpretative Archaeology.* Oxford: Berg.

Trigger, B. G. (1980). Archaeology and the image of the American Indian. *American Antiquity,* 45(4), 662–676.

Trigger, B. G. (1984). Alternative archaeologies: Nationalist, colonialist, imperialist. *Man,* 19, 355–370.

Trigger, B. G. (1989). Hyperrelativism, responsibility, and the social sciences. *Canadian Review of Sociology and Anthropology,* 26, 776–797.

Trigger, B. G. (1995). Romanticism, nationalism and archaeology. In P. Kohl & C. Fawcett (Eds.), *Nationalism, Politics, and the Practice of Archaeology* (pp. 263–279). Cambridge: Cambridge University Press.

Trigger, B. G. (1998). Archaeology and epistemology: Dialoguing across the Darwinian chasm. *American Journal of Archaeology,* 102, 1–34.

Trigger, B. G. (2003). Introduction: Understanding the material remains of the past. In B. G. Trigger, *Artifacts & Ideas: Essays in Archaeology* (pp. 1–30). New Brunswick: Transaction Publishers.

Trigger, B. G. (2006). *A History of Archaeological Thought.* Second Edition. New York: Cambridge University Press.

Wallerstein, I. (1974). *The Modern World-System,* Vol. I. New York: Academic Press.

Wilk, R. (1985). The ancient Maya and the political present. *Journal of Anthropological Research,* 41, 307–326.

Wolle, A.-C. & Tringham, R. E. (2000). Multiple Çatalhöyüks on the worldwide web. In I. Hodder (Ed.), *Towards Reflexive Method in Archaeology: The Example at Çatalhöyük by Members of the Çatalhöyük Teams* (pp. 207–218). Cambridge: McDonald Institute for Archaeological Research.

Wylie, A. (1992). The interplay of evidential constraints and political interests: Recent archaeological research on gender. *American Antiquity,* 57, 15–35.

Wylie, A. (1993). A proliferation of new archaeologies: "Beyond objectivism and relativism." In N. Yoffee & A. Sherratt (Eds.), *Archaeological Theory: Who Sets the Agenda?* (pp. 20–26). Cambridge: Cambridge University Press.

Wylie, A. (2006). Moderate relativism/political objectivism. In R. F. Williamson & M. S. Bisson (Eds.), *The Archaeology of Bruce Trigger: Theoretical Empiricism* (pp. 25–35). Montreal: McGill-Queens University Press.

Zimmerman, L. J., Vitelli, K. D., & Hollowell-Zimmer, J. (Eds.). (2003). *Ethical Issues in Archaeology.* Walnut Creek: Altamira Press.

PART I
OPERATIONALIZING
MULTIVOCALITY

Introduction to Part I

Operationalizing Multivocality

Chapters in Part I introduce case studies that outline the implications of multivocality for archaeological research design, methodology, and interpretation. Drawing upon critical theory, Michael Blakey (Chapter 2) demonstrates how a multivocal approach constituted an integral part of the archaeological research carried out at the New York African Burial Ground. Through a discussion of this research, he reveals how multivocal collaboration and engagement with the public can lead to richer archaeological interpretations and a more ethical archaeological practice. Emphasizing similar ideas, Sonya Atalay (Chapter 3) proposes a decolonizing "Indigenous archaeology" that extends the concept of multivocality beyond the confines of archaeological interpretation. Atalay argues that multivocality must be practiced, through collaboration between all interested groups, during all stages of research. The goal of this practice is to create more culturally sensitive forms of archaeological practice and education. Using Ojibwe oral history, epistemology and worldview, she suggests that notions of multivocality are not restricted to Western intellectual thought. She concludes that archaeology has much to gain by engaging with conceptualizations of multivocality found in other cultures. Matthew Johnson (Chapter 4), in his analysis of the "construction" of the English landscape, emphasizes possible contributions of alternative interpretations of historical archaeological remains. Rosemary Joyce (Chapter 5) outlines the historical context in which an indigenous form of multivocality emerged in Honduran archaeology. She then presents her own interpretation of Honduran archaeology as one of the many voices. Finally, David Kojan (Chapter 6) presents a timely case study from Bolivia, where the creation and manipulation of competing archaeological narratives are inseparably linked to the current political and economic conditions of the country. He argues that all interpretations and narratives of the past must be understood through the power dynamics that shape their creation and use.

   Together, these five chapters demonstrate how anthropological archaeologists can use multivocality as an effective tool for enriching our understanding of the past. They also show how the concept of multivocality, which has its origins in postmodernism/poststructuralism as well as in various social movements, can help archaeologists make their discipline more socially and politically engaged.

Junko Habu
Clare Fawcett
John M. Matsunaga

Chapter 2
An Ethical Epistemology of Publicly Engaged Biocultural Research

Michael L. Blakey

The New York African Burial Ground was rediscovered in 1989 during preparations for the construction of a 34 story Federal office building for the United States General Services Administration (GSA) (Ingle et al. 1990). To mitigate the destruction of cultural resources as required by law, a full-scale archaeological excavation conducted by HCI (Historic Conservation and Interpretation) and John Milner Associates preceded the building project. The excavation and construction site on the Burial Ground is located at Foley Square, in the city block bounded by Broadway, Duane, Reade, and Elk streets in Lower Manhattan, one block north of City Hall.

Archaeological excavation and building construction began during the summer of 1991 and ended in the summer of 1992 when the US Congress called for work on the site to cease in response to the public demand to properly memorialize, and, ultimately, learn about the people buried there. A research team was assembled at Howard University beginning in April of 1992. The task of this team was post-excavation analysis, laboratory work, and interdisciplinary studies. This paper examines the interaction of ethics and theory during the 12 years in which the project's scientific pursuits interfaced with public interests. The research team of the W. Montague Cobb Biological Anthropology Laboratory at Howard University, and eight other universities affiliated with the project have studied the skeletal remains of 419 individuals representing 18th century African captives and their descendants.

The approach taken to the organization and interpretation of data from the African Burial Ground involves four main elements. How these elements of theory have come to guide our particular research program are discussed in this chapter. These theoretic principles are also generalizable and may be extended to a broader range of research projects than are entailed in our study of the African Burial Ground. The four elements are as follows:

1. Critical theory in the vindicationist vein allows the sociocultural and ideological influences on research interpretations to be scrutinized, while seeking socially empowering factual information through scientific and other scholarly research. The fundamental principle rests upon acknowledging that political and ideological implications are intrinsic to science and history, and that choices about these are unavoidable (Blakey 1996, 1998a; Douglass 1999 [1854]). The pervasive

J. Habu, C. Fawcett, and J. M. Matsunaga (eds.), *Evaluating Multiple Narratives: Beyond Nationalist, Colonialist, Imperialist Archaeologies.*
© Springer 2008

incorporation of African diasporic intellectual traditions of this kind into the dialog around New York's African Burial Ground opened a special opportunity for applying this long-standing critical view of historical knowledge to a bioarchaeological study. Many brands of "critical theory" have emerged in recent decades, including neo-Marxist and postmodernist thought in American and European archaeology. The synthesis of criticism that emerges in this case is, in its mainstream, part of the evolved understandings of the social and political embeddedness of history and anthropology among African diasporans (see Drake 1980; Harrison & Harrison 1999). Yet as participants in the intellectual development of a broader "Western" world, such critical thought connects with other intellectual traditions whose experience has led to compatible insights.

2. Public engagement affords the communities, most affected by a research program, a key role in the design and use of research results. A respect for pluralism and the ethics of working with groups of people who historiography puts at risk of social and psychological harm recommends an acknowledgment of this community's right to participate in research decisions. Scholars balance accountability to such communities with responsibility to standards of evidential proof or plausibility that defines the role of scholars. The goal of this collaboration is not simply ethical. By drawing upon broader societal ideas and interests, public engagement affords opportunities for advancing knowledge and its societal significance. The democratization of knowledge involved here is not predicated on the inclusion of random voices, but on democratic pluralism that allows for a critical mass of ideas and interests to be developed for a bioarchaeological site or other research project, based on the ethical rights of descendant or culturally affiliated communities to determine their own well-being.

3. Multiple data sets (or lines of evidence) provide a crosscheck on the plausibility of results. Results may be rejected, accepted, or recombined into newly plausible "stories" about the past based on how diverse results of different methods compete or reconfigure as a complex whole. The required multidisciplinary experts engage in a "conversation" that produces interdisciplinary interpretations of the archaeological population. Diverse expertise provides for recognition of a subject matter that might otherwise go unnoticed by the individuals and in the communities under study. By revealing multiple dimensions of human subjects, this approach can produce characterizations of even skeletal individuals that more nearly resemble the complexities of human experience than are possible in simple, reductionist descriptions.

4. An African diasporic frame of reference was selected as a context for the New York population. This framework provides a connection both to an Atlantic world political economy and a transatlantic cultural history that is more reflective of the causal conditions existing throughout the life cycle of members of this eighteenth century community than was the local Manhattan context of enslavement. The broader diasporic context of the New York population's lives also adds to an understanding of the population as more fully human than is afforded by a local context of enslavement. Non-African diasporic research

might also circumscribe, differently, the scope of time and space required to examine a sufficiently large political economic system and social history to begin to explain how, what, and why its subject came to be.

Critical Theory

African diasporic intellectuals have, since late slavery, acknowledged the intrinsically political implications of anthropology and history with which they were confronted. Indeed, the historical record of American physical anthropology has continued to demonstrate that the physical anthropologists with the most emphatic interest in "objectivity" have nonetheless participated in the creation of racial and racist ideology (Blakey 1987, 1996; Gould 1981; Rankin-Hill & Blakey 1994). White supremacist notions are supported when representations of blacks are so shallow and biological as to denude them of human characteristics and motivations. As racialized "black slaves," African diasporic populations may be removed from culture and history, an objectification that some view as consistent with the ideals of Western science. Here it is both the biological categorization of identity (race) and the omission of history and culture that deny humanity to these historic populations.

While this process dehumanizes the black past, Euro-American history is also transformed to one in which Africans are not recognizable as people. They become instead a category of labor, the instruments or "portmanteau organisms" of whites (see Crosby 1986) that are therefore not readily identified with as the subjects of human rights abuses. These aspects, even of description, transform American history. Douglass, in 1854, asks scholars to simultaneously take sides and be fair to the evidence. This is different from Enlightenment notions of objectivity, because it is accepted that science and history will always be subjective to current biases and interests. How can one take a position and be fair to the evidence? One conceptualization of the purpose of historical research that may not violate either of these goals is the assumption that research into the diasporic past is not simply the pursuit of new knowledge. Indeed, diasporic traditions of critical scholarship have assumed that the search is for the reevaluation of old, politically distorted, and conveniently neglected knowledge about black history.

The research design of the African Burial Ground project asserts that the motivation to correct these distortions and omissions will drive the research effort in part. This understanding of the ideological nature of the construction of history allows our team to scrutinize data more critically than were we to assume ownership of special tools for neutral knowledge. We need to be more circumspect and aware of how our interpretations may be used and influenced by societal interests beyond the academy walls. Our criticism holds, as an assumed goal, the societally useful rectification of a systematically obscured African-American past. The fact that New York's African Burial Ground should not have existed from the standpoint of the basic education of most Americans supports the need for a critical and corrective approach to archaeology. The history of the northern colonies, of New York, is characterized as free and largely devoid of blacks. That, of course, is untrue. The history that denies the presence of blacks and of slavery in places where these actually did profoundly exist is not accidental. Such a history must be deliberately debated. Yet societal interests also influence our alternative interpretations and they may influence policy and social action. We are screwing around with other people's identities. Who are we as individual scientists to decide how to formulate our research plans relative to such potentially powerful societal effects?

Public Engagement

While we are responsible for our epistemological choices, it is perhaps inappropriate for researchers to make those choices in isolation. The epistemological choices – i.e., the choice of ways of knowing the past by virtue of the selection of research questions, theories and analytical categories – are also the justifiable responsibility of the broader communities whose lives are most affected by the outcome of research. This recognition of the potential for a democratization of knowledge merges epistemological concerns with ethical ones. The communities with which we work – living descendants or culturally affiliated groups – have an ethical right to be protected from harm resulting from the conduct of research. The American Anthropological Association Statement on Professional Responsibility and Ethics, the World Archaeological Congress Ethical Statement, and the new ethical principals of the American Association of Physical Anthropologists, which largely recapitulates the former, are key examples of this ethical standard (see Lynott & Wylie 1995 for an extensive discussion of ethics in American archaeology). Communities have a stake in how research is conducted if it might impact them negatively or positively.

The National Historic Preservation Act of the United States allows the public a say in whether research will be done at all and Native American Graves Protection and Repatriation Act (NAGPRA) legislation gives federally recognized Native Americans and Pacific Islanders rights to determine the disposition of their ancestral remains and sacred objects. Many archaeologists and physical anthropologists have resisted these ethical and legal obligations, arguing that the autonomous authority of researchers needs to be protected for the sake of objectivity and the proper, expert stewardship of knowledge about our past. That position is based on assumptions that are inconsistent with our critical theoretical observations of intrinsic cultural embeddedness of science that have informed the activist scholarship in the diaspora. If science is subjective to social interests, it seems fair, at least in the American cultural ethos, to democratize the choice of those interests that scientists will pursue. Since the people most affected are also to be protected, it is least patronizing for anthropologists to enter into a research relationship with descendant communities by which those communities protect themselves by participating in the decisions regarding research design. Indeed, a "publicly-engaged" anthropology of this kind has been proposed by a panel of leading anthropologists who have linked the practice to American values of democratic participation and pluralism

(Blakey et al. 1994; Forman 1994). Hodder (1999) has considered "multivocality" as representing the value of a plurality of perspectives for the development of archaeological programs, and distinguishes pluralism from relativism. At the African Burial Ground, we found useful and exciting paths of inquiry as well as elevated scrutiny of evidential proof when naive objectivity was replaced by ethics. It is interesting to consider that the idea of objective methods capable of revealing universal truths may have served to obscure the need for ethics or accountability to nonscientific considerations in the pursuit of knowledge.

Our project has conceived two types of clientage: the descendant community most affected by our research (the ethical client) and the GSA that funds the research (the business client). While both clients have rights that should be protected, the ethical requirements of the field privilege the voices of descendants. Descendants have the right to refuse research entirely and the researcher's obligation is to share what is known about the potential value of bioarchaeological studies. Our project received permission to present a draft research design to African Americans and others interested in the site. Our purpose was to elicit comment, criticism, and new ideas and questions to which the descendant community was most interested in having answers. The result of this public vetting process is, we believe, a stronger research design with more interesting questions than would have likely come from researchers alone. A sense of community empowerment, in contrast to the preexisting sense of desecration, was fostered by our collaboration. Permission to conduct research according to the resulting design was granted by both clients. Public pressure in support of a more comprehensive research scope than usually afforded such projects resulted from the fact that research questions interested them and that they claimed some ownership of the project. Thus research directions, an epistemological concern, were fostered by public involvement, an ethical concern. The queries produced by the engagement process were condensed to four major research topics:

1. The cultural background and origins of the population;
2. The cultural and biological transformations from African to African-American identities;
3. The quality of life brought about by enslavement in the Americas;
4. The modes of resistance to slavery.

In the application of this approach to an "ethical epistemology" (an ethemology?), experience has shown that conflict, social conflict, can be part and parcel of public engagement. When meeting in a state government auditorium in Harlem while vetting the research design in 1993, the panel of researchers was confronted by some African Americans who objected to our references to slavery in Africa, insisting that slavery had never existed there. We were able to convey familiarity with what we considered to be a reflection of the concern of some African Americans that the Euro-American community's frequent references to African slavery were often meant to suggest that Africans were responsible for the slave trade. That tack gave an apologetic spin that abdicates the responsibility of Europeans and Euro-Americans (the "demand" side of the trade) for American slavery. There was also sensitivity to the all-too-frequent false notion that those brought to the Americas were "slaves" in

Africa rather than free people who had been captured and "enslaved." With recognition of this understanding and of differences and similarities between chattel and African household slavery, our requirement as scholars was, nonetheless, to indicate that we would refer to slavery in Africa because of the material evidence for its existence there. It was the community's right to decide whether or not it would encourage scholars to conduct research on the African Burial Ground or to involve only religious practitioners or provide some other treatment. If the project was to be involved, it was to be involved as scholars and that meant standing on evidence. It is significant too that the diasporic scholars on the panel had knowledge of the kinds of critique (not just emotional sensitivity) that had informed the concern over the suggestions of African slavery and could respond that attempts would be made to maintain an awareness, in the course of our work, of previous misuses by other scholars of the fact of slavery in Africa. This we did.

The project leadership was strongly urged to refer to the Africans of colonial New York as "Africans" or "enslaved Africans" rather than slaves. This recommendation upon deliberation and discussion seemed cogent and not inconsistent with material facts. The critical consideration of the community representatives was that "slave" was the objectified role that Europeans and American whites had sought to impose. The Africans themselves, while clearly subject in large part to the conditions of the role of "slave," had often both previous experience and self-concepts that were as complex human beings "who had their own culture before they came here" and who resisted slavery psychologically, politically, and militarily according to material facts. Thus we agreed that we represented the perspectives of slaveholders by using the dehumanizing definition of the people we were to study as slaves, when "enslaved African" reasonably emphasized the deliberate imposition of a condition upon a people with a culture. Similarly we accepted, as did the State and Federal agencies, the renaming of the "Negroes Burying Ground" to the African Burial Ground for reasons similar to the use of "enslaved Africans." And Sherrill Wilson found it in the course of background research for the National Historic Landmarks Designation of the site that Africans named their institutions "African" in New York City as soon as they obtained the freedom to put such nomenclature on record in the early nineteenth century.

This case is exemplary of the value of the process of public engagement and the deliberation, potential conflict, and reasonable compromise that were often involved. The purpose was to find a synthesis of scholarship and community interests, if a synthesis could be found. These deliberations rest upon trust which is as much established by a demonstration of the integrity of scholarship as it is by the researcher's recognition of the community's ultimate right to determine the disposition of its ancestral remains. Choice of language was one of the most emphatic contributions of the community which did not seem as comfortable with questioning some of the technical aspects of methodology. Invasive methods were discussed and accepted as required to answer the important question of origins that has long been keenly important to African Americans. Family roots and branches were deliberately severed by the economic expediencies and psychological control methods of slavery.

Another community emphasis of importance to the course of the research project was the insistence on including African and Caribbean research in our geographical and cultural scope and on extending the temporal parameters back to the Dutch period when, despite the lack of historical reference, the cemetery might have been used. These ideas helped move the project's research questions and choice of expertise toward the African and diasporic scope that become immensely important for recognizing the specific artifactual, genetic, and epidemiological effects of the cemetery and its population. Furthermore, our team's adherence to the observations of African suppliers of a Euro-American driven transatlantic trade in human captives positioned us properly to receive a senior delegation of the Ghanaian National House of Chiefs who regretfully acknowledged the involvement of some past leaders.

An example of conflict with the project's business client, the GSA, is found in the project's adherence to agreements that the Federal Agency had made on the scope of research, including DNA and chemical studies, that it would begin to reverse 5 years into the study. There seemed to be other attempts to contain or reduce the project by limiting the scope of newsletter mailing or the project and community input into memorialization projects such as the interpretive center. In each case the project leaders returned to the public forum and were brought as community advisors to legislators in New York and on Capital Hill to make these efforts transparent to the public. Congressmen and community members were able to reiterate their support by letter and verbally to the GSA, which over the course of the project indicated that it was turning the project around and getting it back on track four times, interspersed each time by at least a year of obstruction by a variety of means, usually the elimination of funding. As a partly academically based project, it was possible to continue with alternative funding to meet with the descendant community and government leaders without fear of loss of the next contract, and the often overwhelming evidence of GSA's inconsistency with its legal requirements to which it had previously agreed would ultimately bring the agency back to the public to restart the project from the point where it had been when the impediments were put into effect. Although many aspects of the research design (Howard University & John Milner Associates 1993) were ultimately not funded, the integrity of the researchers' relationship to the ethical client was maintained by standing with the community and insisting that the GSA carry through with its commitments. The GSA was not allowed to summarily disregard its legal obligations or promises to the black community once its building had been built, and would have to return to fund aspects of the research and memorialization that it had tabled, sometimes over a period of years. This project's leadership refused to give our business client anything other than our best and honest advice.

Were this project not linked to community interests there might have been fewer conflicts with the federal agency. On the other hand, community engagement (and to some extent the presence of what Congressman Savage called the "obstinacy" of the governmental agency) defined much of the significance of the project that would represent descendant community empowerment. Part of that empowerment came to be shown by the community's resolve and effective opposition to desecration by a white leadership of a large federal governmental agency of the United States (see Harrington 1993). On the other hand, the project's ability to withstand attempts to arbitrarily end the project is the result of having a strong base of support in the general public and among legislators representing them. Funding, even under these terms, was adequate for a broad scope of work demonstrated in the current report and two others.

Finally, the project was designed to utilize a biocultural and biohistorical approach and rejected race estimation in favor of culturally salient categories of ethnic origin using DNA, craniometry, archaeological artifacts and features, as well as the available historical record. We had no need of reinforcing the concept of race through our research especially when that concept obscures the cultural and historical identity of those who are made subject to its classification. Moreover, new molecular technologies and specialists in African mortuary data could put us on the trail of ethnic groups with discernable histories. Having acquired the project against the competitive efforts of a forensic team that emphasized its customary use of racing methodology, an effort in their defense was successfully solicited in which over 50 physical anthropologists wrote to the GSA, usually supporting the forensic approach to racing (Cook 1993; Epperson 1997, 1999).

Indeed, a number of these letters and comments suggested that the use of DNA, chemistry, and cultural traits such as dental modification could be of no value in determining origins. Without the backing of the descendant community that was far more interested in social and cultural history than racial classification, the project would not have been able to, as it did, say "no" to the vast majority of physical anthropologists who demonstrated a lack of support to the project's business client.

The essential point here is that the questions and approaches that have driven the research of the New York African Burial Ground Project were produced by a public process of empowerment that involved distinct supporters and detractors. What we have been able to accomplish for present evaluation and future development has been the result of protracted struggle with those who customarily expect to control this kind of contracted research to create a research enterprise that is not repugnant to the African-American community. But it is also a project of unusual epistemological complexity. As a result, the project has had an impact upon both the scientific community and public discussions of human rights and reparations for slavery (see Blakey 1998a,b, 2001; La Roche & Blakey 1997). Six documentary films and frequent and lengthy textbook references to the New York African Burial Ground Project (Johnson 1999; Parker Pearson 1999; Thomas 1998 and others) also suggest that the project has raised interesting issues for a broad range of people.

Multiple Data Sets

Multidisciplinary expertise was repeatedly shown to be essential in our attempts to answer the project's major questions regarding the origins, transformations, quality of life, and modes of resistance. Examining a question such as the origin of the population with different sets of data such as genetics, anthropometry, material culture, history, and chemistry was valuable because:

1. Verification of the plausibility of findings on the part of a particular specialized method or set of data is provided in the form of complementary or conflicting results from an alternative data set. Contrasting results were at least as useful as complementary data because these would raise new questions and possibilities about interpretation or the need for methodological development. Biological data (such as molecular genetics) have often been privileged over cultural and historical data. We found genetics data, read in isolation of other information, to lead to erroneous conclusions relative to more verifiably accurate cultural and historical evidence. We do not privilege the biological data, but are benefited from the discussion among the differing results that led us to mutually plausible conclusions. Metaphorically, one voice allowing the floor with impunity can easily make false representations without there being any means of evaluation or accountability. Where there are several voices in a dialogue about facts, the standards of plausibility are elevated by the accountability that the facts generated by each method have to one another. This sort of "discussion" among different data sets become a means, if not of objectivity, of raising standards of plausibility and of fostering a dialectical process by which new research directions would emerge.

2. Multidisciplinary research allows us to recognize more diverse dimensions of the individual biographies and community histories than any one discipline could allow us to "see" in the data. By assessing layers of origins data, for example, we construct the population in terms of its demography, pathology, genetics, cultural influences on burial practices, environmental exposures in teeth, religious history, and art that allow the construction of a more complex human identity at the site. A fraction of these disciplines would have produced a fraction of the richer human qualities we worked to understand because observations are largely limited to the specialized knowledge and research tools required to make them.

3. This disciplinary breadth, inclusive of biology, culture, and history, makes possible the kind of political economic analysis in which we are interested as biocultural anthropologists. The biological data are interpreted in relation to the population's social, political, and economic history. Yet some studies will rely on evolutionary theory while remaining historical in their attempt to discover cultural origins with biological evidence. There needs to be a "tool kit" of theories for purposes of different research questions. The break with tradition here is that such an approach is not in search of a unifying theory that physical anthropology and human evolution are not synonymous.

Diasporic Scope

The descendant community had been forceful in its insistence upon our examination of the African backgrounds for the New York population. Their idea was that these were people with a culture and history that preceded their enslavement and which continued to influence them even in captivity. We found the African and Caribbean connections important for understanding the site in many ways. We would require archaeologists, historians, and biologists with expertise and experience in research in all three areas.

Similar to the value of multidisciplinary resources of the project, the diasporic scope of expertise allowed us to find meaningful evidence where narrower expertise could not have "seen" it. The use of quartz crystals as funerary objects required an African archaeological background whereas Americanist archaeologists might have assigned them no meaning (see Perry 1999); the heart-shaped symbol, believed to be of Akan origin and meaning (see Ansa 1995), was assumed to have a European, Christian meaning in the absence of anyone who could recognize an Akan adinkra symbol. Thus the geographical and cultural connections to the site are enlarged by the diasporic scope of the researchers.

Bioarchaeological projects are often limited to very localized special and temporal contexts of interpretation. Were this project to have limited its scope of interpretation to New York City's history (or to the cemetery itself) the African Burial Ground would have revealed a New York population understood for the immediate conditions of its members' enslavement, or less. A larger international context reveals a cultural background for these captives, an ebb and flow of migration between different environments and social conditions, shifting demographic structures related to a hemispheric economy, and the interactions of people and environments that changed over the course of the life cycle to impact their biology in multiple unhealthy ways. By understanding these African captives as people from societies of their own who were thrust into enslavement in an alien environment, perhaps their human experience can be more readily identified. This at least was the expressed goal in meetings of descendant community members that informed the research design. And of course the desire to reach back and critically examine that experience is motivated by the scope of interests of an African diaspora "concept" that has traditionally included a vindicationist approach to black history that stands against Eurocentric historical apologetics.

A variety of other, specific theories (or explanations relating specific observations to generalizable systems within which they have meaningful implications for us) have been applied to explain particular phenomena observed at the African Burial Ground. The above approaches, however, form the most general framework of our analyses. The meta-theoretical approach described above comprises a process for generating the questions we ask, for assessing the reasons why we are asking those questions, and for making choices about theory with which the information is organized to answer those questions. They are also perhaps the most unique to our situation in which these approaches emerged as special opportunities to resolve problems and contradictions met with at the site. The principles and processes I have described are often likely to be, nonetheless, generalizable and can be usefully extended for bioarchaeological work in many kinds of situations, not to be limited to this site or to African diasporic bioarchaeology.

Final Comment

It has been rewarding to see, now about a quarter century after Joan Gero and I organized the first session on "The Socio-politics of Archaeology" at the Society for American Archaeology meetings in Minneapolis (see Gero et al. 1983) and with the further inspiration, of the first World Archaeological Congress in Southampton in 1986, the need of practitioners of our field to grapple with the fact of our humanity has begun to be taken seriously enough to produce new ways of knowing the past. One hopes for qualitative change. As for New York's African Burial Ground, our project anthropologists have shared the pleasure of engagement with a community in a battle for the dignity of a desecrated and belittled cemetery, a place that would be established as a new United States National Monument in the summer of 2006.

References

Ansa, K.O. (1995). Identification and validation of the Sankofa symbol. *Update*, 1, 3.

Blakey, M.L. (1987). Skull doctors: Intrinsic social and political bias in the history of American physical anthropology; with special reference to the work of Ales Hrdlicka. *Critique of Anthropology*, 7, 7–35.

Blakey, M.L. (1996). Skull doctors revisited. In L. Reynolds & L. Lieberman (Eds.), *Race and Other Misadventures: Essays in Honor of Ashley Montagu in His Ninetieth Year* (pp. 64–95). New York: General Hall, Inc.

Blakey, M.L. (1998a). Beyond European enlightenment. In A.H. Goodman & T.L. Leatherman (Eds.), *Building a New Biocultural Synthesis: Political-Economic Perspectives on Human Biology* (pp. 379–405). Ann Arbor: University of Michigan Press.

Blakey, M.L. (1998b). The New York African Burial Ground project: An examination of enslaved lives, a construction of ancestral ties. *Transforming Anthropology*, 7(1), 53–58.

Blakey, M.L. (2001). Bioarchaeology of the African Diaspora in the Americas: Its origins and scope. *Annual Review of Anthropology*, 30, 387–422.

Blakey, M.L., Dubinskas, F., Forman, S., MacLennan, C., Newman, K.S., Peacock, J.L., Rappaport, R.A., Velez-Ibanez, C.G., & Wolfe, A.W. (1994). A statement to the profession: the American Anthropological Association Panel on Disorders of Industrial Societies. In S. Forman (Ed.), *Diagnosing America: Anthropology and Public Engagement* (pp. 295–311). Michigan: University of Michigan Press.

Cook, K. (1993). Black bones, white science: The battle over New York's African Burial Ground. *Village Voice*, 4 May, 23–27.

Crosby, A. (1986). *Ecological Imperialism: the Biological Expansion of Europe 900–1900*. Cambridge: Cambridge University Press.

Douglass, F. (1999) [1854]. Claims of the Negro ethnologically considered, commencement speech at Western Reserve University, Cleveland, OH. In P.S. Foner (Ed.), *Frederick Douglass: Selected Speeches and Writings* (pp. 282–297). Chicago: Lawrence Hill Books.

Drake, St.C. (1980). Anthropology and the Black experience. *The Black Scholar*, 11, 2–31.

Epperson, T.W. (1997). The politics of "race" and cultural identity at the African Burial Ground excavations, New York City. *World Archaeological Bulletin*, 7, 108–117.

Epperson, T.W. (1999). The contested commons: archaeologies of race, repression, and resistance in New York City. In M.P. Leone & P.B. Potter, Jr. (Eds.), *Historical Archaeologies of Capitalism* (pp. 81–110). New York: Plenum.

Forman, S. (Ed.). (1994). *Diagnosing America: Anthropology and Public Engagement*. Michigan: University of Michigan Press.

Gero, J., Lacy, D., & Blakey, M. (Eds.). (1983). *The Socio-Politics of Archaeology*. Research Report No. 23. Amherst: University of Massachusetts, Department of Anthropology.

Gould, S.J. (1981). *The Mismeasure of Man*. New York: Norton & Company.

Harrington, S.P.M. (1993). Bones and bureaucrats. *Archaeology*, 46(2), 28–38.

Harrison, F.V., & Harrison, I. (1999). *African American Pioneers in Anthropology*. Chicago: University of Illinois Press.

Hodder, I. (1999). *The Archaeological Process: An Introduction*. Oxford: Blackwell Publishers.

Howard University & John Milner Associates. (1993). *Research Design for Archeological, Historical, and Bioanthropological Investigations of the African Burial Ground (Broadway Block) New York, New York.*

Ingle, M., Howson, J., & Edward, R.S. (1990). *A Stage 1A Cultural Resource Survey of the Proposed Foley Square Project in the Borough of Manhattan, New York, New York.* Edwards and Kelcey Engineers, Inc., and the General Services Administration. Newton, NJ: Historic Conservation and Interpretation, Inc.

Johnson, M. (1999). *Archaeological Theory: An Introduction*. Oxford: Blackwell Publishers.

La Roche, C.J., & Blakey, M.L. (1997). Seizing intellectual power: The dialogue at the New York African Burial Ground. *Historical Archaeology*, 31, 84–106.

Lynott, M.J., & Wylie, A. (Eds.). (1995). *Ethics in American Archaeology: Challenges for the 1990s*. Washington D.C.: Society for American Archaeology.

Parker Pearson, M. (1999). *The Archaeology of Death and Burial*. College Station: Texas A&M University Press.

Perry, W. (1999). *Landscape Transformations and the Archaeology of Impact: Social Disruption and State Formation in Southern Africa*. Normal, IL: Illinois State University.

Rankin-Hill, L.M., & Blakey, M.L. (1994). W. Montague Cobb: Physical anthropologist, anatomist, and activist. *American Anthropologist*, 96, 74–96.

Thomas, D.H. (1998). *Archaeology* (3rd edition). Fort Worth: Harcourt College Publishers.

Chapter 3
Multivocality and Indigenous Archaeologies

Sonya Atalay

In July 1844, an Ojibwe orator told a Jesuit priest: *"My brother you have come to teach us there is only one way, for all people, to know the Great Spirit...My brother, there are many species of trees, and each tree has leaves that are not alike"* (cited in Delage et al. 1994:319).

In this statement, the orator speaks of an important aspect of traditional Anishinaabe[1] culture: an appreciation for a diversity of ideas and multiple ways of understanding cultural knowledge – in this case, spiritual knowledge. He equates knowledge with trees in a forest, recognizing and appreciating that the diversity of those trees is responsible for the beauty of our woodland homeland. In this chapter, I explore several concepts that relate to this statement – those of multivocality and the diversity of knowledge practices. I first provide a brief overview and introduction to some of the concepts and concerns of Indigenous archaeology approaches. This is followed by a brief practical example in which I examine the relevance of multivocality in Ojibwe epistemologies, philosophies, and practices as they relate to public education of the Ojibwe past in a museum display.

Beyond Nationalist: Global Applicability of Indigenous Archaeologies

The theoretical and methodological tenets and practices of Indigenous archaeology are currently being defined. As with many contemporary approaches within social science fields, Indigenous archaeology is not defined by one coherent theory or method. Rather, it includes many different experiences and approaches that have manifested themselves in a range of different practices. To reflect this, throughout this chapter I sometimes refer to the plural "Indigenous archaeologies" in discussing these approaches; while for simplicity and ease of language, at other times, I refer simply to Indigenous archaeology. While focus and specifics may vary, one common thread among Indigenous archaeologies that I have observed is an incorporation of, and respect for, the experiences and epistemologies of Indigenous groups globally.

J. Habu, C. Fawcett, and J. M. Matsunaga (eds.), *Evaluating Multiple Narratives: Beyond Nationalist, Colonialist, Imperialist Archaeologies.*
© Springer 2008

Just as "Westerners" do not maintain a monolithic, homogenous culture with a single ideology or way of viewing the world, Indigenous people do not hold a common worldview or shared experience with archaeology, approaches to history, and cultural heritage. Those practicing a form of Indigenous archaeology build on the diverse experiences and views of Indigenous people to examine topics such as ethics and human rights, reburial and repatriation, decolonization, community collaboration, culturally effective dissemination of research, and field methodology. Approaches to Indigenous archaeology are being developed by Indigenous people and those working in collaboration with them. Some of the defining characteristics of Indigenous archaeology include: collaboration with local communities; development of research questions and agendas that benefit local groups that are developed and approved by them; respect for and adherence to local traditions when carrying out field and lab work; utilization of traditional practices of cultural resource management; combining indigenous methods with western scientific approaches; and a recognition and respect for the unbroken connection of the past with the present and future. Although born from and developed in conjunction with indigenous perspectives and experiences, the applicability of Indigenous archaeology approaches is not limited to Indigenous land and people, but rather holds relevance for archaeological practice more broadly.

Indigenous archaeology approaches are not simply critique and practice carried out by Indigenous people – one need not be a Native person to follow an Indigenous archaeology paradigm. It is also not necessarily archaeology located on an Indigenous land base – it may or may not take place on Native lands. Indigenous archaeologies do not include such essentialist qualities. Archaeology on Indigenous land, conducted by Native people without a critical gaze that includes collaboration; that does not incorporate Indigenous epistemologies and Native conceptions of the past, history, and time; or that neglect to question the role of research in the community would be a replication of the dominant positivist archaeological paradigm. A noncritical archaeology that is not based on or informed by the experiences and epistemologies of Indigenous people, even if carried out by Native people on Indigenous land, would be, to use Trigger's terms (1984), a *nationalist* archaeology – one that seeks to examine a particular Indigenous region or cultural group to contribute to nationalist concerns. In my view, approaches to Indigenous archaeology are not nationalist because they are not simply concerned with carrying out archaeological research on Native land using mainstream archaeological methods and theories. Rather, they attempt to bring to the table new tools and concepts based on Indigenous experiences. These have relevance outside of Indigenous settings for archaeologists working with local communities, descendent groups, and stakeholders.

Thus, Indigenous archaeology is not marginal in its applicability, but rather has implications for mainstream archaeological practice globally. It offers the potential of bringing to archaeology a more ethical and engaged practice, one that is more inclusive and rich without sacrificing the rigor and knowledge production capacity that make archaeology such a powerful tool for understanding past lifeways.

Beyond Colonialist and Imperialist: Toward a Decolonizing Archaeology

As discussed above, in my view the aims of Indigenous archaeology approaches are primarily to avoid replicating mainstream (Western) archaeological practice, to investigate Indigenous concepts and knowledge related to history and cultural heritage management, and to incorporate such knowledge into mainstream archaeology (see Atalay 2006a, 2008, for discussions of how to accomplish this). Incorporating these indigenized practices, which may relate to theory, method, fieldwork, and education/pedagogical strategies, adds multivocality not only to archaeological interpretation, but also to all aspects of archaeological practice. The need to move beyond a multivocality of interpretation is discussed more fully later in this chapter.

The incorporation of indigenized practices into mainstream archaeology is an important point of consideration when examining traditions of nationalist, colonialist, and imperialist forms of archaeology. Through investigating and incorporating indigenized (and any number of other) concepts of knowledge (re)production about the past, it becomes possible to move beyond a colonialist or imperialist archaeology that disperses the methods and ideologies of mainstream Western (American and British) archaeology to some form of "other." The foundation in Indigenous concepts and experience coupled with the political aspirations of supporting Indigenous sovereignty and maintaining certain aspects of control over cultural knowledge production bring Indigenous archaeology approaches away from a colonialist or imperialist paradigm and into another realm. This is one that I believe is best termed a *de*colonizing archaeology, part of a wider global project of decolonization.

Before moving more specifically to a discussion of decolonizing practices and the involvement of multivocality with these efforts, I'd like to turn briefly to the development of Indigenous archaeologies and the decolonizing aspects of these approaches in order to demonstrate how their development is deeply rooted in Indigenous activism, and is part of a larger whole of internal efforts toward positive change for Indigenous communities. In his 1984 article "Alternative Archaeologies: Nationalist, Colonialist, Imperialist" (and in other work since then), Trigger discusses the ways that contemporary politics influences views of, and research into, the past. The rise and growth of Indigenous archaeology offers yet another demonstration of this situation. Indigenous people, marginalized and victimized by the early development and ongoing daily practice of anthropology, archaeology, and other social sciences have begun finding ways to speak back to the power of nationalist, colonialist, and imperialist interpretations of the past. A growing number of Indigenous people from around the globe have received archaeological training and field experience, and the number of those working professionally as archaeologists in some capacity is increasing. Education and training of Indigenous people in the field of archaeology range from extensive field school and professional experience to those who hold bachelor's, master's, and doctoral degrees.

Many work in tribal archaeology programs, as tribal cultural resource management officers, tribal historic preservation officers, and a smaller but still growing number are employed in museums or work within academia.

The activism and influence of Indigenous people, both those within and outside the field of archaeology, had a strong impact on the direction of the discipline. Simultaneously, the research and efforts of non-Indigenous archaeologists, many of whom worked closely with Indigenous groups, or on issues of Marxism, feminist approaches, and postprocessual concepts brought to archaeology a much needed change in perspective geared toward respect and the understanding of multivocality. Activism within Indigenous communities together with changes in mainstream archaeological practice created a *critical mass*, of sorts, and resulted in positive changes in interactions between archaeologists and Native People.

While some of this was the result of working together, in other cases it was heated debate, often in discussions involving the Native American Graves Protection and Repatriation Act (NAGPRA) that led to dialogue, and eventually greater interaction and improved archaeological practices. The passing of national legislation related to repatriation, particularly NAGPRA in 1990, had a dramatic and very positive influence on the relationships between archaeologists and Native people. Both the public support behind NAGPRA and the resulting consultation with Native Americans in regards to museum collections led to a greater number of positive interactions and relationships with archaeologists – many of which were unexpected on both sides.

These contemporary events led to the rise of Indigenous archaeology and brought a much needed change in perspective and direction in the ways many archaeologists engaged in research. This is most clearly evident in the evolving changes in the relationships between archaeologists and Indigenous, local, and descendent communities, the multiple and diverse publics of archaeological research, and the various stakeholders involved. Changes in archaeological theoretical perspectives involving postprocessual concepts of multivocality and plurality paved the way for greater receptivity, respect, and appreciation of the Indigenous activism that attempted to bring concepts and experiences of Indigenous people into archaeological practice. The Indigenous activism that drove these changes was part of a larger push toward asserting sovereignty and self-determination, and a wider project of decolonization. All of these were internal developments that were not part of a colonizing or imperial process, but were in reaction against and in opposition to such oppressive forces.

New Tools for Building a Multivocal Archaeology

One of the primary points of concern in my own research is the decolonizing aspects of Indigenous archaeology approaches (Atalay 2006a,b). I'd like to explain more fully what I mean by decolonization, and more specifically and importantly for the purposes of this volume, the multilayered role of multivocality in decolonizing efforts. In an important and oft quoted essay, Audre Lorde (1984) states that "the master's tools will never dismantle the master's house." If we consider that, in many ways, mainstream (Western) archaeology has oppressed and disenfranchised Indigenous people from holding sovereignty over their own past and heritage, then efforts to decolonize archaeology and to build an Indigenous archaeology have been understood by some (Indigenous and non-Indigenous, archaeologists and non-archaeologists) as aiming to introduce new tools that will either dismantle the discipline or exclude non-Indigenous archaeologists from studying the heritage and history of Indigenous peoples. On the contrary, I argue that the goal of researching and developing Indigenous archaeology approaches is not to dismantle Western archaeological practice (Atalay 2006a, 2008). The discipline of archaeology is not inherently good or bad; it is the application and practice of the discipline that has the potential to disenfranchise and be used as a colonizing force. Rather than dismantling, archaeology requires critical reflection and positive change if it is to remain relevant and effective. Indigenous archaeology approaches offer a set of tools to use in building positive change from within the discipline; but these are tools, concepts, epistemologies, and experiences for remodeling, not dismantling.

In response to Audre Lorde's thoughts about the role of the "master's tools," Henry Louis Gates, Jr. (1998:30) stated that, "you can only dismantle the master's house using the master's tools." I would argue that, for the discipline of archaeology the way forward lies between the views of Lorde and Gates, Jr., and multivocality plays a critical role in the scenario. There is no doubt that archaeology was built upon and remains deeply entrenched in a Western paradigm of history, culture, and the past, and it is thoroughly steeped in Western ways of viewing the world. Such Western paradigms include a reliance on economic models of optimal decision making that minimize the influence of spiritual or symbolic meanings; accumulation of knowledge production in the hands of a small elite (who set the research agenda and benefit most from its products); divorcing the people and places of the past from communities and situations in the present; and a strong privileging of written and material evidence over oral accounts and traditional knowledge. These can be contrasted with Indigenous paradigms that, in building on Native experiences and knowledge, recognize the high priority placed on things beyond "rational" comprehension; the importance of creating and sharing knowledge with the community; the critical connection of the past with the present and the interrelationship and holistic nature of these; and the power and importance of oral tradition and indigenous knowledge.

However, sole reliance on a Western paradigm with regard to producing and reproducing archaeological knowledge need not remain a standard practice. To bring greater diversity to the discipline, those following an Indigenous archaeology approach are attempting to move archaeology beyond its nationalist, colonialist, and imperialist roots in order to find new tools for understanding past cultures and lifeways by gaining insight from indigenous approaches and knowledge structures. As stated earlier, the attempt is to incorporate Indigenous experiences and epistemologies into current mainstream archaeological practices. The goal is not to replace Western concepts with Indigenous ones, but to create a multivocal archaeological practice that benefits and speaks to society more broadly. In my view, it is precisely this form of multivocality that Indigenous archaeologists are calling for. This view of multivocality does not simply involve addressing multiple perspectives at the level of interpretation of a particular site or region. It is a more comprehensive approach to multivocality that attempts to find ways of combining Western and Indigenous theoretical and methodological concepts that begin at the planning stages of research, and works to create diverse approaches to long-term management of archaeological resources, as well as both the tangible and intangible aspects of heritage.

In thinking about multivocality as an Indigenous archaeologist, I do not aim to simply present Indigenous interpretations of the past or to make room for multiple perspectives at the interpretative table. Rather, it is a much deeper level of multivocality that is attempted which will have a more fundamental effect on the daily practice of archaeology at all levels – from the planning stages to the final sharing and presentation of research results. It is at this level of multivocality that decolonization efforts become central. Part of the methodology of decolonization is to research Indigenous traditional knowledge and practices and to utilize them, as Cavender-Wilson (2004:75) describes, "for the benefit of all humanity." As with Western ways of knowing, understanding, and teaching about the world, there is also a great deal of knowledge and wisdom in Indigenous forms of knowledge production and reproduction, and these have the power to benefit our own Indigenous communities as well as others globally. A decolonizing archaeology holds as one of its goals the work of bringing these concepts to the academy and working toward their legitimization as part of mainstream research strategies. More specifically, some Indigenous archaeologists are engaged in the struggle to put these concepts into practice in our own scholarship, producing models that others can follow.

Integral to decolonizing efforts is the realization and acknowledgment that Western ways of knowing are not in any way superior or natural – they are produced in specific contexts and are reproduced through daily practice. As such, these ways of knowing and understanding the world can be disrupted, changed, and improved upon. In the same light, it is also important to recall that all aspects of human life and culture, knowledge, and the practices associated with its production and reproduction are not static, but are constantly changing. Situated within the context of a global decolonizing practice, effective ways of regaining traditional Indigenous knowledge, epistemologies and practices are being examined through Indigenous archaeology approaches. When appropriate for sharing outside of a Native context, such knowledge, epistemologies, and practices are being brought to the foreground and put forth as models (Atalay 2006a, 2008).

Some might utilize the resulting methods and theories within Indigenous communities, while others see the value of incorporating certain aspects into archaeological practice more broadly. As part of decolonizing efforts and in working toward a multivocal archaeology, Indigenous archaeology situates itself to work from the place of the "local"; to acknowledge specific critiques and concerns of Indigenous people and descendent populations; to research them, name them, deconstruct them; and finally to offer a positive plan of forward movement toward a more ethical practice. This kind of ethical practice finds respect for humanistic concerns, spiritual landscapes, material and ancestral remains, and the heritage issues that bind all of these together.

Multivocality in Native American Epistemologies

In Western thought multivocality has played an important role in postmodernism, and within archaeology some postprocessual approaches, such as Hodder's (1999) reflexive methodology, hold multivocality as a central tenet. Certain, although not all, Indigenous cultures also maintain a strong epistemological tradition of multivocality when dealing with history and knowledge about the past. In my approach to Indigenous archaeology, I attempt to actively move away from the idea of simple binaries that categorize knowledge and ideas, and rely instead on a pluralistic approach based on my own tribe's (Ojibwe) epistemological view. Ojibwe cultural heroes are often trickster figures who, rather than embodying pure good or evil, personify multiplicity. One example of this in Ojibwe culture is the cultural hero Nanaboozhoo. Among many Indigenous cultures there are trickster figures similar to Nanaboozhoo. This figure, and many like him, embodies multiplicity. The cultures from which they originate often find balance and knowledge in the struggle and space of ambiguity that he embodies. This acceptance of ambiguity is interesting and useful for thinking of multivocality in archaeology.

The acceptance of multiplicity is not only seen in Ojibwe cultural heroes, but is found throughout the Ojibwe worldview. There is an understanding that multiple and conflicting interpretations are acceptable and need not be worrisome. Multivocality is expected, and stems from the standpoint or perspective of the viewer, teller, or one who experiences. When using an Ojibwe worldview in thinking about the past, one doesn't need to choose the best or correct interpretation, as knowledge about the past is more closely related to the concept of *understandings* that stem from perspective.

Peter Nabokov (2002) emphasizes the importance of a diversity of interpretation and multivocality in American Indian concepts of history among many North American groups. In the case of the Ojibwe, this concept is echoed in the orator's quote from the beginning of this chapter, and it is present in other aspects of Ojibwe daily life as well. Nabokov illustrates the ways in which multiple accounts of Indian pasts from a range of tellers are the norm. He states:

> By identifying the multiple, often quarreling interest groups within any society, and by making each of their claims the measure of any given history's intended relevance or "scale"…, we arrive at oral tradition's defining benefit and unending pleasure: multiple versions (2002:47).

Nabokov relates the experiences of Luci Tapahonso, a Navajo oral historian, who explains that Navajo oral histories often begin with words such as "the way I heard it was…" Tapahonso explains that one variation of a tribal history might *privilege* a certain group's role in an account, but it does not discount other versions. She states that it, "adds to the body of knowledge being exchanged" to "enrich the listener's experience" (Nabokov 2002:47–48).

Multivocality: Beyond a Seat at the Interpretive Table

While there are similarities between Western and Indigenous concepts of multiplicity, there are also differences. When multivocality is brought within the sphere of research, particularly archaeological research, Indigenous experiences and perspectives have the potential to enrich the way multivocality is currently practiced within a Western tradition – particularly with respect to collaboration in all aspects of research, identifying the dangers of multivocality, and pointing to the importance of public education about multiple perspectives.

In an effort to decolonize research and indigenize the academy, Indigenous scholars (Tuhiwai-Smith, Mihesuah, Cavender Wilson) have called for research to be carried out in collaboration with Native communities to produce research that is viewed as relevant and useful to those communities. Collaboration with communities is an important component of my approach to Indigenous archaeology (Atalay 2006a), and one that is critical to the concept of multivocality. With the importance of collaborative and participatory research in mind, multivocality becomes important long before the interpretive process begins. It is also a critical component in all aspects of archaeological knowledge production and reproduction. Developing the research design, asking research questions, funding projects, sharing the knowledge that is created with a wider community (knowledge stewardship), and overall heritage management are all intimately tied to, and involve the concept of, multivocality.

Indigenous experience has brought to the foreground the need for local and descendent communities and other stakeholders to become involved through the use of a multivocal model not only at the interpretive stage, but also from the outset of research. Comprehensive multivocality in participatory research designs bring to bare important issues related to arguments of local versus national and global "world" heritage; who has rights and privilege to interpret the past; and the long term management of tangible and intangible heritage. Yet beyond this is the broader question of, "who has the right and privilege to carry out archaeological research, to excavate, to obtain funding, and to be involved in knowledge production and reproduction?" To adequately and ethically respond to such a question, multiplicity of approach becomes crucial at all levels of research, not only at the point of interpretation. It is with this point that Indigenous experience brings a much needed addition to the current postprocessual view of multivocality, which has concerned itself primarily with the multivocality of interpretation.

There are also ways in which multivocality can undermine marginal groups, and Indigenous experiences help to bring this critical point of consideration to the foreground. While Indigenous archaeology has tended to focus primarily on researching and incorporating alternative ways of producing and reproducing knowledge about the past, history, and heritage management, I find it is also critical to consider ways of ensuring that multiple (alternative) "ways of seeing" are viewed as valuable and legitimate. Is it enough for Indigenous people to have a seat at the multivocal table if all voices are considered equally valid and there is no concern for evaluating which interpretations are the strongest, supported by evidence, and appropriately fit the data? If we rely on multivocality to mean that all voices are equally valid, then doesn't multivocality, in some ways, constitute a loss of power for Indigenous (and other "marginal") groups, who no longer have any claim to truth or greater legitimacy? Wylie (2002:190) discusses a similar point in relation to feminist critiques of science. She refers to the work of Lather (1991) and Mascia-Lees et al. (1989), who each in different ways point out that aspects of postmodernism (including multivocality) may be "dangerous for the marginalized" (Lather 1991:154). Along the same line of argumentation, Mascia-Lees et al. (1989:14–15) state that, "In the postmodern period, theorists "stave-off" their anxiety by questioning the basis of the truths that they are losing the privilege to define." In the same paper, Mascia-Lees et al. point to other feminist scholars, such as political scientist Nancy Hartsock (1987) and Sarah Lennox (1987), who make similar points. They summarize this aspect of Hartsock's (1987) work stating, "…she [Nancy Hartsock] finds it curious that the postmodern claim that verbal constructs do not correspond in a direct way to reality has arisen precisely when women and non-Western peoples have begun to speak for themselves and, indeed, to speak about global systems of power differentials." Mascia-Lees et al. (1989:15) highlight a similar point raised by Sarah Lennox (1987), summarizing Lennox as follows: "…postmodern despair associated with the recognition that truth is never entirely knowable is merely an inversion of Western arrogance. When Western white males – who traditionally have controlled the production of knowledge – can no longer define truth, she argues, their response is to conclude that there is not a truth to be discovered." So while Indigenous views of the past often include aspects of multivocality that in traditional practice have no conflict with concepts of plurality, it is also critical to be cognizant of and bring to the foreground the ways in which multivocality, when placed in the proper historical context with Western modernism and postmodernism, can be harmful or detrimental to Indigenous views and interpretations in the ways outlined by feminist scholars above.

Furthermore, there is the question of public understanding and acceptance of multivocality. In traditional Indigenous contexts, where entire communities subscribed to concepts of multivocality with reference to understanding and interpreting the past, the concern for refuting dominant, often hegemonic, interpretations did not hold relevance. However, when placed in the current context in which the majority of public audiences have been taught to accept a univocal view and have most often not been trained to evaluate multiple arguments, it becomes critical to question the impact that multivocality holds for public audiences. If the same (Western) voices, interpretations, and worldviews continue to be perceived as true or legitimate, then there is little effectiveness in a multivocal approach as alternative voices are in danger of being seen as quaint or superfluous. Unless we do more to educate the general public, particularly children, about the value and importance of multivocality, then it will remain either nearly impossible to gain legitimacy for views and approaches that are not mainstream, or pointless to put these interpretations forward since they will not carry authority for a public that is searching for univocal answers. It is no longer enough for Native people or any other disenfranchised group to simply have a place at the table when interpretation takes place.

A more comprehensive approach is needed that includes all aspects of research and involves changing the mindset of people on a much broader scale as to what is expected from archaeological knowledge production.

In terms of reaching the public, teaching a tolerance for ambiguity and multivocality is as critical as researching and implementing a multiplicity of approaches. Public archaeology thus plays a central role in any pursuit of multivocality as it becomes our responsibility as archaeologists concerned with multivocality not to teach what the *right* interpretation is, but rather to help people understand that many interpretations are potentially valid, and that it is our cultural worldview that determines how we evaluate, and what we respect and choose as valid. It is the tolerance of multiplicity in practice that becomes important. Such pursuits of educating the public can occur on many levels, but would most effectively involve advocacy on the part of archaeologists at the K-12 educational level. Finding the most productive strategies for doing this at the local and national level, on school boards and through local classroom visits, is one of my ongoing research projects and something I hope to present and publish in the near future.

Since starting research in the area of Indigenous archaeology, I've been asked by both Native community people and archaeologists if Indigenous archaeology refers to archaeology carried out by only Indigenous people. In presenting Indigenous archaeology concepts I've been called "colonialist" and accused of trying to replace the current Western approach to archaeology with an Indigenous one. With a concern for implementing multivocality in mind, these become critical points for consideration. The replacement of one power structure with another without changing the way power is perceived and enacted is pointless. Similarly, offering a seat at the interpretive table in the absence of true appreciation and respect for other worldviews can become an empty, even dangerous gesture if it removes the concern for evaluating arguments and fitting data with interpretation. Of course the question then becomes: who decides which data and evaluation techniques are legitimate? These are the issues that must be further considered and grappled with, and will only be worked out through further multivocal dialogue. They will not be solved simply by replacing one power structure with another; they will involve multivocality far before the point of interpretation, and they are most likely to build on a newfound strength through a combined or blended approach of Western and Indigenous forms of knowledge.

Diba Jimooyoung: Telling our Story

This chapter was originally written as a theoretical piece examining the role of multivocality in Indigenous archaeology. However, as this edited volume focuses on case studies that examine multivocality in a particular setting, I'm including an example of multivocality in practice within an Indigenous context to illustrate some of the points introduced above. The Ziibiwing Cultural Center of the Saginaw Chippewa Indians of Michigan developed and curated an exhibition that beautifully illustrates the points made in this chapter quite clearly. The permanent display at the Ziibiwing Cultural Center is called *Diba Jimooyoung: Telling Our Story*. The building of the cultural center and the development of the *Diba Jimooyoung* exhibit were part of the collaborative efforts by Native people of one tribal community (the Saginaw Chippewa [Ojibwe] of Michigan). The exhibit tells the history of this community from the distant past to contemporary life. The physical space of the museum is organized around Ojibwe cosmological principles – clockwise, as the Earth turns, as the Earth turns around the Sun, and as the Moon turns around the Earth. As you enter the museum you physically follow the Ojibwe path of the universe. The museum is bilingual (Anishinabemowin and English) and as you proceed through the displays you hear discussions and presentations in Anishinabemowin and then in English. All text panels are also multilingual. The opening display is a life size replica of the Sanilac Petroglyphs of Michigan, a rock art site in the tribe's traditional territory that has several hundred engraved petroglyphs (Fig. 3.1). This rock art site is managed by DNR but is now co-managed by the tribe. Tribal historians, spiritual and community leaders, and elders were brought out to the site to interpret the carvings. The tribe utilizes the site on a regular basis to give spiritual teachings and for ceremonial events.

Of the several hundred carvings on the Sanilac Petroglyphs, several were chosen by the community collaborative team for depiction and interpretation in the *Diba Jimooyoung* exhibit. One carving chosen was that of a spiral (Fig. 3.2). The text panel next to the spiral reads: "...touch this to connect with the teaching."

Fig. 3.1 Replica of the Sanilac petroglyphs of Michigan displayed in the *Diba Jimooyoung* permanent exhibit at the Ziibiwing Cultural Center

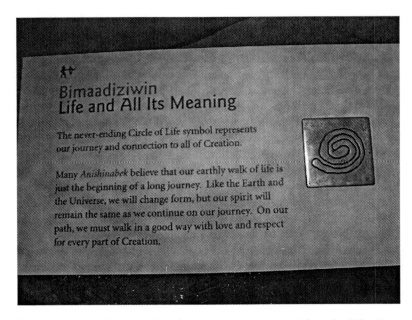

Fig. 3.2 Replica of spiral petroglyph and accompanying text panel from the *Diba Jimooyoung* permanent exhibit at the Ziibiwing Cultural Center

The panel also presents the interpretation of the spiral, stating that it describes the connection of the past to the present and our ongoing connection with all living beings. One important point of this spiral is its representation of the past coming alive in us in the present. Another image featured on the Sanilac replica, as well as in a text panel, is that of an archer (Fig. 3.3). The interpretation of this petroglyph is that our Ojibwe ancestors placed the rock art images for us to find in the future, during a time when we need their wisdom and teachings. The teachings from these petroglyphs are being shot by the archer into the future.

The Sanilac replica is not only teaching spiritual lessons, but also combines these with archaeologically based information about how the petroglyphs were made – displaying both males and females making petroglyphs. This technique of combining archaeological data with important cultural information is repeated throughout the exhibit. These views are combined together so that the visitor (both Ojibwe community members and non-Native visitors) learns about Ojibwe history, culture, worldview and spirituality from an Ojibwe perspective. Through this process, Ojibwe perspectives are made more accessible to those who don't view the world through this set of beliefs and practices. Ojibwe worldviews and beliefs are priviledged, but are constantly combined with western science and concepts of time and space to help reach and educate the viewer. There are also constant reminders of the important role of multivocality in the Ojibwe worldview, as well as reminders that Western knowledge systems are not natural or exclusively correct.

These presentations of the Ojibwe view of multivocality are most clearly displayed in the section following the Sanilac replica, in the section called "Our Creation." As

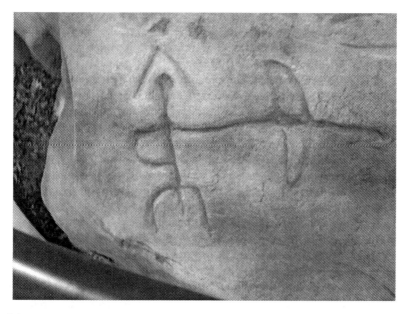

Fig. 3.3 Replica of archer petroglyph from the *Diba Jimooyoung* permanent exhibit at the Ziibiwing Cultural Center

Fig. 3.4 Banner marking entrance to the "Our Creation" section of the *Diba Jimooyoung* permanent exhibit at the Ziibiwing Cultural Center

you enter this section the first thing you see is a large banner hanging above the exhibit. You must pass under this banner to enter the remainder of the *Diba Jimooyoung* displays. On the center of the banner is the Sanilac spiral, which the visitor learned about in the previous display, and the words (in both Anishinabemowin and English): "All Creation Stories are True" (Fig. 3.4). The visitor then passes into the Our Creation display where the Ojibwe creation story is presented briefly. It describes our creation story in a panel and has several rattle-shakers on display that relate to the creation story. These are described using labels with information on dates and the artist's name clearly presented, but are brought into a worldview that is distinctly Ojibwe through the telling of the story using a speaker's voice from an overhead voice box. Visitors may also visit the "Creation Theatre," a small domed movie theatre that presents a more-detailed version of the creation story with different emphasis by a different speaker.

I've highlighted here some of the primary examples of the multivocality present throughout the Diba Jimooyoung exhibit. The museum provides an alternative interpretation to the standard one found in most natural history museums that present a Western view of the Ojibwe based on archaeological materials. However, an important component of the displays is to illustrate that the Anishinaabe version of our own history is not at complete odds with the archaeological version. In fact, there is complementarity between them that is presented quite effectively in the exhibit. In each of the displays that follow, including a diorama depicting seasonal activities; Ojibwe countings of time and season; the seven Ojibwe prophesies and spirituality more broadly; boarding schools; treaties; and even the importance of NAGPRA, stories are told from a distinctly Ojibwe perspective. In many cases these are combined with archaeological data and are presented by men, women, and children – many of whom mention the ambiguity and multiplicity of beliefs among Ojibwe people.

As the visitor exits the *Diba Jimooyoung* exhibit, she leaves through the same door from which she entered, and is again presented with the same Sanilac Petroglyph replica. Of course, having moved through the exhibit and learning of Ojibwe history, the meaning of this display is much different for the viewer, and the panel describing the Sanilac replica at the exit points this out explicitly. It reminds the visitor that Ojibwe people valued this sacred place in the past and used it to send messages to contemporary Ojibwe people in the present. The spiral petroglyph symbolizes the connection of past to present, and the petroglyph site is itself a way of connecting the past to the present. Through text, symbol, voice, and physical experiences of the body, as it is guided through the displays, the Diba Jimooyoung exhibit manages to effectively give a site and the objects and symbols associated with it renewed and multiple meanings for the viewer.

In these and many ways not highlighted in this brief example, the museum illustrates the points I've tried to make throughout this chapter about Anishinaabe views of multivocality and epistemological views on history, heritage, and the past. The Anishinaabe acceptance and expectation of multivocality are present throughout the displays in the Ziibiwing Cultural Center's museum. It is this embracing of multivocality that gives the museum strength. It is also these same views that I see as being present in the concepts of Indigenous Archaeology.

Conclusion

What I've attempted to do in this chapter, in postcolonial terms, is to point out the need to *de-center* mainstream archaeological practices, and place at the center, at least momentarily, Ojibwe concepts of multivocality in producing and reproducing knowledge of the past *for* people living in present Indigenous and local communities.

I argue here that Indigenous archaeology approaches need not be nationalist, colonialist, or imperialist in nature. They fall into a category that Trigger (1984) didn't discuss in his 1984 paper, a category that many, including myself, couldn't even envision at the time – they are part of a *decolonizing* archaeology. Decolonizing archaeology does not mean discounting science or Western epistemologies, such as multivocality. It means struggling to build bridges and develop tools to build a more tolerant society that allows different epistemologies to exist and play a role.

Indigenous experiences call for the need to develop collaborative methods for archaeological research and find ways to put multivocality into practice – not only in interpretation, but through community developed research projects that include culturally sensitive methods of education.

Knowledge of the past can be utilized in a variety of ways – producing and reproducing history can be an act of resistance, a reworking of the master narrative of the past, and/or something that informs us on the image that a community (or certain members of it) has of itself through emphasis on certain aspects of the historical narrative. In these ways, Indigenous archaeological practices find no conflict with the concept of multivocality. I would argue, in fact, that Indigenous archaeology is, by its very nature, multivocal and at once decolonizing and democratizing of archaeological knowledge in its collaboration with local people. These are illustrations of the ways in which the leaves of many trees can best be appreciated to build a rich forest of knowledge about the past, in any part of the world, in all time periods, and by archaeologists who are as diverse as the pasts that they hope to explore.

Note

[1] Anishinaabe, which means *original person*, is formed of an alliance of three related groups: Ojibwe, Ottawa, and Potawatomi. Anishinaabe people refer to this alliance as the "Three Fires." The people of the Three Fires speak a related language (Anishinabemowin) and had common cultural and kin ties.

References

Atalay, S. (2006a). Indigenous archaeology as decolonizing practice. *American Indian Quarterly*, 30(3), 280–310.

Atalay, S. (2006b). No sense of the struggle: creating a context for *survivance* at the National Museum of the American Indian. *American Indian Quarterly*, 30(4), 597–618.

Atalay, S. (2008). Pedagogy of decolonization: advancing archaeological practice through education. In S. Silliman (Ed.), *Collaborative Indigenous Archaeology at the Trowel's Edge: Exploring Methodology and Education in North American Archaeology*. Tucson: University of Arizona Press and the Amerind Foundation (in press).

Cavender-Wilson, A. (2004). Reclaiming Our Humanity: Decolonization and the Recovery of Indigenous Knowledge. In D. A. Mihesuah & A. C. Wilson (Eds.), *Indigenizing the Academy: Transforming Scholarship and Empowering Communities* (pp. 69–87). Lincoln: University of Nebraska Press.

Delage, D., Tanner, H. H., & Chazelle, P. (1994). The Ojibwa-Jesuit Debate at Walpole Island, 1844. *Ethnohistory*, 41(2), 295–321.

Gates, Jr., H.L. (1998). Interview with Henry Louis Gates, Jr. *Progressive*, 62(1), 30.

Hartsock, N. (1987). Rethinking Modernism. *Cultural Critique*, 7, 187–206.

Hodder, I. (1999). *The Archaeological Process: An Introduction*. Malden: Blackwell Publishers.

Lather, P. (1991). Deconstructing/deconstructive inquiry: The politics of knowing and being known. *Education Theory*, 41, 153–173.

Lennox, S. (1987). Anthropology and the politics of deconstruction. Paper presented at the 9th Annual Conference of the National Women's Studies Association, Atlanta, GA, June.

Lorde, A. (1984). *Sister Outsider: Essays and Speeches*. Trumansburg: Crossing Press.

Mascia-Lees, F. E., Sharpe, P., & Cohen, C. B. (1989). The postmodernist turn in anthropology: cautions from a feminist perspective. *Signs*, 15, 7–33.

Nabokov, P. (2002). *A Forest of Time: American Indian Ways of History*. Cambridge: Cambridge University Press.

Trigger, B. G. (1984). Alternative archaeologies: nationalist, colonialist, imperialist. *Man*, 19(3), 355–370.

Wylie, A. (2002). *Thinking from Things: Essays in the Philosophy of Archaeology*. Berkeley: University of California Press.

Chapter 4
Making a Home: Archaeologies of the Medieval English Village

Matthew H. Johnson

Introduction

This paper discusses how we might evaluate different narratives of the English landscape (Fig. 4.1). Although such archaeology is characteristically presented in an atheoretical and particularistic way, it is, of course, embedded in a discourse of Englishness; so British colonial archaeology on the one hand and the W. G. Hoskins and O. G. S. Crawford tradition of local empirical studies are both key discourses, even if they rarely cross-reference each other. I will therefore look at how recent postcolonial views of landscape might help us critically evaluate different traditions (including the tradition of local empirical studies) with respect to a particular archaeological problem – the creation of the medieval English village.

The last 20 years or so have seen an explosion in explicit discussions of English and British national identity. These discussions have taken place across a wide spectrum. They range from a general level of popular accounts of cultural identity by journalists, cultural commentators, and others (Ackroyd 2002; Bassnett 1997; Dimbleby 2005; Paxman 1999; Strong 1999), through to the more specific and academic level of the archaeology and political and cultural history of "the English" or "the British" (a few of many examples are Colley 1992; Johnson 2003; Miles 2003; Pryor 2003). The specific viewpoints taken by this literature to the question of Englishness and Britishness vary, from the celebratory, essentialist and (in most cases) banal, to the explicitly theoretical, multicultural, and reflexive.

However, what is not in doubt is the explosion in overt discussion of English and Britishness. This explosion is all the more remarkable in that it can be argued to be a new development in the style and tone of national cultural discourse. It should be stressed that Englishness has habitually been a set of values that, traditionally, was implicit and inflected rather than overtly stated. As such, it stands in some contrast to the (perhaps superficially) more overt and strident nationalist discourses of other nation-states whose relationship to archaeology Bruce Trigger has done so much to elucidate. I have discussed elsewhere Stephan Collini's characterization of this implicit and inflected nature, exploring the implications for academic discourse of his characterization of national discourse as one of "muffling inclusiveness" (Collini 1991; Johnson 2003).

J. Habu, C. Fawcett, and J. M. Matsunaga (eds.), *Evaluating Multiple Narratives: Beyond Nationalist, Colonialist, Imperialist Archaeologies.*
© Springer 2008

Fig. 4.1 The English landscape: part of the village of Selborne and the Hampshire/Sussex countryside beyond, looking east from the summit of Selborne Hanger

These discussions of national identity were referenced in graphic and visual form in a recent policy document produced by English Heritage, entitled *Power of Place*. English Heritage is the organization responsible for the conservation and understanding of the "historic environment" in England (it has counterparts in Historic Scotland and, for Wales, Cadw). It is sponsored by and advises the government; its duties are defined by government legislation. *Power of Place* attempted to lay down guidelines and recommendations for the "historic environment" over the next 10 years. In doing so, it was informed by a commissioned survey of attitudes of English people towards "heritage," and in its turn has seen many of its recommendations fed into subsequent Government legislation. More broadly, the context of *Power of Place* was the challenge of the mobilization of cultural capital with reference to perceived political need: in other words, of understanding and enhancing the role of the historic environment with reference to the changing social and political imperatives of modern England.

In the first years of the twenty-first century, these imperatives are explicitly ones of social inclusion, diversity, and of the potentials and issues of a multicultural society. As such, then, they might be held to directly address the questions of multivocality raised by this volume. The most obvious influence of these new imperatives on *Power of Place* was in the choice of pictures, in particular the front and back cover. The front cover was a lively, bustling street scene from a market in Brixton in south London – clearly chosen to convey an urban and "multicultural" feel.

The back cover, on the other hand, was taken not from street level but from the air, and gave a view of a traditional English village, with the classic features of church, village green, pub, and houses. My concern in this paper is to look more closely at this back cover, and what it means or might be held to mean.

The Making of the English Village

In many ways, the topic of the English village provides an interesting reverse case for the concerns of this volume in exploring issues of multivocality. The academic study of the English village remains anything but multivocal: a brief scan of the pages of the *Journal of the Medieval Settlement Research Group* or of *Medieval Archaeology* reveals an area of the discipline that remains insistently traditional, empiricist, and univocal, in contrast to, for example, the study of contemporary settlement in other areas of the world such as the former British and other European colonies, and in contrast also to British prehistory (see Johnson 2007 for a wider discussion of this point). In theoretical terms, the underlying assumptions of historic rural settlement remain at a culture-historical phase in terms of their underlying theory, with only hesitant attempts at, for example, quantification and understanding of variability in the sense proposed by the New Archaeology (Roberts & Wrathmell 2000, 2002 are landmark publications in this respect). The starting point for this discussion, then, is the question: why is the English village an area of archaeological enquiry which has been almost untouched by issues of multivocality and multiple narratives?

The scholarly study of the English village as a legal entity, with the customary practices and relations between tenant and landlord that lay behind them, goes back to the Victorian period, and finds its context in an emergent practice of documentary history that itself must be understood contextually within nineteenth century political concerns. These concerns were inevitably implicated in a nationalist and progressive view of history. Writers such as the legal historian Maitland wrote within a late nineteenth century consciousness of the village and associated elements on the legal and economic landscape – the "township," the "manor" – as one of the constituent elements of national identity.

The origins of the English village were dated by Victorian scholars to the Anglo-Saxon period, after the fall of the Roman Empire but before the Norman Conquest. As such, it also fell into place in a progressive view of history, as one of the key elements in a legal definition of the social order defined by historians as "feudalism." The focus of documentary historians was thus on often legalistic discussions of the relations between landlord and peasant, and between villagers. It was this ongoing discussion that Marx drew on in his characterization of feudalism as a stage in human history, though historians such as Maitland and others in no way saw themselves as Marxists (Maitland 1897; for discussion of this context see Austin 1990).

However, the archaeological study of the medieval origins of the village took off much later. It was bound up, historically, with a discourse of Englishness that emerged after the Second World War and in particular in the 1950s. Two books serve as a landmark in this development, O. G. S. Crawford's *Archaeology in the Field* (1953) and the historian W. G. Hoskins' *The Making of the English Landscape* (1955). Crawford is more famous in conventional histories of archaeology for his efforts as a prehistorian, but he laid down a method for the understanding of the rural landscape which, I would argue, survives unamended today in many field and interpretive methods and their underlying theory, and which forms part of the often unspoken research culture of both professionals and amateurs. He discussed the combination of the evidence of early maps, other documentary sources, fieldwalking, field observation, and air photographs. For Crawford, the field archaeologist assembled this material painstakingly acquired "by book and by foot," with excavation forming only a small part of such an ensemble of techniques: the whole he gave a national association by calling it "a modern, and primarily a British invention" (Crawford 1952:52–53). The analogy Crawford used was that of the landscape as palimpsest, or ancient document written and written over again; the task of the archaeologist was to recover the imperfectly erased traces of earlier scripts on that palimpsest.

Hoskins popularized the methods outlined by Crawford and others, and related them to a powerful story which he told in passionate and emotive terms. His most famous book *The Making of the English Landscape* became a bestseller and did more than any other book before or since to communicate a consciousness and appreciation of the English historic landscape to a popular as well as academic audience (its impact is discussed by, amongst others, Thirsk 2000 and Muir 1998).

For Hoskins, the English landscape was much older than hitherto appreciated. Following Maitland and the succeeding orthodoxy of the period, he saw the creation of the village in implicitly racial/ethnic terms as an Anglo-Saxon phenomenon. That is, he assumed that it was brought to eastern and central Britain by Anglian and Saxon settlers from Germany and Denmark in the centuries following the breakup of the Roman Empire after AD 400. Hoskins speaks in memorable terms of Germanic settlers "making a home" (1955:30) in what he sees as the uncleared, primordial forests of central and eastern England. Hoskins' vision of the English landscape was explicitly Romantic, nostalgic and celebratory: *The Making of the English Landscape* implicitly traces a curve in its narrative with only brief discussion of prehistoric and Roman landscapes, concentration on the medieval foundation and early modern transformation of villages, rounded off by a denunciation of industrialization. He was disgusted by modernity, only reluctantly admitting, for example, that Victorian railway embankments made excellent viewing platforms for the landscape: "true that the railway did not invent much of this beauty, but it gave us new vistas of it" (1955:206).

Culture and Nationalism in the 1950s

Hoskins' vision was articulated within a pattern of English nationalism that was characteristic of the post-war period, and which continues to exert an exceptionally powerful influence over intellectual and popular patterns of thinking today (Sinfield

1989, 2000, for example, discusses its grip on 1950s culture, and Easthope 1999 traces its continuing influence as a hegemonic discourse today). This national pattern can be characterized in four ways.

First, it was overtly populist and in many cases socialist. Hoskins and his contemporaries taught working men's and extra-mural groups across the country; the intellectual thrust and style of *The Making of the English Landscape*, with its clear and direct prose and Romantic allusions, came in part from a strong ethic of and commitment to education for all. Hoskins was a Liberal politically, but he came from a relatively humble social background, and professed to loathe both the English class system and what he called "the stinking Tories and their Affluent Society" (private letter, 1963, cited in Millward 1992:68). Many of the early researchers of deserted medieval villages, most obviously Maurice Beresford and John Hurst, were part of the great upswell in socialist conviction expressed via the election and subsequent reforms made by the 1945–1951 Labour Government, and their research was part of a desire to rediscover and understand the material conditions of the lives of medieval peasants (Gerrard 2003:103–105). Such a "radical" discourse was largely articulated in terms of class, often pushing gender and racial/ethnic issues into the background.

Second, it was backward-looking. David Matless (1998) has shown how different twentieth century visions of the English landscape, though they varied in their specific premises one from another, found their place within a discourse that was resolutely anti-modernist and conservationist in tone. For Matless, these discourses of an "organic England" stood (and continue to stand) in opposition to modernist and reformist currents in political and cultural life. Hoskins shared such an analysis (most famously in the concluding passages of *The Making of the English Landscape* where politicians, bureaucrats and modernizers of every hue are berated), but at least overtly denied anything could be done about it, proclaiming in characteristically grumpy fashion that all one could do was turn away from the present and contemplate the past "before all is lost to the vandals."

Third, it was discursively and emotionally rooted in the rural landscape, and in particular in a particular vision of the English village. From Wordsworth onwards, and before then the Renaissance translation of Classical ideas of the rural retreat into vernacular discourse, ideas of Englishness have been located in the countryside, to the extent that World War II propaganda posters only had to evoke an image of the rolling fields of the Sussex Downs for their message to be self-explanatory; the caption read: "Your Britain – Fight For It Now!" (Dimbleby 2005:58). In such a scenic nationalism, the essence of Englishness was and continues to be rooted not in an overt political ideology, but in an aesthetics, an ineffable portrayal of a quintessential scene.

Fourth, and most fundamentally for the purposes of this paper, this was a vision of a landscape of ancestors and forebears. Hoskins' England was a country of his ancestors. He writes of his discovery that "my great-great-grandfather Richard Thorn," traced his ancestry in turn to "Robert Atte Thorne in 1332" and back beyond this to "the first moorland peasant who broke up the ground around the solitary thorn-tree, perhaps in the closing years of the twelfth century or the first years of the thirteenth century. First the ancient tree gave its name to the farm, then the farm gave its name to the owners;

and still there are Thorns in Chagford ... These things delight me when I come across them. This is the immemorial, provincial England, stable, rooted deep in the soil, unmoving, contented, and sane. These are my forebears, who have made me what I am whether I like it or not" (Hoskins 1954:xx). Hence his lack of interest in prehistory – in *The Making of the English Landscape*, for example, his prose sparks up when he comes to the Anglo-Saxons. In *Devon* (Hoskins 1954), a study and gazetteer of the county in western England which he refers to as the home county of his forefathers, prehistory was discussed as a cold, mysterious place, where it was impossible to feel any kind of emotional link – and hence, Hoskins implies, any interest in or understanding of the prehistoric past.

Ancestral Villages

In many ways, the above account of English landscape archaeology is a photo-negative of the arenas in which multivocality has traditionally been played out: it remains insistently univocal, a single hegemonic discourse if you will, right up to the present. As I was revising the final draft of this paper, a publicity flyer arrived on my desk announcing a new series of books co-sponsored by English Heritage: "ENGLAND'S LANDSCAPE. A series of eight books offering a new and authoritative view of *the* evolution of *the* landscape of England" (italics added). This univocality works in several senses.

The village is part of the life of "our ancestors." The question of who "we" are is taken for granted, as part of the muted, inflected nature of English nationalism – in many ways, the word "we" is the most obscure and jargon-laden piece of intellectual fuzziness in the English language; or to put it in a slightly different way, it is a two-letter piece of ideology. Hoskins and his contemporaries were not consciously racist; indeed, Hoskins goes out of his way to condemn jingoistic nationalism on several occasions in his writing (for example, Hoskins 1960:131). However, they were part of a contemporary mental climate in which a common "English" culture was assumed. Hoskins' guidebooks to individual counties, most obviously *Devon* (which some consider to be his greatest book), are clearly written with a specific audience in mind – the middle-class traveler from another part of England, in many cases seeking "refreshment" from cosmopolitan life. Postcolonial critics, in particular Paul Gilroy, Stuart Hall, and others in Black British studies, have talked of this post-war understanding of Britishness as "assimilationist": anyone, regardless of gender or skin color, is welcome to assimilate into this core set of values and assumptions about what national culture is (Gilroy 1987; Sinfield 1989, 2000).

This assumption of a single culture in which the English village is a symbol of ancestry went along with parallel projects in twentieth century cultural and literary life, about which much has been written. Two obvious examples are John Betjeman and J. R. R. Tolkein. Betjeman combined the careers of poet and architectural critic, and was made the official Poet Laureate; his poems are much more than an uncritical celebration of the English countryside, but they take that celebration as their base-line nevertheless (Matless 1998). Tolkein's explicit purpose in *The Hobbit* and *The Lord of the Rings* was to write an origin myth for the English (White 2001; the selection of the New Zealand landscape for the recent films could thus be viewed as the ultimate colonialist appropriation of landscape).

Evaluating Alternative Interpretations

Much of the anxiety about multivocality in archaeology has stemmed I think from a desire to avoid a slippage into a disabling relativism. As Bruce Trigger has insisted, archaeologists need to be able to evaluate different accounts of the past even if a diversity of indigenous and other perspectives is acknowledged and even celebrated. In that spirit, I will now look at how and why research has changed our Hoskins-derived view of the village landscape, and which elements have remained inviolate.

Where major changes in the model have been proposed, they have occurred in prehistory. Hoskins' model of Anglo-Saxons making a home by cutting through the primeval forest surviving from prehistoric times has been revised. Decades of work on the landscape after 1955 have shown extensive remains of prehistoric landscapes (this shift in perspective is summarized in Aston 1983 and exemplified by Fleming 1988). Interestingly for the purposes of this paper, then, the model has shown itself to be open to critical evaluation, to be responsive to evidential constraints, at precisely the point where for many it has a lesser social/political meaning. English nationalism takes as its reference points the historic development of the landscape from the Anglo-Saxon period onwards; it is difficult to argue that Neolithic and other prehistoric landscapes hold the same emotional and popular power.

At the same time as the chronology of landscape clearance has been revised, so has our understanding of the mechanics of the making of the English village. The Wharram project, which arose from the desire to study the archaeology of the medieval village and subsequently ran for over 40 years, studied a single English village, Wharram Percy on the Yorkshire Wolds. Wharram showed that, first, many features in the village landscape are prehistoric in origin – the medieval village did not sweep all before it, but rather was laid out within the interstices of linear boundaries of prehistoric and Roman origin; second, that the village itself was not an organic creation of early Anglo-Saxon date, but rather appears to be a planned episode of much later (though still uncertain) date – an apparently deliberate creation from several earlier foci rather than growth from around the village church; and third, that the Monty Pythonesque interpretation of peasant houses as flimsy, filthy hovels rebuilt every generation has to be questioned. The old view of the village as an importation of Anglo-Saxon migrants has been abandoned.

However, I would argue that all these revisions have taken place within the framework of the Hoskins tradition rather than confronting the tradition itself. I draw here from Kathleen Biddick's (1993:23) discussion of Hoskins' primeval forests, in which she asks: "to what voice, to what gaze, to what desire does this passage refer?" The context of Biddick's comment deserves a gloss. It serves as an epilogue to an essay which makes the point that most research has taken the framework of the English village for granted rather than questioning it. Thus, at Wharram, excavations took place within the toft and croft boundaries. But these boundaries were, of course, active creations, part of an early medieval social process that created the categories of peasant and lord, secular and religious, male and female. So, rather than investigating the process by which the physical structure of the English village created and enforced these categories, existing archaeological traditions of field practice reinforce the categories themselves as obvious, natural and taken for granted.

This failure to address the very processes of the creation of a material and social order has happened, I suggest, because of the construction of the English village as ancestral. Cultural anthropologists tell us that what is laid down by the ancestors is taken for granted, "natural," and that it lies beyond the bounds of critique. It is so familiar that it needs no explanation or justification. As a result, British prehistory, with a tenuous and questionable link to the present that can be argued but is controversial (Pryor 2003), is full of people doing interesting things in the landscape. It is a landscape full of ancestors, but the ancestors are constructed anthropologically, as having another culture. By contrast, in accounts of the English village, people just seem to eat, sleep, herd cattle, and harvest grain. These people, being "our ancestors" in a 1950s view of Englishness, were orthodox Christians, but religion was something that was done decently and quietly on Sundays, rather than infusing the landscape and way of life as a whole.

The Relevance of Multivocality

For a present generation, then, the relevance of multivocality is largely a potential one, yet to be applied. Characteristically for myths that stand close to the heart of English nationalism, dissenting voices are not denounced, but rather ignored and muted. Biddick (1993) merely poses the question rather than providing a sustained answer, but it is striking, and characteristic of national discourse, that her paper has been actively excluded from the "mainstream" literature; it was removed from a reader on medieval peasants at the insistence of a prominent though anonymous British medieval historian. Biddick has subsequently discussed how this experience led her to reflect on her "outsider" status as an archaeologist, a woman, and an American (Biddick 1998). Her experience was echoed by that of Paula Weideger, an American journalist who wrote a sharp critique of that most British of institutions, The National Trust, a charity that acts as guardian and custodian of many of the great houses and landscapes of England. Weideger found that her critique of the Trust, with which this author is largely in agreement though it is now a little dated, had been dismissed as the disrespectful rantings of a strident American before they had even been published (as discussed in the preface of her book: Weideger 1994). It is instructive to note that spokespeople for The National Trust do often appear more at ease citing traditional inheritance (even if unintentionally), perhaps at the expense of others. Fiona Reynolds, Director of The National Trust, for example, gave Hoskins' *The Making of the English Landscape* as her preferred book to take on a desert island (alongside the compulsory Shakespeare and Bible: www.bbc.co.uk/radio4/factual/desertislanddiscs_20020407.shtml). Her favorite recordings to take with her included a classic of English landscape appreciation – a spoken recording of Wordsworth's *Lines Composed Above Tintern Abbey*.

This lack of multivocality has led, I suggest, to a tangibly poorer and impoverished account of the historic landscape. Since the 1950s, landscape historians and archaeologists have labored harder and harder, but have become less and less confident in their ability to give a convincing account of landscape change and in their ability to explain and account for that change. In many ways, this loss of confidence can be likened to the "taphonomic retreat" in other areas of archaeology (Johnson 1997 develops this parallel). If theoretically much of the archaeology of the English village is still at the stage of "culture history," then the standard critique of the New Archaeology can be leveled at much of its output (Johnson 2007).

It is much more difficult to be positive rather than negative – to sketch out what archaeologies of the English village which are responsive to issues of multivocality might look like. One point that is worth making is that in many ways they would be very simple, very direct, and very close to the "bread-and-butter" evidence of the archaeological record. For example, we might ask about:

1. An exploration of the different patterns of movement around the village. What were the different daily routines and experiences of women, men, and children as they moved around the landscape of the village and the fields beyond?
2. A consideration of different ways of experiencing the landscape spiritually. Hitherto, peasants simply eat, sleep, procreate, and die – their spiritual life has been seen as the preserve of the religious historian.

One point that stands out is that these questions take us away from issues apparently important for ancestral reasons (was the village an Anglo-Saxon creation?) back towards the empirical strengths of archaeology. Archaeologists can only grapple tenuously with Maitland's definition of "manorialisation," but they can and do know exactly where peasants walked to and from the fields. Archaeologists' coarse-grained chronologies cannot date the replanning of Wharram to the period of the historically attested Danish invasions or later, but they can and do know about daily, weekly, and seasonal rhythms of activity – cyclical rather than linear time. Archaeologists have a limited grasp of the subtleties of Christian doctrinal debates, but they can and do know how the tolling of the church bell would have been heard in the fields, and where and how the bodies of medieval peasants were laid to rest at the end of their lives. In this way, then, a more anthropological and multivocal archaeology of the English village would actually dovetail with the traditional strengths of archaeological enquiry; they are certainly not an esoteric addition to it.

Conclusion

In proposing responses to some of the questions posed by the introduction to this volume (and by Bruce Trigger's work) I am arguing that we as archaeologists can contribute to a redefinition of Englishness and Britishness which attempts to be socially inclusive rather than assimilationist. More specifically, I hope to have demonstrated that archaeological thinking can take a lead in introducing multivocality to what many scholars would perceive as a stubbornly traditional area of study. The sociopolitics of the archaeology of the English village, in particular its place within a construction of English nationalism, have frequently acted to remove any possible discussion of multivocality from "mainstream" discourse. However, my argument is that multivocality is nevertheless highly relevant, in part because these alternative understandings contribute tangibly and effectively to the development of a more critical, more anthropologically aware, and more empirically rigorous, archaeology of the English village. By embracing multivocality the local and particular can become meaningful on a much larger scale.

Acknowledgments Many of these thoughts arose from the reaction to my keynote address to the Australian Archaeological Association in November 2003; the audience, many of whom came from a background dealing with issues of "indigenous archaeology," found the *Power of Place* images a source of fertile debate. I also thank the editors of this volume for inviting me to contribute, and Rebecca Johnson for comments on a first draft.

References

Ackroyd, P. (2002). *Albion: the Origins of the English Imagination*. London: Chatto and Windus.

Aston, M. (1983). The making of the English landscape – the next 25 years. *Local Historian* 15, 323–332.

Austin, D. (1990). The 'proper study' of medieval archaeology. In D. Austin & L. Alcock (Eds.), *From the Baltic to the Black Sea: Studies in Medieval Archaeology* (pp. 9–42). London: Unwin Hyman.

Bassnett, S. (Ed.) (1997). *Studying British Cultures*. London: Routledge.

Biddick, K. (1993). Decolonising the English past: readings in medieval archaeology and history. *Journal of British Studies* 32(1),1–24.

Biddick, K. (1998). *The Shock of Medievalism*. Durham: Duke University Press.

Colley, L. (1992). *Britons: Forging the Nation, 1707–1837*. New Haven: Yale University Press.

Collini, S. (1991). Genealogies of Englishness: literary history and cultural criticism in modern Britain. In C. Brady (Ed.), *Ideology and the Historians* (pp. 128–145). Dublin: Lilliput Press.

Crawford, O. G. S. (1953). *Archaeology in the Field*. London: Phoenix House.

Dimbleby, D. (2005). *A Picture of Britain*. London: Tate Publishing.

Easthope, A. (1999). *Englishness and National Culture*. London: Routledge.

Fleming, A. (1988). *The Dartmoor Reaves: Investigating Prehistoric Land Divisions*. London: Batsford.

Gerrard, C. M. (2003). *Medieval Archaeology: Understanding Traditions and Contemporary Approaches*. London: Routledge.

Gilroy, P. (1987). *"There Ain't No Black in the Union Jack": The Cultural Politics of Race and Nation*. London: Hutchinson.

Hoskins, W. G. (1954). *Devon*. London: Collins.

Hoskins, W. G. (1955). *The Making of the English Landscape*. London: Hodder & Stoughton.

Hoskins, W. G. (1960). *Two Thousand Years in Exeter: An Illustrated Social History of the Mother-City of South-Western England*. Exeter: Townsend.

Johnson, M. H. (2003). Muffling inclusiveness: notes towards an archaeology of the British. In S. Lawrence (Ed.), *The Archaeology of the British: Explorations of Identity in Great Britain and its Colonies 1600–1945* (pp. 17–30). London: Unwin Hyman.

Johnson, M. H. (2007). *Ideas of Landscape*. Oxford: Blackwell.

Maitland, F. W. (1897). *Domesday Book and Beyond: Three Essays in the Early History of England*. Cambridge: Cambridge University Press.

Matless, D. (1998). *Landscape and Englishness*. London: Reaktion.

Miles, D. (2003). *The Tribes of Britain*. London: English Heritage.

Millward, R. (1992). William George Hoskins, landscape historian (1908–1992). *Landscape History* 14, 65–70.

Muir, R. (1998). *Approaches to Landscape*. London: Macmillan.

Paxman, J. (1999). *The English: Portrait of a People*. London: Penguin.

Prior, F. (2003). *Britain BC: Life in Britain and Ireland before the Romans*. London: HarperCollins.

Roberts, B. K., & Wrathmell, S. (2000). *An Atlas of Rural Settlement in England*. London: English Heritage.

Roberts, B. K., & Wrathmell, S. (2002). *Region and Place: A Study of English Rural Settlement*. London: English Heritage.

Sinfield, A. (1989). *Literature, Politics and Culture in Post-War Britain*. Oxford: Blackwell.

Sinfield, A. (2000). *British Culture of the Postwar: An Introduction to Literature and Society*. London: Routledge.

Strong, R. (1999). *The Spirit of Britain: A Narrative History of the Arts*. London: Hutchinson.

Thirsk, J. (Ed.) (2000). *The English Rural Landscape*. Oxford: Oxford University Press.

Weideger, P. (1994). *Gilding the Acorn: A Critical History of The National Trust*. London: Simon & Schuster.

White, M. (2001). *Tolkein: A Biography*. London: Little, Brown.

Chapter 5
Critical Histories of Archaeological Practice: Latin American and North American Interpretations in a Honduran Context

Rosemary A. Joyce

The editors of this volume cite Bruce Trigger's "Alternative archaeologies" paper as the beginning point of a reconsideration of contemporary Anglo-American calls for increased multivocality in archaeology, situating multivocality as (potentially) yet another imperialist move on the part of a powerful global archaeological elite, and as (again, potentially) leading to an inability on the part of archaeologists to argue against problematic interpretations offered under the guise of "multivocality." As an advocate of multivocality in archaeology who also insists that we have a standpoint from which to critically examine alternative interpretations, I obviously would like to argue that such an approach has a powerful potential for local archaeological communities, and is not solely a product of the divisive identity politics of Anglo-American societies. But before even attempting to make such a claim for the country which provides my case study, Honduras, where I have worked continuously for 20 years, I think it is necessary to broaden the terms of debate further, to acknowledge other ways of conceiving of the history and sociopolitics of archaeology that have significant effects on shaping the reception of Anglo-American theoretical conceits. For Latin America, histories of nation-making following republican liberation from Spanish colonial power in the early nineteenth century already engaged the material remains of past peoples before Euro-American antiquarians entered the scene.

The South American scholar Augusto Oyuela-Caycedo (1994) suggests that the history of Latin American archaeology may be understood in terms of a sequence of development from "Proto-State" archaeology, to "State" and finally "National" archaeology. In his concept of Proto-State archaeology, the issues raised by archaeology are peripheral to government interests. Oyuela-Caycedo suggests there was diverse participation by individuals with different backgrounds and training, without local regulatory oversight and primarily as an elite activity. Local elites engaged in archaeology in the proto-states of Latin American sometimes employed explicit nationalist discourses about archaeology, but just as often did not. Oyuela-Caycedo links the growth of state regulatory agencies, formal training, and cultural resource inventories to his second, "State" phase, with development of state interests in archaeology. Depending on the timing of development, these state interests may be related to nation-building, or may concretize around the development of culture resources of global significance for economic ends. National archaeology, which in

J. Habu, C. Fawcett, and J. M. Matsunaga (eds.), *Evaluating Multiple Narratives:*
Beyond Nationalist, Colonialist, Imperialist Archaeologies.
© Springer 2008

Oyuela-Caycedo's view is as yet unrealized in Latin America, would see a diversification of national institutions beyond those of the state, fostering research, and dissemination of research results to a broader public, or publics, within individual countries.

Oyuela-Caycedo characterized Honduran archaeology in 1994 as being in his Proto-State stage. His description of the characteristics of this stage matches many features of the practice of archaeology in Honduras through World War II. However, legislation aimed at regulating archaeology in Honduras was passed as early as 1845, and in 1900 was strengthened sufficiently that it discouraged most foreign researchers for at least 20 years (Agurcia 1984). Elsewhere, I have suggested that Honduran archaeology from at least the 1950s through the 1990s better conforms to Oyuela-Caycedo's definition of State archaeology, in which international participation in archaeology dominates, but is legislatively controlled, while national archaeologists begin to emerge as participants at all stages and levels of research (Joyce & Henderson 2002). During this period, we can document Honduran-initiated calls for creation of alternative archaeological interpretations, today closely related to a developing conceptualization by Honduran intellectuals of their contemporary civil society as multicultural, and to calls by Honduran groups – both descendant communities and other localized factions – for greater control both of their own histories and of the means of production of those histories – including archaeological sites and materials.

A Brief History of Honduran Archaeology

To understand this argument, it would be helpful to briefly review the development of archaeology in the territory that today is Honduras. Honduras actually occupies a very visible position in most histories of archaeology in the Americas, as its iconic Classic Maya site, Copan, was a locale of transition from early exploration, through the work of museum-affiliated and independent antiquarians, to institutionalized academic research (Hinsley 1984, 1985; Willey & Sabloff 1974). In this canonical history, the move from the early speculations of John Lloyd Stephens (1841) to the extremely detailed historical and socioeconomic models of late twentieth century research on Copan epitomizes the development of a specifically Americanist archaeology, engaged in by practitioners located primarily in United States universities.

But there are other histories of Honduran archaeology, even at Copan, that can be explored. Oswaldo Chinchilla (1998) has recently demonstrated that the anglophone archaeological lineage of research at Copan beginning with John Lloyd Stephens was preceded in the early nineteenth century by a Guatemalan research project that crossed national borders in the Central American Republic in pursuit of a specifically local history. The Honduran historian Dario Euraque (1998), documenting the role of US archaeologists during the period of transition from museum- to university-based research, reminds us that there was an elite Honduran tradition of interest in a material past that was intimately bound up with, and in fact influenced the direction of, the projects of US archaeologists.

We can link even early stages of what later becomes a pervasive Maya-centrism in Honduran archaeology (Joyce 1993) to a denial of cultural variability as part of nineteenth century strategies of nation building (Euraque 1998; Joyce & Henderson 2002). The form this takes in early Honduran archaeology is the adoption of a diffu-sionist perspective in which Copan and Maya culture in Honduras was viewed as an extension of a foreign (Guatemalan-Mexican) culture, naturalizing and establishing a deep historical precedent for Honduras as a marginal place, receiver of civilizing influence. For recent decades, I would argue that world systems and other forms of core/periphery models, which relate Honduras to Mesoamerica as a dependent periphery, have perpetuated this perspective (Joyce & Henderson 2002).

In the nineteenth century, Copan, as the epitome of Maya writing, calendar sys-tems, and art, was a particularly potent symbol in the nationalist discourse Euraque (1998:87) calls "mayanization," in which

> the Honduran state began to encourage the creation of an official national identity. This had as a goal, among other things, to educate the public through official discourse about the indigenous past and its role in the historic evolution of the country. This discourse presumes the inevitable collapse of the "remains" of the indigenous civilizations, but also the rescue of the monumental "ruins" that remained, inert, throughout the territory of the country. Therefore, a first approximation of the notion of "mayanization" recognizes this process simply as an official emphasis on rescuing ruins as an ancestral legacy of a "nationality" constructing itself (my translation).

Euraque (1998:87, 89) notes that mayanization accomplished the erasure of the pres-ence of living indigenous groups, especially the large Lenca population of western Honduras. Simultaneously, new nationalist symbols drew explicitly on the Lenca past. The fundamental unit of Honduran currency was renamed the "lempira" during monetary reform in the 1920s, commemorating not a Maya, but a Lenca leader defeated during Spanish invasions in the sixteenth century. The interest groups that promoted Lempira over the Honduran hero of independence, Morazan, were tied to the multinational business community of the Honduran north coast (Euraque 1996a). As archaeology reemerged as a practice in the country between World War I and World War II, members of the business community of north coast Honduras were also significant brokers in the struggle for prestige between foreign institutions that drove the next phase of research in Honduras, providing logistical support, access to sites, and reports of sites and artifacts. The interests of these local Honduran actors – with roots in extra-national communities – sometimes promoted the discourse of mayanization, but just as often were promoting histories of multiple indigenous groups thought to have inhabited the north coast of Honduras prior to Spanish colo-nization, including the Lenca, "Jicaque" (now known as Torrupan or Tol), and Paya (Pech). That North American archaeologists reduced these diverse histories to a sin-gle Maya/non-Maya dichotomy placed them in the position of ignoring what in ret-rospect is clearly an intense interest in localized histories related to the sense of regional distinction that Euraque (1996a,b) documents.

North American institutions had begun to take an active role in archaeological research in Honduras by 1890, interrupted for 20 years by the reaction to the passage of stronger antiquities legislation in 1900 (Joyce & Henderson 2002). Archaeology was becoming professionalized elsewhere in Latin America at this time as well (Díaz-Andreu 1998; Oyuela-Caycedo 1994), but the trajectory of development in

Honduras was distinctive, especially in terms of the involvement of North American archaeologists and institutions. The role of Harvard's Peabody Museum in the early professionalization of Honduran archaeology has been well documented (Hinsley 1985; Joyce 2001b). An important effect of the affiliation of archaeologists with established North American institutions was that research materials were retained and could serve as a starting point for later projects, facilitating but in the process perpetuating an emphasis on work in select areas, and leading to a neglect of others. While there continued to be legislative control of archaeology in Honduras, there was no institutional center articulating Honduran interests in the country's past until the establishment of the Instituto Hondureño de Antropología e Historia (IHAH) (Honduran Institute of Anthropology and History) in 1952, based on legislation passed in 1946 (Joyce 2001a; Veliz 1983). From the beginning IHAH served to identify Honduran interests that were not necessarily shared by foreign archaeologists. Not coincidentally, the first research by a Honduran archaeologist was carried out at Copan at this time, by Jesús Nuñez Chinchilla, first head of IHAH, who also published discussions of the multiple indigenous groups in the country and reported on "non-Maya" materials around Copan.

Whether because of a disinclination to deal with new regulatory requirements, or for other reasons, foreign archaeological research in Honduras came to a halt after World War II and did not resume until the French Archaeological Mission undertook projects at several sites, not including Copan, in the late 1960s (Baudez 1966). This work culminated in the first full length study of a single archaeological site other than Copan: Los Naranjos, on Lake Yojoa at the southern end of the lower Ulua Valley (Baudez & Becquelin 1973). Claude Baudez, the principal archaeologist involved in these projects, had previously worked in Costa Rica, and brought to Honduran archaeology a perspective that included attention to relations with Lower Central America as well as Mesoamerica, and that did not limit interesting aspects of Honduran prehistory to those that connected with the Maya civilization that dominated North American researchers' attention.

In 1968, the IHAH was renewed when it was chartered as an autonomous institution. This legal status gave IHAH control over its personnel and facilities and effectively allowed it to function as an investigative unit for the first time. With the restructuring of IHAH, international researchers began to work again throughout the country. North Americans in this new wave of research were likely to be working directly for IHAH as staff members of projects intended to mitigate development impacts (e.g., Hasemann et al. 1982; Henderson 1984; Hirth et al. 1981). Other archaeological projects began as collaborations between foreign and Honduran archaeologists operating in new organizational structures that bridged government, and local and international nongovernmental sponsors (e.g., Hasemann et al. 1977; Lincoln 1979; Robinson et al. 1979; Sheehy 1976, 1978; Sheehy & Veliz 1977). Copan became the first Honduran site identified as a UNESCO World Heritage property, placing archaeologists, both national and international, in a position of responsibility to transnational interests (Joyce 2003a, 2005).

Honduran archaeology was wrenched from a descriptive project rooted in the culture historical paradigm of North American museums and universities prior to

World War II, to a global archaeology engaged with demands of cultural resource management, cultural tourism, and the rebuilding of national citizenship after a transition to constitutional democracy, under late twentieth century ideals of cultural pluralism recognizing the presence of descendants of multiple ethnic groups, both indigenous and nonindigenous. Simultaneously, the field of foreign practitioners in Honduran archaeology broadened dramatically, to include French, German, US, Mexican, Guatemalan, Australian, and Japanese archaeologists trained in extremely different approaches to archaeological research. This structural situation has created conditions for divergent interpretations of research by global and local archaeologists working together to meet regulatory mandates producing a clear example of multivocality, not as a consequence of an abstract theoretical engagement, but as an entailment of sociopolitical and intellectual hybridity.

Honduran Sites of Archaeological Interpretation

I will illustrate this contemporary situation of multivocality in Honduran archaeology by discussion of two sites where the meaning of archaeological materials has been under active negotiation by archaeologists and others who work from completely different understandings of what constitutes significance. As befits its role as icon of Honduran national identity, Copan is one of these sites. The second site is Cerro Palenque, where in the 1980s I conducted dissertation research amid active cow pasturage (Joyce 1991). In the 1990s, this site was identified as a prospect for development as a national park, leading the Honduran government to compensate the landowners for their use rights. Today, the park is about to be developed for the local public with funding from the World Bank. What makes these sites significant for our theme is that their development as world heritage and national monuments, and as parks intended for international, national, and local visitation, has been guided over the last decade by explicitly articulated concerns with multicultural national identity like those associated in the anglophone world with emphases on multivocality. They thus provide an excellent case study of how far multivocality and pluralism may be said to be attributes of Anglo-American disciplinary concerns, how they travel when they are concerns of national elites in a Latin American republic, and what they have to say about the question of the objectivity of archaeological interpretations.

Touring Copan

Copan was one of the earliest reported scientifically excavated Maya sites, explored during the mid- to late-nineteenth century. As the UNESCO citation (UNESCO – Maya Site of Copan 2007) listing it as a World Heritage site in 1980 stresses, a case can even be made for Copan being one of the first Classic Maya sites seen by Europeans:

Discovered in 1570 by Diego García de Palacios, the ruins of Copán, one of the most important sites of Mayan civilization, were not excavated until the 19th century. Its citadel and imposing public squares characterize its three main stages of development, before the city was abandoned in the early 10th century.

Copan was nominated for the UNESCO list as "an outstanding example of a type of building or architectural or technological ensemble or landscape which illustrates (a) significant stage(s) in human history" "directly or tangibly associated with events or living traditions, with ideas, or with beliefs, with artistic and literary works of outstanding universal significance" (UNESCO – The Criteria for Selection 2007). As I have detailed elsewhere (Joyce 2005), the site's significance has been actively contested during the 1990s as international archaeologists working at the site, Honduran ethnographers and archaeologists working elsewhere in the country, and Honduran cultural heritage officers, debated a revision of the management plan mandated as a condition of the site's UNESCO recognition.

For the archaeologists working at the site, the significant story the site has to tell is that of the sequence of rulers documented in monumental art and inscriptions and their deeds. Tourist experiences of the site are shaped by this international archaeological narrative as well, as it is registered both in popularly read works, like Linda Schele and David Freidel's *Forest of Kings,* and in guidebooks (Joyce 2003b; compare Mortensen 2001). Guidebooks foreground a narrative that focuses attention on rulership and hierarchy, even though the archaeology conducted at this site includes almost unprecedented excavation of a range of house compounds, as well as the reconstruction for tourism of a number of middle-range residences. Even when commenting on the latter sector of the site, the archaeological narrative shared by international tourists and enshrined in cultural heritage designation would appear to leave little room for multivocality or pluralism:

> The first view of the ruins is breath-taking as you gaze over the acres of courts and plazas surrounded by buildings and studded with heroic sculptured monuments. *Ceremonial centers such as this one were the focal point for Mayan society* (Hunter 1974:74; emphasis added).

> Linda Schele and David Freidel wrote, in 'A Forest of Kings', that 'In the course of a lifetime, 18 Rabbit transformed the center of Copan into a unique and beautiful expression of Maya royal power that endured to the present, unfailingly touching the most dispassionate of modern visitors' (quoted in ABC de Honduras 2002:52).

> Of some 40 residential compounds... about half have been investigated... The most important building in the group is the House of the Bacabs, also called the Palace of the Scribes, a large elite residence...The residence was occupied by Mac Chaanal, a royal scribe, and his family... Inside the structure an elaborately carved stone bench was discovered during excavation...The beautifully carved full-figure glyphs on the bench record the date AD 781, the time when the residence was dedicated; Yax Pac, Copan's reigning ruler, participated in the rites (Kelly 1996:273–274).

And yet, through dramatic demonstrations by indigenous groups who took over the visitor's center in October 1998, and again in September 2000, Copan has been given a somewhat different interpretation for both national and international audiences (Joyce 2005):

"This is a sacred place. That's why we have a right to the benefits that come in, because all the revenue goes to the government and the people have no resources" (Chorti Indian Jose Rufino Perez, quoted in an unsigned story from *Out There News* 1999).

The significance expressed by the Chorti Maya and their other indigenous allies frames the site as a sacred place, part of a direct inheritance whose exploitation should profit the descendant population. This historical narrative of connection is precisely the kind of alternative that archaeologists in Honduras, like those elsewhere in Central America, rarely articulate and often find uncomfortable. It is central to my second site of interpretation, Cerro Palenque.

A Fortress in History

The designation of Cerro Palenque as a site for development was driven directly by a concern to demonstrate to Honduras' pluralistic population the reality of a pluralistic past, articulated by Rodolfo Pastor Fasquelle, a Honduran historian who in the mid-1990s was briefly Minister of Culture and thus ultimately responsible for policy directions at the Honduran Institute of Anthropology and History.

In 1995, Pastor Fasquelle suggested that new national archaeological parks should complement Copan by providing recognition to other aspects of the country's Precolumbian heritage (personal communication, 1995). Los Naranjos and Cerro Palenque, the proposed sites for development, were located in territory arguably associated with the predecessors of Honduras' Lenca population, located close to the north coast economic center, San Pedro Sula, where a regional history museum incorporating archaeology and history was then being created with Pastor Fasquelle's participation. In a press conference held in the ballcourt of Cerro Palenque, he encouraged the archaeologists present (including me) to describe the ancient residents as separate from the Maya of Copan, constituting local Lenca antecedents for the region.

During the same press conference, Pastor Fasquelle also asserted that Cerro Palenque – a site whose archaeological remains I interpreted as indicating occupation from ca. AD 400 to 1,100 – was a significant place during the sixteenth century AD, identifying it as the location of a definitive battle between local natives and Spanish invaders. This was an interpretation he had presented previously in a regional history (Pastor Fasquelle 1989). This alternative interpretation was apparently part of the basis for his enthusiasm for developing the site as a regional archaeological park, safeguarding its status as a national monument.

While I did not contradict this statement at the time, I was troubled by it and by Pastor Fasquelle's apparent failure to give credence to my scientific opinion, embodied in a book I knew he had read. The idea that the site was occupied during a time of war had been promoted previously by the archaeologist Doris Zemurray Stone (Joyce 2001c), a North American whose father was a banana company entrepreneur, and who grew up in the economic community of north coast Honduras that Euraque (1996a,b) wrote about. Stone (1941) suggested that Cerro Palenque, with its hilltop location, must have been a fortress like the famous hilltop site in central Honduras where Lempira died, described in sixteenth century documents. She and others have noted that "palenque" itself means "palisaded place" in archaic Spanish, drawing the inference that colonial Spanish visitors named the site to commemorate an actual fortified place (rather than reflecting a post hoc rationalization of a visible masonry site, as is the apparent case for the Classic Maya site, Palenque, Chiapas, Mexico).

I felt certain that we knew where the ultimate battle of the Spanish conquest in the Ulua River valley had happened, and that Cerro Palenque was not the location. Then in the course of ongoing documentary research on the sixteenth century (in collaboration with Russell N. Sheptak and Kira Blaisdell-Sloan), we made an identification that had previously eluded us, and realized that Santiago, the modern community at the base of Cerro Palenque can be identified as tributary to the leader whose defeat was the turning point in the early colonization of the region. Documents from the sixteenth century described this battle as taking place at a palisaded town on the river. Rather than being a closed question, it appears there are multiple candidates for the town where this leader made his last stand, and one of them was indeed at Cerro Palenque – not within the zone sampled by my archaeological excavations, and thus not subject to my verification or falsification.

Clearly, bringing Cerro Palenque forward in time to the period that began the formation of the modern multicultural state gave it a different significance than the one I could offer, which dealt with the site as a place in the late stages of the Classic Maya states-system of the tenth-century AD. The Honduran historian's preference for a connection based on interpretation of documentary evidence was in part structured by his goal of creating a history for the localized indigenous population of the north coast. Archaeological research is never exhaustive, nor can interpretation ever be so, so there will always be an unavoidable subjectivity in the choice of the partial stories we tell, grounded in the materials we have at hand. The credible interpretation may change at the turn of a page. But in my experience, interpretations rarely change dramatically within the discourse of our discipline; it is precisely the multivocality enforced by dialogue with others outside the discipline that reframes the terms of engagement.

Limits of Interpretation

In 1995, Hondurans had experienced barely a decade of government by electoral representation. The minister's goal was to promote development of multisited archaeology to provide a basis for a specifically Honduran identity as a multicultural society, including the descendants of Spanish colonists and those of seven separate indigenous groups – the Lenca, Chorti Maya, Torrupan, Pech, Chorotega, Sumo, and Tawahka – and the Afro-Caribbean Garifuna, whose rights had been codified with the ratification of the 1989 *Convention concerning Indigenous and Tribal Peoples in Independent Countries #169* of the International Labor Organization (ILO) in 1994 (England & Anderson 1998; Mortensen 2001). While the Maya archaeology of Copan serves to place Honduras in the first rank internationally, non-Maya archaeology has been pressed into service to demonstrate that Honduras has always been pluralistic.

Official recognition of the civil status of the descendants of indigenous peoples was quickly integrated in tourism information. An English-language brochure (Honduran Institute of Tourism 1995) lured visitors with the prospect of meeting multiple friendly natives:

> There are some interesting people we'd like you to meet. Let us introduce you to nine different cultural groups which speak half a dozen languages, their beautiful crafts and fascinating customs and history...The Lenca, our largest cultural group, inhabits much of western Honduras. They preserve interesting vestiges of the old ways...

A letter in another tourist publication, signed by the minister of tourism, Norman García, reproduced a similar description:

> Eight different ethnic groups are part of our rich cultural heritage. The Chorti near Copan, the Tolupanes in the department of Yoro, and the Tawahka, Pech, and Miskito in the La Mosquitia region all maintain ancient customs and speak their own native language. Traditional art and culture live on in the daily rituals of colorful Lenca markets... (Honduran Institute of Tourism 1998:6).

Newspaper coverage of the award of the Juan Carlos I prize by the government of Spain to the Honduran Institute of Anthropology and History made the link between archaeology and identity explicit, while citing a notably diverse range of archaeological projects in non-Maya sites, some challenging the precedence of Maya culture:

> Currently, the Instituto has programs such as the Ruins of Copán, the Caves of Talgua (where recently evidence of a people earlier than the Mayas was discovered) ... it operates programs of exploration in Cerro Palenque, Yarumela, and at Los Naranjos... To know who we are, to enter into our collective experience as a nation, to understand our roots and to be conscious of our culture is as essential as to breathe the oxygen that guarantees our survival. In a world where free trade, economic globalization, television, the information super highway and electronic capitalism tend to make us uniform, it is vital that we know ourselves and understand what are the traits that distinguish us from the rest... It is a question of achieving the identity that is our own, to develop a legitimate pride in our culture and to bring that specificity to the contemporary world (my translation; "Museo de Antropología e Historia Museo: cinco años en la promoción del rescate del patrimonio cultural" 1999).

Where does the objectivity of archaeology fit into this discourse of national pluralism and differentiated identities (with its self-evident slipperiness signified by the changing numbers of constituent groups described in different popular media)? The pressure to identify the inhabitants of past sites in terms of contemporary ethnic groups is by no means new. What is new is the consequences of such identification, realized by both national elites and these groups themselves, who are struggling to advance claims for sufficient agricultural land to support themselves, dramatizing their economic needs with requests for a portion of income from archaeological tourism. Even the advocates of pluralism in Honduras can find themselves at odds with claims made by the newly empowered pluralistic groups. Commenting on Afrocentric claims by Honduran Garifuna, Rodolfo Pastor Fasquelle argued that:

one cannot invent oneself according to one's whim or preference. To try to pass as African is just as questionable for a Garifuna as it would be for [then President] Carlos Roberto Reina to dress like a Lenca or for me to presume to be a Briton or a Pech Indian just because I have these ancestors. Like all other Hondurans, the Garifuna are mestizos... (in an editorial in *La Prensa*, cited in England & Anderson 1998:3)

Archaeological interpretation in this setting is potentially an adjudication of land claims, and few archaeologists are well prepared to think about their "objective" statements of stylistic identity and population movement from that perspective. In Mesoamerican archaeology, where most of the active archaeologists in Honduras were trained, the conflation of linguistic identity with material cultural style to produce ethnic groups is standard practice. Arguably, archaeological interpretation needs to be more precisely framed in terms of what is known and indeed knowable, but is that enough?

It is certainly, in my experience, not effective. When I first began working in Honduras, I struggled to explain to local people around San Pedro Sula that we did not know who the makers of the sites and painted pottery we found had been; we did not know the language they spoke, or what they called themselves. My emphasis on the need to refrain from over-interpretation simply delegitimized me in the eyes of the most elite people with whom I engaged, and for the rural people who I encountered in the field, meant I offered nothing in place of legends of giants and *duendes*, the magical owners of the fields. Nor did I displace the automatic assumption shared by both classes that the Maya, now vanished from the scene, were to be credited with the ancient "civilization."

And to a certain extent, I was not being entirely honest in these conversations, because I certainly have well-founded opinions about who these people actually were. I thought, and continue to think, that they most likely came from towns composed of speakers of several languages, based on patterns of naming of single towns with multiple names in the sixteenth century documents. I thought, and continue to think, that they probably included a majority speaking dialects of Lenca, but that this did not cause them to recognize themselves as the same, since sixteenth century documents note the existence of many distinct named populations that identified themselves in distinction to others who also spoke variants of Lenca. I thought, and think, that these people were more likely to identify with others of their kin groups than to identify with a town government or regional political unit encompassing many towns. In order to communicate this vision of the past to the contemporary people with whom I am engaged in dialog, I would need to begin the conversation by explaining that in those times there was no nation, no state, and thus no possibility of a pluralistic precedent for the modern Honduran state.

I think that interpretation – which is, without a doubt, a direct outcome of a commitment to value multivocality – is worth adding to the mix of interpretations already loose on the Honduran landscape. But I do not think I can argue that it is inherently privileged, and should replace either the traditional Maya-centric view propounded by international archaeologists, or the vision of a useful past in which Honduras was occupied by the ancestors of many of its present cultural groups. I do not think my view is more objective, or for that matter, too subjective: I think it is normal, a consequence of a subjective frame that causes me to attend to material as evidence for different defensible propositions than those of others situated differently. Like Rodolfo Pastor Fasquelle, I also reserve my right to contest strongly any interpretations offered that actually violate observable material conditions about histories of change and continuity. But those interpretations come, in my experience, as often from proponents of single authoritative views as from those who encourage multiple perspectives.

References

ABC de Honduras. (2002). *Destination Honduras, 1998–1999: The Official Visitor and Business Guide to Honduras*. San Pedro Sula: ABC de Honduras, Grupo Nacion GN, S.A.

Agurcia F. R. (1984). La defensa del patrimonio cultural en Honduras: El caso de la arqueología. *Yaxkin*, 7(2), 83–96.

Baudez, C. (1966). Niveaux ceramiques au Honduras: une reconsideration de l'evolution culturelle. *Journal de la Societe des Americanistes de Paris*, 55, 299–341.

Baudez, C., & Becquelin, P. (1973). *Archéologie de los Naranjos, Honduras*. Etudes mesoaméricaines 2. Mexico, D.F.: Mission Archeologique et Ethnologique Française au Mexique.

Chinchilla M., O. (1998). Archaeology and nationalism in Guatemala at the time of independence. *Antiquity*, 72, 376–387.

Díaz-Andreu, M. (1998). Nacionalismo y arqueología: del Viejo al Nuevo Mundo. *Arqueología*, 20, 115–138.

England, S., & Anderson, M. (1998). Authentic African culture in Honduras? Afro-Central Americans challenge Honduran Indo-Hispanic Mestizaje. Paper prepared for presentation at the XXI Latin American Studies Association International Congress. Chicago.

Euraque, D. A. (1996a). La creación de la moneda nacional y el enclave bananero en la costa caribeña de Honduras: ¿en busca de una identidad étnico-racial? *Yaxkin*, 14, 138–150.

Euraque, D. A. (1996b). *Reinterpreting the Banana Republic: Region and State in Honduras, 1870–1972*. Chapel Hill: University of North Carolina Press.

Euraque, D. A. (1998). Antropólogos, arqueólogos, imperialismo y la mayanización de Honduras: 1890–1940. *Yaxkin*, 17, 85–101.

Hasemann, G., Van Gerpen, L., & Veliz, V. (1977). *Informe Preliminar, Curruste: Fase 1*. San Pedro Sula: Patronato Pro-Curruste-Instituto Hondureño de Antropología e Historia.

Hasemann, G., Dixon, B., & Yonk, J. (1982). El rescate arqueológico en la zona de embalse de El Cajón. Reconocimiento general y regional 1980–1981. *Yaxkin*, 5(1), 22–36.

Henderson, J. S. (Ed.). (1984). *Archaeology in Northwestern Honduras: Interim Reports of the Proyecto Arqueológico Sula*, 1. Ithaca: Latin American Studies Program-Archaeology Program.

Hinsley, C. (1984). Wanted: One good man to discover Central American history. *Harvard Magazine*, 87(2), 64A–64H.

Hinsley, C. (1985). From shell-heaps to stelae: Early anthropology at the Peabody Museum. In G. W. Stocking, Jr. (Ed.), *Objects and Others: Essays on Museums and Material Culture* (pp. 49–74). History of Anthropology, Vol. 3. Madison: University of Wisconsin Press.

Hirth, K., Urban, P., Hasemann, G., & Veliz, V. (1981). Patrones regionales de asentamiento en la región de El Cajon: Departamentos de Comayagua y Yoro, Honduras. *Yaxkin*, 4, 33–55.

Honduran Institute of Tourism. (1995). *Brochure*. Tegucigalpa, Honduras: Honduran Institute of Tourism.

Honduran Institute of Tourism. (1998). *Brochure*. Tegucigalpa, Honduras: Honduran Institute of Tourism.

Hunter, C. B. (1974). *A Guide to Ancient Maya Ruins*. Norman: University of Oklahoma Press.

Joyce, R. A. (1991). *Cerro Palenque: Power and Identity on the Maya Periphery*. Austin: University of Texas Press.

Joyce, R. A. (1993). Construction of the Mesoamerican frontier and the Mayoid image of Honduran polychromes. In M. Miller Graham (Ed.), *Reinterpreting Prehistory of Central America* (pp. 51–101). Niwot: University Press of Colorado.

Joyce, R. A. (2001a). Instituto Hondureño de Antropología e Historia. In T. Murray (Ed.), *Encyclopedia of Archaeology: History and Discoveries, vol. III* (pp. 669–671). Denver: ABC-Clio.

Joyce, R. A. (2001b). Peabody Museum, Harvard University. In T. Murray (Ed.), *Encyclopedia of Archaeology: History and Discoveries, vol. III* (pp. 1006–1010). Denver: ABC-Clio.

Joyce, R. A. (2001c). Stone, Doris Zemurray (1909-). In T. Murray (Ed.), *Encyclopedia of Archaeology: History and Discoveries, vol. III* (pp. 1212–1214). Denver: ABC-Clio.

Joyce, R. A. (2003a). Archaeology and nation building: a view from Central America. In S. Kane (Ed.), *The Politics of Archaeology and Identity in a Global Context* (pp. 79–100). Colloquia and Conference Papers 7. Boston: Archaeological Institute of America.

Joyce, R. A. (2003b). Confessions of an archaeological tour guide. A paper presented in the session "Ethical Interactions: National Modernities, Tourism and the Archaeological Imaginary" (L. M. Meskell, organizer) at the World Archaeological Congress, Washington DC.

Joyce, R. A. (2005). Solid histories for fragile nations: Archaeology as cultural patrimony. In L. M. Meskell & P. Pels, (Eds.), *Embedding Ethics* (pp. 253–273). Oxford: Berg.

Joyce, R. A., and Henderson, J. S. (2002). Who do we work for now? Imperialism, nationalism, globalism: Archaeology in Honduras, 1839–2002. Revised version of a paper presented in the Willey Symposium, "Archaeologists Abroad," at the annual meeting of the Society for American Archaeology, Denver.

Kelly, J. (1996). *An Archaeological Guide to Northern Central America*. Norman: University of Oklahoma Press.

Lincoln, C. (1979). Architectural test excavations at Travesia, Honduras. *Human Mosaic*, 13, 15–24.

Mortensen, L. (2001). Las dinámicas locales de un patrimonio global: arqueoturismo en Copán, Honduras. *Mesoamerica*, 22(43), 103–134.

Museo de Antropología e Historia: cinco años en la promoción del rescate del patrimonio cultural. (1999). *La Prensa* (Online), 20 January, 1999. Honduras. http://www.laprensahn.com/socarc/9901/s20001.htm

Out There News (1999). Copan: Chorti Indians Stake Their Ground. London (February 19, 2007); http://web.archive.org/web/19991013185306/http://www.megastories.com/mitch/map/copan.htm

Oyuela-Caycedo, A. (1994). Nationalism and archaeology: a theoretical perspective. In A. Oyuela-Caycedo (Ed.), *History of Latin American Archaeology* (pp. 3–21). Aldershot: Avebury.

Pastor Fasquelle, R. (1989). *Biografía de San Pedro Sula: 1536–1954*. San Pedro Sula: DIMA.

Robinson, E., Hasemann, G., & Veliz, V. (1979). An archaeological evaluation of Travesia, Honduras. *Human Mosaic*, 13, 1–14.

Sheehy, J. (1976). Preclassic artifacts from Choloma, Cortes, Honduras. *Las Fronteras de Mesoamerica*, Sociedad Mexicana de Antropologia, XIV Mesa Redonda, 2(1), 221–228.

Sheehy, J. (1978). Informe preliminar sobre las excavaciones en Travesía en 1976. *Yaxkin*, 2(3), 175–202.

Sheehy, J., & Veliz, V. (1977). Excavaciones recientes en Travesía, Valle de Sula. *Yaxkin*, 2(2),121–124.

Stephens, J. L. (1841). *Incidents of Travel in Central America, Chiapas, and Yucatan*. London: John Murray.

Stone, D. Z. (1941). *Archaeology of the North Coast of Honduras*. Peabody Museum Memoirs 9(1). Cambridge, MA: the Peabody Museum of Archaeology and Ethnology.

UNESCO World Heritage Centre – Maya Site of Copan. (2007). Paris, France (January 30, 2007); http://whc.unesco.org/en/list/129

UNESCO World Heritage Centre – The Criteria for Selection. (2007). Paris, France (January 30, 2007); http://whc.unesco.org/en/criteria/

Veliz, V. (1983). Síntesis histórica de la arqueología en Honduras. *Yaxkin*, 4 (1&2), 1–8.

Willey, G. R., & Sabloff, J. (1974). *A History of American Archaeology*. San Francisco: W. H. Freeman and Co.

Chapter 6
Paths of Power and Politics: Historical Narratives at the Bolivian Site of Tiwanaku

David Kojan

Introduction

On January 23, 2006, Evo Morales was formally inaugurated as Bolivia's new president in the capital city of La Paz. Primarily because of his political allegiance with President Hugo Chavez of Venezuela and his outspoken opposition to US policy and corporate interests, Morales' election and inauguration received significant international press coverage. But for many Bolivians, his "spiritual" inauguration the day before at the archaeological site of Tiwanaku represented the watershed moment in recent Bolivian political life. Evo Morales is the first indigenous president of Bolivia, and the first indigenous national leader in South America since the defeat of the Inca Empire by a small Spanish army almost 500 years ago. Since the sixteenth century, the majority Indian population of New Spain, and later Bolivia has been suffering under a variety of oppressive colonial systems ruled by the minority white and *mestizo* elites. So dominant have the structures of power been, that right up until Evo Morales' election and inauguration, an Indian head of state in Bolivia seemed a fundamental impossibility.

At the event Morales – now known simply "Evo" to all Bolivians – was barefoot, dressed in the traditional Andean *manta* and *chucu*,[1] and made offerings to *Pachamama*[2] as he was ritually purified and vetted for office by Aymara *yatiri*.[3] He processed through the central part and four quarters of Tiwanaku and across the large pyramid of the *Akapana* before receiving his blessings and addressing the assembled audience from the steps of the *Kalasasaya* temple (Fig. 6.1). While the city of La Paz is the focal point of Bolivia's colonial power, Tiwanaku is seen as the center of the more ancient pre-conquest power. At the event were international heads of state, local residents of the town of Tiwanaku, tourists from around the world, and thousands of Bolivians who came to see their new president sworn into office on the steps of Tiwanaku.

The historical moment of the Evo inauguration at Tiwanaku offers a window into the creation, manipulation, and dynamism of archaeological narratives and the impacts that they have in the contemporary world. In particular, this moment illustrates two key aspects of archaeological narratives and the concept of multivocality. First, the existence of diverse stakeholders and understandings of the past is a fact of

J. Habu, C. Fawcett, and J. M. Matsunaga (eds.), *Evaluating Multiple Narratives:*
Beyond Nationalist, Colonialist, Imperialist Archaeologies.
© Springer 2008

Fig. 6.1 Evo Morales at his "spiritual" inauguration at Tiwanaku, January 22, 2006 (printed with permission of Nick Buxton. Copyright Nick Buxton)

the social world, and therefore multivocality needs to be viewed as a key component of the practice of all archaeology rather than a methodology to be adopted or rejected according to the predilections of individual archaeologists. Second, all historical narratives are intimately tied to the contemporary dynamics of social, political, and economic power, and thus any consideration of multiple understandings of the past must also take into account the issues of authority and power that underlie them.

Paths to Tiwanaku

As with any examination of an historical moment, the inauguration of Evo Morales at Tiwanaku does not hold one single meaning or interpretive perspective. Instead, it points to the complex and fluid intersection between our understandings of the past and the contemporary social world in which these narratives are created. We can see in this moment the tensions between competing historical narratives, and we can glimpse the historical silences that remain outside traditional archaeological narratives. Rather than a series of signposts along a linear historical narrative, there are many multiple paths leading up to, and extending away from this historical moment. There are also hidden paths that impact the contemporary world, yet remain outside of our traditional view. That many of these paths are divergent and contradictory provides a window onto the state of Bolivian nationalism, Andean archaeology, and the formation of historical narratives generally.

By any measure, Tiwanaku is an important archaeological site. Located on the Bolivian Altiplano at an elevation of almost 13,000 ft. above the sea level, it is physically impressive both in the large area that it covers and in the scale of the structures that comprise it. It is argued from artifactual evidence that the site was part of a large sphere of influence that ranged from the Pacific coast of southern Peru to the southern Altiplano of Bolivia (Albarracin-Jordán 1996a,b; Janusek 2002; Kolata 1993, 1996; Vranich 1999). The early date of its fluorescence – approximately AD 500, or nearly a thousand years before the rise of the Inca Empire and the arrival of the Spanish conquistadores – further marks the site's importance (Fig. 6.2).

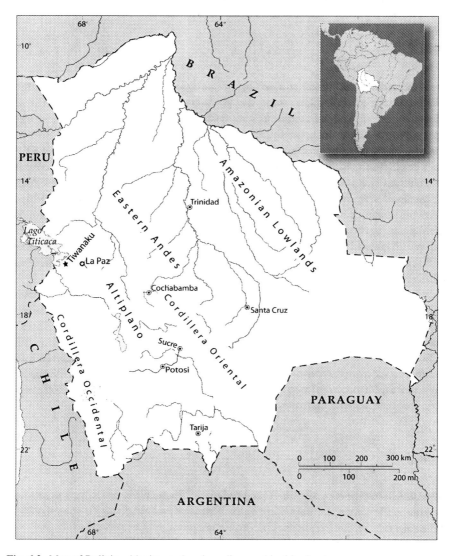

Fig. 6.2 Map of Bolivia with sites and regions discussed in this chapter

Tiwanaku is primarily composed of a variety of monumental structures; including a large constructed pyramid known as the *Akapana*, a large raised platform adjacent to a sunken temple, and several other massive raised structures. The central part of the site and the section most photographed and visited by tourists is actually a "reconstruction" of dubious fidelity that was undertaken by the Bolivian government in the 1960s under the direction of Carlos Ponce Sanginés. This monumental portion of the site was surrounded by many smaller structures that may have housed thousands of permanent or transient residents who once occupied the site (Kolata 1996). The archaeological site of Tiwanaku is located next to the modern town of Tiwanaku and other modern villages scattered throughout the valley.

Path 1

From the path of traditional archaeological narratives, the site of Tiwanaku and the inauguration that took place there are affirmations and symbols of a particular understanding of Andean culture history. In this narrative, Tiwanaku is an archaeological puzzle whose massive stones and statuary, abundant pot sherds and faunal remains, earth features and human burials are pieces of evidence that we study to learn about the past lifeways and cultural achievements of the people who constructed and lived at this site two millennia ago. Although from this perspective Tiwanaku is only one of a series of cultural horizons to rise and fall in the Andean mountain chain, the well-marked archaeological path identifies in Tiwanaku the main ingredients of the concepts of "civilization" and "complex societies" (see, for example, Stanish 2001). Plant and animal domestication, monumental architecture, craft specialization, increasing social hierarchy, and other markers of advancement are the main themes of Tiwanaku's archaeological narrative.

In traveling this path, the Evo inauguration seems to represent the supreme achievement of the archaeological approach specifically, and the scientific method generally. The knowledge gained from almost a century of archaeological investigation at Tiwanaku has made the site the most powerful and recognizable symbol of Bolivian history. The archaeologists in the audience at the Evo inauguration – taking a break from their research projects – must have felt a sense of pride that this important archaeological site and a hundred years of research there was being highlighted on an international stage.

Path 2

From a different perspective the inauguration at Tiwanaku is an explicit symbol of Bolivian nationalism. In this telling of the historical narrative, the Tiwanaku culture represents the primordial roots of the Bolivian nation. It is as if the modern Bolivian nation-state is the latest (and inevitable) incarnation of this ancient civilization. From its image on Bolivia's currency, to the large statues that adorn a central plaza in the capital city of La Paz, to its ubiquitous place on store fronts, billboards, and public buildings, Tiwanaku is the focal point of Bolivian nationalism (Kojan & Angelo 2005). As with political theater around the world, the Evo inauguration at Tiwanaku can be seen as a simple appeal to the most potent symbol of Bolivian national identity. In this narrative, Tiwanaku is not so much a site of archaeological research, but a locus of national power and identity.

A closer examination of the archaeological "ruins" from which Evo addressed the world is telling. The steps of the Kalasasaya on which he stood and was seen in newspapers around the world is not an intact archaeological site, but a rather imaginative "reconstruction" built in the 1960s as a tool and symbol of Bolivian nationalism. Carlos Ponce Sanginés, who masterminded the reconstructions, was an avowed nationalist who plainly saw his primary responsibility as an archaeologist to help construct a narrative of Bolivian primordial identity (Kojan & Angelo 2005). In this sense, the inauguration did not take place on an in situ archaeological site, but rather on a twentieth-century monument to Bolivian nationalism.

Path 3

For most of the audience at the Evo inauguration, Tiwanaku is not primarily seen as an archaeological site, or even a locus of national identity, but as a physical embodiment and symbolic representation of Bolivia's indigenous cultural heritage. From this reading of the site, Evo's election and inauguration is above all else a reclaiming of Tiwanaku and Bolivia by the majority Indian population of the country. For the first time since the defeat of the Incan empire at the hands of the Spanish invaders, a South American country is now being ruled by an indigenous leader. Evo – a coca farmer turned protest leader – draws much of his support from the historically disenfranchised segment of Bolivia's population (Fig. 6.3).

This was a watershed event for Bolivia's 75% Indian population, who have been under the often oppressive rule of a minority white and *mestizo* elite since Pizarro's *conquistadores* toppled the Inca Empire in 1532. Above all, Tiwanaku's past is an indigenous Andean one. The Evo inauguration was especially powerful for many of the Aymara people in attendance who trace their own cultural patrimony to the site of Tiwanaku. Supporters of this perspective sometimes argue that Tiwanaku is more than 10,000 years old, and that archaeological claims for a much younger date are simply part of the continuing colonial attempt to separate Indian people from a sense of their own heritage. In many ways, this moment was a reclaiming of Tiwanaku and its history. Mamani (1996) argues that nationalists and non-Indian elites have systematically co-opted important sites and symbols of indigenous heritage like Tiwanaku for their own purposes – part of the widespread efforts at colonial control and subordination enacted by separating colonized peoples from markers of their own historical heritage. The image and reality of an indigenous man being sworn in as president by indigenous spiritual leaders at this locus of Indian heritage is a powerful and long-awaited moment for many Bolivians.

Fig. 6.3 An Evo supporter at the inauguration holds a large coca-leaf symbol. Coca is a potent symbol of indigenous identity in the Andes, and the fact that Evo, a coca farmer, has been a significant source of pride for much of Bolivia's population, and a source of considerable consternation to the US government (printed with permission of Nick Buxton. Copyright Nick Buxton)

Path 4

Most newspapers, television stories, conservative radio shows and left-leaning blogs reported the Evo inauguration as a symbolic show-down over globalization and the conflict between poor countries like Bolivia on one side, and the US and corporate interests on the other ("Bolivia Takes on the Superpower" 2006; "Enter the Man" 2006; Evitar 2006; Shultz 2006). Over the last decade Bolivia has emerged as a focal point for the debate over globalization. From protests over the US-led coca eradication program; to the "Water Wars" which nixed Bechtel Corporation's control of a local water district; to the "Gas Wars" of 2003 which led to the resignation of Bolivia's president and the eventual election of the principal leader of these protests, Evo Morales; Bolivia has become for many a laboratory in which the debates over globalization are tested and interpreted by observers around the world (Finnegan 2002).

From this perspective, the inauguration is a victory celebration and a show of force by the opponents of corporate interests and the supporters of Latin America's poor. Tiwanaku becomes a stage for a contemporary dispute over politics, economic power, and social authority, and a crucible in which these power struggles are tested. The archaeological site is not simply a backdrop for these festivities, but is situated as a kind of active participant in them. Tiwanaku embodies the primordial roots of this struggle, communicating the resolve of the opposition movement and the fleeting nature of corporate interests.

One could similarly view the Evo inauguration at Tiwanaku as a media event to draw international attention and monetary aid to Bolivia, a tourist spectacle to publicize the central tourist attraction in Bolivia, a show of political force to the political and ideological opposition of Evo Morales, or any number of other potential readings of the events of this past January. In all of these narratives, Tiwanaku plays a key role as stage, social symbol, material evidence, or political participant.

The Social Reality of Multivocality

Whatever one thinks about the existence of multiple interpretations of the past, for every known archaeological site, historical period, or event there are always contested understandings. Whether archaeologists embrace these multiple understandings as important and dynamic expressions of the past, or flinch at them as chaotic, "unscientific" or "mythological" readings of the past matters very little. This multiplicity exists and will continue to do so regardless of how archaeologists or any other party feel about it. Of course, what archaeologists can affect is the manner in which we understand, communicate, and acknowledge the existence of these multiple narratives.

In recent archaeological discourse the concept of multivocality has been primarily pushed to the foreground by Ian Hodder (1997) and other scholars (Chadwick 2003; Colwell-Chanthaphonh & Ferguson 2006; Gnecco 1999) who are exploring ways that archaeologists can include alternative voices in our research. Hodder argues that archaeologists should engage with alternative, nonarchaeological narratives of the past as a way of expanding the relevance of our study of history, and to include groups and individuals that have been traditionally excluded from "official" interpretations of the past. In this sense of the term, "multivocality" becomes a largely methodological problem about how we can integrate multiple voices into the daily work of archaeological research. I understand multivocality in a broader sense as simply the idea that there are always multiple interpretations of the past. Whether these interpretations arise from archaeological research, oral histories, popular media, religious scripture or any other source, the past is always a varied and contested terrain.

The sources and motivations of historical narratives are as diverse as the narratives themselves. The meanings of Tiwanaku and its significance in the world are not fixed, but are fluid and contingent. Individuals and groups with stakes in the history or archaeology of Bolivia will understand Tiwanaku in different ways and shift their own perspective of the site to fit their current needs and desires. As with the Evo inauguration, the site can be seen as an archaeological puzzle, a symbol of Bolivian national identity or a source of tourism revenue. But these perspectives are highly malleable. An archaeologist who would normally bristle at the nationalist romanticization of an important archaeological site like Tiwanaku might appeal to the important symbolism of the site in order to help protect it against development or in an application for research funding. A local businesswoman who makes her living from the tourist influx to the site may have felt pangs of ethnic pride seeing Evo standing in front of the *Kalasasaya* gate. Cultural identity, political coercion, societal authority, economic incentive, spiritual belief, and material evidence are just a few of the factors that contribute to differing understandings of the past. If this interrogation is pushed far enough one can argue that every stakeholder for a given historical moment has a unique understanding of that moment.

Power and Historical Narratives

For professional archaeologists perhaps the most challenging implication of multi-vocality is that our own interpretations, often constructed from years of careful thought and hard toil, in the end, merely represent one voice telling stories about the past. One reason that archaeology (and archaeologists) has been rather slow to apply many of the postcolonial critiques to our own field is that it is in the very marrow of our identity that we represent the standard bearers of historical objectivity. All narratives are not created equal, this reasoning holds. Archaeological interpretations are based on evidence and testable hypotheses that are open to challenge and refutation, while other stories about the past are just that – stories. The idea, for example, that archaeological interpretations of Tiwanaku should be considered in the same way as notions that the site was built 10,000 years ago, or that the massive stones are so large that they could only have been placed there by space aliens or time travelers flies in the face of our basic professional identity. Our professional narrative holds that archaeological narratives have become accepted and desired in the world because they have prevailed over other inferior historical narratives. And such a professional image is not without some validity. Archaeological research, among other accomplishments, is partially responsible for supporting the longevity of the indigenous occupation of the Americas and Australia, for debunking the ethnocentric western belief that Europe represents the origin of all cultural advancement, and for confronting religious dogma in the disguise of "intelligent design."

However, at least 25 years of scholarship makes clear that archaeological interpretations of the past are extremely vulnerable to a multitude of forces in the contemporary context from which they emerge. Trigger (1984) paved the way for western archaeology to seriously consider the proposition that sociopolitical factors always exert themselves in interpretations of the past. With his insightful examples of nationalist, colonialist, and imperialist archaeologies, he convincingly demonstrated that archaeological narratives are never developed in an interpretive vacuum, but are heavily influenced by the social and historical conditions in which they are written. Trigger observed, for example, that Chinese nationalism heavily influenced the development and practice of archaeology in that country; that archaeology in Sub-Saharan Africa was initially aimed at establishing the innate inferiority of indigenous cultures as a legitimization of colonial rule; and that archaeology in the former Soviet Union was primarily directed at furthering the hegemonic control of the Russian center over the ethnic hinterlands.

Motivated by a diverse set of influences, including the postcolonial and feminist critiques of anthropology, hermeneutics, and neo-Marxist theory, a generation of theoretical scholarship and the documentation of specific case studies have substantiated and greatly expanded Trigger's observations, demonstrating that all archaeological interpretations are squarely embedded in the social, economic, and political contexts in which they are fashioned (see, for example,Conkey 2005; Deloria 1992; Gathercole & Lowenthal 1990; Hodder 1986; Kohl & Fawcett 1995; McGuire 1999; McNiven & Russell 2005; Schmidt & Patterson 1995; Watkins 2000, 2003). Recent studies also make the critical observation that archaeology can play an integral role in shaping the attitudes, policies, and physical landscapes in ways that have very real consequential impacts on the lives of individuals and communities today (Arnold 1990, Abu El-Haj 1998; Kojan & Angelo 2005; Thomas 1991). It is a demonstration of the malleability and potency of historical narratives that even as they are produced by contemporary power dynamics they are simultaneously turned around to become tools of social control themselves. Mamani (1996) argues that Bolivian archaeology and its precolonial past have both been systematically co-opted by the country's white and *mestizo* elites as a mechanism of social and political disenfranchisement of the Indian majority. Abu El-Haj (1998, 2002) identifies a similar pattern in the practice of archaeology in Israel/ Palestine in which markers of Jewish heritage and antiquity are monumentalized, while the material evidence of Palestinian history is left in silent ruin or even destroyed. In North America, thousands of Indian bodies are warehoused in museums and storage facilities as markers and reminders of the colonial control and subjugation of the continent's indigenous population (Deloria 1992; Watkins 2000).

Such studies repeatedly suggest that despite professional efforts to approach our subject from a detached and objective perspective, archaeologists are active agents in the processes of nationalism (Kohl 1998; Trigger 1995), neocolonialism (Mamani 1996; McNiven & Russell 2005), globalization (Kojan & Angelo 2005), as well as social justice and human rights (Ferguson et al. 2000). The degree to which archaeologists are granted and hold authority, and to which archaeological narratives are believed or trusted above others, is a matter of contemporary power dynamics, not an inherent quality of the past. In fact, the very motivation to separate "objective" interpretations of the past from their wider social, political, and economic context is itself rooted in a power system that seeks to uphold the authority of the Western "scientific" narratives above all other forms of understanding of the past (Colwell-Chanthaphonh & Ferguson 2006; Dumont 2003; Wylie 2000).

The researching, writing, retelling, and critiquing of historical narratives is thus not a neutral process, but is intimately bound up with contemporary dynamics and relationships of power. Differing understandings of the past are not the inexplicable result of irrational cultural beliefs or practices, as traditional philosophies of science would have us believe (see Dawkins 2006 for the most recent iteration of this argument and Colwell-Chanthaphonh & Ferguson 2006 for a recent refutation). Rather, I would argue that we can only comprehend and appreciate the existence of multiple understandings of the past through an examination of the contemporary concerns of cultural identity, economic necessity, political autonomy, social identity, and other factors of great importance to individuals and communities today.

The Aymara Indians who see Tiwanaku as an integral part of their cultural past do so out of a contemporary feeling of pride in their identity and as a symbolic reminder of their longevity in the physical and historical landscape of Bolivia (Kojan & Angelo 2005; Mamani 1996). Whether this narrative is backed up by specific archaeological research is of secondary and relatively inconsequential concern. The political supporters of Evo Morales and the organizers of his spiritual inauguration are clearly making strong reference to the deep past of Bolivia with their decision to hold the event at Tiwanaku. But the specific "past" that is being referenced is one that serves their needs here in the twenty-first century. Positioning Evo on the steps of the *Kalasasya* temple is a direct reference to the *Inti Raymi* solstice festival celebration, which is itself constructed as a creative reenactment of the ancient celebrations imagined to have taken place at the site. Evo is thus gaining contemporary political and spiritual power from his placement at Tiwanaku (see Silverman 1999 for a similar, though more cynical use of archaeological symbolism). The fact that there is little hard evidence to suggest that any such ritual ever took place in ancient Tiwanaku, or that the *Kalasasaya* itself is a modern imaginative construction of the original structure, mattered very little in this moment. What matters in this context is the power that we ascribe to Tiwanaku's past today. The blog writers (Shultz 2006, for example) who see Tiwanaku and its past as a symbol of the antiglobalization movement are certainly not claiming that such debates were taking place a thousand years ago – this is a twenty-first-century concern being played out on the stage of the past.

And what of the archaeologists who work diligently to uncover the past of Tiwanaku? Certainly the abstract past as examined from the material evidence at Tiwanaku and other archaeological sites around the Andes plays a large role in our understanding. But so too, other contemporary factors, both obvious and unexamined, play an important role in establishing archaeological narratives. Feminist critiques of archaeology, for example, have established the vulnerability of archaeological narratives to individual and societal values, norms, and biases (see for example, Conkey 2005; Wylie 1992)

Large-scale political factors also influence our work. Gero and Root (1990), for example, examined the use of archaeology in the pages of National Geographic magazine and concluded that these stories have consistently been used to bolster a sense of American nationalism and imperialism. Blakey (1990) has shown how American representations of archaeological research communicate a marked racial message that privileges a dominant white identity over other racial and ethnic groups – a clear translation of contemporary social hierarchies on the interpreted past. Archaeology has regularly been appropriated by political regimes as legitimizations of often heinous acts of violence and genocide. Under Nazi Germany, archaeological "research" was a major focus and was used to help establish the (fictional) antiquity of the "Germanic" people – an argument that was ultimately used to justify the persecution of Roma, Jews, homosexuals, and other minority groups (Arnold 1990). And in much of Latin America, colonial and postcolonial debates about the role and treatment of Indians in the modern world have played out in the pages of archaeological scholarship as interpretations about the origin and development of precolonial societies. Patterson (1995) shows that changing political attitudes among the dominant white and *mestizo* elites toward Indian populations in Latin America have led to fundamentally different archaeological interpretations.

As social beings embedded in our own cultural and historical contexts we cannot consider narratives of the past without invoking dynamics of power. When presented with stories about the past, we immediately begin to ask questions about the present: What kind of narrative is it? How does this story align with our own belief systems? A narrative that substantiates a closely held belief is received very differently than one that threatens such a belief. We immediately ask questions about who is presenting the narrative – is it an archaeological interpretation or an indigenous creation story? We might also ask question about facts and evidence. All of these questions refer to interpretations of the past but they all exist in the present moment and focus on contemporary issues.

Foucault reminds us that power exists and is enacted through discourse. Power exists in the practice of everyday life, and most especially in appeals to authority and knowledge production. He famously argued that "power produces reality" – it determines what we imagine to be possible and we in turn create our social world in that image (Foucault 1977: 194). In this sense, the writing, retelling, and critiquing of historical narratives are very direct expressions and manifestations of power. They are attempts to define and delimit the story of who we are and where we come from. We develop these stories about the past not for neutral or abstract purposes, but to affect an impact in the world. In the 1960s, when the jumbled stones and stelae of Tiwanaku failed to meet the requirements of a nationalist agenda, large parts of the site were "reconstructed" to make the site an appropriately inspiring and "readable" one.

Whether we have a conscious intention to change some aspect of our social world – as with the "reconstruction" of Tiwanaku – or believe that we are engaged in an objective search for truth with little real-world impact, matters very little according to Foucault. In fact, power is most effectively exercised not in conflict, but in agreed-upon and sweeping acts of knowledge transmission. When our understandings of the past are least controversial or problematic, that is when contemporary structures of power are being enacted most strongly.

In this sense power is manifested not only in the historical narratives that we repeat or disagree over, but also in the repression and silencing of alternative understandings of the past. In the multiple understandings of the Evo inauguration there is at least one significant commonality: the centrality of Tiwanaku goes unquestioned. Whether we enter the moment of Evo's inauguration from the perspective of a Bolivian nationalist, a professional archaeologist, or an active opponent of globalization, Tiwanaku remains a fixed and solid entity – a reference to the past whose meanings can be shifted, but whose singular importance goes unquestioned.

A more subtle, but no less potent expression of contemporary power are the silences and erasures of the many pasts that remain outside of the dominant Tiwanaku-centered narratives. In one sense, the different views of the Evo inauguration and their conceptualizations of Tiwanaku and its past are multiple and alternative readings of the past. But at another level they are all elevating a single archaeological site and a single past above all others. When viewed from another angle the "multiple" narratives of Tiwanaku blur together into a single master narrative that holds this site and all that it symbolizes at the center (Kojan & Angelo 2005). Although the attendees and observers of the Evo inauguration differed in their understanding of that day's events and the history that Tiwanaku represents, few had any doubt that they were standing at the focal point of Bolivian history and society. The idea that the monuments of Tiwanaku like the *Kalasasaya* and *Akapana* were occupied for a relatively short period of history, probably by a relatively small number of elite individuals in one corner of the Andean Altiplano, was likely not considered or perhaps actively repugnant to those assembled on January 22. On that day, as with every other day, the innumerable archaeological sites of the eastern Andes, or the histories of the lowland Amazonian peoples, or the cultures of southern Bolivia were not even in play to be disagreed over. Elsewhere, I have written about this process of selection and silencing in Bolivian archaeology (Kojan & Angelo 2005) in which the narrative of Tiwanaku consistently emerges as *the* central focus of Bolivia's deep history. The focus on Tiwanaku at the expense of alternative narratives is itself rooted in the political and economic history of South American colonialism and contemporary economic, political, and social power dynamics (Kojan 2002).

The eastern Andes, for example, is today a region with extensive archaeological evidence of precolonial occupation, yet its history remains well outside the cannon of official Bolivian history. This silencing traces its roots to the early Spanish Conquest when the colonial powers quickly took control of this lucrative coca-producing region by forcibly removing the indigenous inhabitants and importing foreign laborers with little connection to the land (Klein 1993; Kojan 2002; Larson 1988). This pattern continues even today as the Bolivian government and foreign companies reap large profits from the eastern part of the country, while the region is still considered a peripheral frontier zone with little significant history. Even as the coca farmers and miners of eastern Bolivia protested and died in the streets of La Paz, and elected one of their own to the presidency, their history remains a silenced one. From this perspective, it is an ironic twist of fate that Evo Morales took his spiritual inauguration at Tiwanaku, which overshadows the history of his own region and has come to symbolize the dominant story of Bolivia.

Trouillot (1995) argues that the silencing of particular narratives is especially targeted at readings of the past that challenge or undermine the legitimizing ideas of contemporary power structures. In his analysis of Haitian history, he writes that we are almost incapable of considering historical narratives that contradict our accepted understanding of the past and its path to the present. So fundamental are our narratives of the past to an understanding of our present condition, that when the two come into conflict, we erase the contradictory histories from our collective memory. Power produces reality.

On Relativism and Social Engagement

If we accept the idea that there are always multiple understandings of the past, and that these understandings are significantly rooted in contemporary power dynamics as important interlocutors between the past and the present, what are archaeologists to do? As historical agents ourselves, inexorably bound to these power dynamics, how are we to evaluate the legitimacy of any historical narrative? If we let the singular authority of archaeological interpretations slip even incrementally, what standards are we left with to determine the validity of the multitude of these perspectives?

It would be a mistake to infer that because all historical narratives are intrinsically bound to contemporary dynamics of power that we are left only with a hyper-relativist position, as Trigger (1989b) fears in which all narratives are seen as equally plausible. As Wylie (2002: 191) identifies, such a position is in itself the ultimate checkmate by those with power over those without. By foreclosing any claim to empirical evidence or reason, those in power create a system in which their own position can never be questioned on empirical or ethical grounds. Power in its rawest form becomes the only thing that matters. If all stories about the past are seen as equally valid, then archaeology can never be used to challenge existing power structures.

However, if archaeologists are guilty of adopting an extreme relativist position, it is not in reference to our interpretation of past material culture, but in our appreciation for the contemporary uses and impacts of our work in the world and in lives of living people. I would argue that we have been much too relativist and passive in examining the political context in which our work occurs.

Before 1953, when Bolivia finally ended the colonial *encomienda* system, which granted control of all Bolivian land to the descendants of the conquistadores and functionally made serfs of the majority Indian population, archaeological research in Bolivia progressed for half a century with little word about the plight of the descendants of the people under study (Mamani 1996). In 2003, as protesters were marching and even dying in the streets of La Paz, archaeological field work in Bolivia continued almost unabated. In some cases, resourceful archaeologists negotiated their way around road blocks to get to their field sites. The widespread excavation, study, display, and storage of thousands of Indian bodies and graves continue to this day with very little public dialogue about the professional ethics and community attitudes about such practices. Bolivia is the second poorest country in the Americas, with alarmingly high rates of maternal mortality, infant mortality, malnutrition, and infectious diseases, yet as a profession we treat such human realities as a mere backdrop to our archaeological research.

In specific cases, foreign archaeologists have helped to establish agricultural projects (Erickson 1988), local museums (Hastorf 2006), and health care centers in the Bolivian communities in which they work, but these have largely been undertaken as unique personal efforts, rather than acts of professional engagement typical of the field as a whole.

It is only very recently that archaeologists have undertaken to examine the social, political, and economic context and impacts of our work (Trigger 1989a; Ucko 1990). The prevailing attitude within western archaeology seems to be that we are only responsible for creating convincing narratives, and that whatever impact our work has in the world is the responsibility of others. Who those "others" remain unnamed. It is true that we cannot anticipate or control every potential use of our work and the interpretations that we produce. Any field of knowledge can be co-opted or manipulated for purposes that we do not support. But I would argue that we have a responsibility to think about the wider power structure in which we live and work and to take the impacts of our work into account.

The lesson of multivocality is not that we should redouble our efforts toward perfect objectivity in order to overcome the political, social, and economic motivations for, and implications of, archaeological research. Theoretical analysis and a growing number of case studies on the vulnerability of archaeological interpretations to contemporary forces make clear that we can never separate our work from these ubiquitous aspects of the social world – the dynamics of power and identity are present in all representations of the human experience. The forces of nationalism, economic disparities, authority, and identity will always exert themselves in historical narratives, even if we imagine that they do not – or I should say, *especially* if we imagine that they do not. When we imagine that we are not significantly influenced by our own present-day systems of power, authority, and social hierarchy, then these factors wield all the more influence. They appear to be natural outcomes of the histories that we write, rather than as structures to be studied, critiqued, and challenged.

The lesson that I take from multivocality is that we must make the implications and impacts of our field as an integral part of our research. To hope against our better judgment that in this generation we will finally achieve an objective or bias-free reading of the past is at this point to engage in a large degree of self-deception. We must base and evaluate the historical narratives that we produce not only on the material evidence that archaeologists have traditionally examined, but also in terms of the impact that those narratives have in the world. Which individuals, parties or causes do particular historical narratives support or refute? Who is being helped by the work that we do, and who is being hurt by it? Does our work support the aims and desires of those who already wield considerable power and authority in the world, or does it challenge such hierarchies?

Conclusion

If we accept the fundamental observation that archaeological interpretations are rooted in the present moment and defined by contemporary social, political, and economic motivations, then we must also recognize that there is no external position in examinations of the past. We are all, archaeologists included, embedded in a contingent consideration of the past. In this sense, each of us is part of the historical narratives that we write, circulate, and rework. We are all invested agents in our own understandings of the past – even a past as seemingly far removed from our present moment as that represented by the massive stones and buried artifacts of Tiwanaku.

To understand the multiple narratives of Tiwanaku (or any other site), we must also seek to understand the contemporary world in which these narratives exist. And if we are sincere in a desire to allow multiple voices on the past to emerge in public discourse, we must immerse ourselves in the contemporary political, social, and economic struggles that play a significant role in producing these narratives in the first place. As archaeologists, we cannot presume to speak for any party other than ourselves – that would be both an abdication of our professional responsibility to say what we believe to be true, as well as a recapitulation of existing power dynamics (Conkey 2005; Spivak 1988). But as Abu El-Haj (1998) writes, the practice of archaeology creates a material culture of its own. The multiple understandings of the *Kalasasaya* that supported Evo Morales at his inauguration, the nationalist identity of Bolivia that is legitimized by Tiwanaku, the silenced histories that remain hidden from our consideration, and the continued racial and economic discrepancies that exist in contemporary Bolivia are all to a large or small degree the products of archaeological practice. If we want to comprehend the emergence and persistence of multiple understandings of the past then we need to engage with the real contemporary forces that help shape them. And if we are interested in helping to facilitate social change in the world, then we need to take these understandings seriously.

Acknowledgments Thanks to Dante Angelo for his invaluable contributions to many of the ideas in this paper. An earlier collaboration on these issues was published in the *Journal of Social Archaeology* (Kojan & Angelo 2005).

Notes

[1] A *manta* is a traditional Andean ceremonial cloth. A *chucu* is a traditional ceremonial Aymara hat.

[2] *Pachamama* is the traditional Andean mother earth goddess – one of the most powerful and important deities in the Aymara panteon.

[3] Aymara is the largest Indian language and cultural group of Bolivia. *Yatiri* are Aymara spiritual specialists.

References

Abu El-Haj, N.A. (1998). Translating truths: nationalism, the practice of archaeology, and the remaking of past and present in contemporary Jerusalem. *American Ethnologist*, 25(2), 166–188.

Abu El-Haj, N.A. (2002). *Facts on the Ground: Archaeological Practice and Territorial Self-fashioning in Israeli Society*. Chicago: University of Chicago Press.

Albarracín-Jordán, J. (1996a). Tiwanaku settlement system: the integration of nested hierarchies in the Lower Tiwanaku Valley. *Latin American Antiquity*, 7, 183–210.

Albarracín-Jordán, J. (1996b). *Tiwanaku. Arqueología Regional y Dinámica Segmen-taria*. La Paz: Plural Editores.

Arnold, B. (1990). The past as propaganda: totalitarian archaeology in Nazi Germany. *Antiquity*, 64(244), 464–478.

Blakey, M. (1990). American nationality and ethnicity in the depicted past. In P.W. Gathercole & D. Lowenthal (Eds.), *The Politics of the Past* (pp. 38–48). London: Unwin Hyman.

Bolivia takes on the superpower. (2006). *The Economist*, 378(8461), 10.

Chadwick, A. (2003). Post-processualism, professionalization and archaeological methodologies. Towards reflective and radical practice. *Archaeological Dialogues*, 10(1), 97–117.

Colwell-Chanthaphonh, C., & Ferguson, T. (2006). Memory pieces and footprints: multivocality and the meanings of ancient times and ancestral places among the Zuni and Hopi. *American Anthropologist*, 108(1), 148–162.

Conkey, M. (2005). Dwelling at the margins, action at the intersection: feminist and indigenous archaeologies. *Archaeologies*, 1(1), 9–59.

Dawkins, R. (2006). *The God Delusion*. New York: Houghton Mifflin.

Deloria, V. (1992). Indians, archaeologists, and the future. *American Antiquity*, 57(4), 595–598.

Dumont, C. (2003). The politics of scientific objections to repatriation. *Wicazo Sa Review*, 18(1), 109–128.

Enter the man in the stripey jumper. (2006). *The Economist*, 378(8461), 40.

Erickson, C. (1988). Raised field agriculture in the lake Titicaca Basin: putting ancient agriculture back to work. *Expedition*, 30(1), 8–16.

Evitar, D. (2006). Evo's challenge in Bolivia. *The Nation*, 282(3), 11.

Ferguson, T., Anyon, R., & Ladd, E. (2000). Repatriation at the Pueblo of Zuni: diverse solutions to complex problems. In D. Mihesuah (Ed.), *Repatriation Reader* (pp. 239–265). Lincoln: University of Nebraska Press.

Finnegan, W. (2002). Leasing the rain: the world is running out of fresh water, and the fight to control it has begun (Letter from Bolivia). *The New Yorker*, 78(7), 43–52.

Foucault, M. (1977). *Discipline and Punish: The Birth of the Prison*. London: Allen Lane.

Gathercole, P.W., & Lowenthal, D. (Eds.). (1990). *The Politics of the Past*. London: Unwin Hyman.

Gero, J., & Root, D. (1990). Public presentations and private concerns: archaeology in the pages of National Geographic. In P.W. Gathercole & D. Lowenthal (Eds.), *The Politics of the Past* (pp. 19–37). London: Unwin Hyman.

Gnecco, C. (1999). Archaeology and historical multivocality. A reflection from the Colombian multicultural context. In G. Politis & B. Alberti (Eds.), *Archaeology in Latin America* (pp. 258–270). London: Routledge.

Hastorf, C. (2006). Building the community museum at Chiripa, Bolivia. In H. Silverman (Ed.), *Archaeological Site Museums in Latin America* (pp. 85–98). Gainesville: University Press of Florida.

Hodder, I. (1986). *Reading the Past*. Cambridge: Cambridge University Press.

Hodder, I. (1997). Always momentary, fluid and flexible: towards a reflexive excavation methodology. *Antiquity*, 71(273), 691–700.

Janusek, J.W. (2002). Out of many, one: style and social boundaries in Tiwanaku. *Latin American Antiquity*, 13(1), 35–61.

Klein, H.S. (1993). *Haciendas and Ayllus: Rural Society in the Bolivian Andes in the Eighteenth and Nineteenth Centuries*. Stanford: Stanford University Press.

Kohl, P.L. (1998). Nationalism and archaeology – on the constructions of nations and the reconstructions of the remote past. *Annual Review of Anthropology*, 27, 223–246.

Kohl, P.L., & Fawcett, C.P. (1995). Archaeology in the service of the state: theoretical considerations. In P.L. Kohl & C.P. Fawcett (Eds.), *Nationalism, Politics, and the Practice of Archaeology* (pp. 3–18). Cambridge: Cambridge University Press.

Kojan, D. (2002). Cultural identity and historical narratives of the Bolivian Eastern Andes: An archaeological study. (Doctoral dissertation, University of California, Berkeley).

Kojan, D., & Angelo, D. (2005). Dominant narratives, social violence and the practice of Bolivian Archaeology. *Journal of Social Archaeology*, 5(3), 383–408.

Kolata, A. (1993). *The Tiwanaku: Portrait of an Andean Civilization*. Oxford: Blackwell.

Kolata, A. (Ed.). (1996). *Tiwanaku and its Hinterland: Archaeology and Paleoecology of an Andean Civilization*. Washington, DC: Smithsonian Institution Press.

Larson, B. (1988). *Cochabamba 1550–1900: Colonialism and Agrarian Transformation in Bolivia*. Durham: Duke University Press.

Mamani, C. (1996). History and prehistory in Bolivia. What about the Indians? In R.W. Preucel & I. Hodder (Eds.), *Contemporary Archaeology in Theory* (pp. 632–645). Oxford: Blackwell.

McGuire, R. (1999). Class confrontations in archaeology. *Historical Archaeology*, 33(1), 159–183.

McNiven, I., & Russell, L. (2005). *Appropriated Pasts: Indigenous Peoples and the Colonial Culture of Archaeology*. Walnut Creek: AltaMira Press.

Patterson, T. (1995). Archaeology, history, indigenismo, and the state in Peru and Mexico. In P.R. Schmidt & T.C. Patterson (Eds.), *Making Alternative Histories: The Practice of Archaeology and History in Non-Western Settings* (pp. 69–86). Santa Fe: School of American Research Press.

Schmidt, P.R., & Patterson, T.C. (1995). Introduction. In P.R. Schmidt & T.C. Patterson (Eds.), *Making Alternative Histories: The Practice of Archaeology and History in Non-Western Settings* (pp. 1–24). Santa Fe: School of American Research Press.

Shultz, J. Evo mania. Bolivia (January 22, 2006); http://www.democracyctr.org.

Silverman, H. (1999). Archaeology and the 1997 Peruvian hostage crisis. *Anthropology Today*, 15(1), 9–13.

Spivak, G.C. (1988). Can the subaltern speak? In L. Grossberg & C. Nelson (Eds.), *Marxist Interpretations of Literature and Culture. Limits, Boundaries and Frontiers* (pp. 271–313). Urbana: University of Illinois Press.

Stanish,C. (2001). The origin of state societies in South America. *Annual Review of Anthropology*, 30, 41–64.

Thomas, N. (1991). *Entangled Objects: Exchange, Material Culture and Colonialism in the Pacific*. Cambridge, MA: Harvard University Press.

Trigger, B. (1984). Alternative archaeologies: nationalist, colonialist, imperialist. *Man*, 19(3), 355–370.

Trigger, B. (1989a). *A History of Archaeological Thought*. Cambridge: Cambridge University Press.

Trigger, B. (1989b). Hyperrelativism, responsibility, and the social sciences. *Canadian Review of Sociology and Anthropology*, 26, 776–797.

Trigger, B. (1995). Romanticism, nationalism, and archaeology. In P.L. Kohl & C.P. Fawcett (Eds.), *Nationalism, Politics, and the Practice of Archaeology* (pp. 263–279). Cambridge: Cambridge University Press.

Trouillot, M.-R. (1995). *Silencing the Past: Power and the Production of History*. Boston: Beacon Press.

Ucko, P. (1990). Forward. In P.W.Gathercole & D. Lowenthal (Eds.), *The Politics of the Past* (pp. ix–xxi). London: Unwin Hyman.

Vranich, A. (1999). Interpreting the meaning of ritual spaces: the temple complex of Pumapunku, Tiwanaku, Bolivia. (Doctoral dissertation, University of Pennsylvania).

Watkins, J. (2000). *Indigenous Archaeology. American Indian Values and Scientific Practice*. Walnut Creek: AltaMira Press.

Watkins, J. (2003). Beyond the margin: American Indians, First Nations and archaeology in North America. *American Antiquity*, 68(2), 273–285.

Wylie, A. (1992). The interplay of evidential constraints and political interests: recent archaeological research on gender. *American Antiquity*, 57(1), 15–35.

Wylie, A. (2000). Questions of evidence, legitimacy, and the (dis)unity of science. *American Antiquity*, 65(2), 227–237.

Wylie, A. (2002). *Thinking from Things: Essays in the Philosophy of Archaeology*. Berkeley: University of California Press.

PART II
EVALUATING MULTIPLE NARRATIVES IN VARIOUS REGIONAL AND HISTORICAL SETTINGS

Introduction to Part II

Evaluating Multiple Narratives in Various Regional and Historical Settings

The various chapters in Part II examine the political and ideological implications of multiple interpretations developed in diverse regional and historical settings. All the case studies discussed here deal with multiple interpretations that have emerged, or may emerge, outside the theoretical framework of contemporary Anglo-American archaeology. The Japanese case study presented by Junko Habu and Clare Fawcett (Chapter 7) reveals the tensions between (1) local archaeologists' efforts to be independent from the academic hierarchy within Japan, (2) their attempts to accommodate multiple interpretations of the past including those supported by local residents, and (3) the potential danger of getting incorporated into a neo-nationalistic narrative. Behind these tensions is the particular history of Japanese archaeology, in which "archaeology as science" has developed, not in the context of processual archaeology, but as a tool to negate the ultra-nationalistic ideology of the Second World War period. Minkoo Kim (Chapter 8) stresses the difficulty of importing the practice of multivocality from Anglo-American archaeology directly into the Korean context. Neil Silberman (Chapter 9) explains how sites and museums developed for the tourist market, many of which have "interactive" computer-based presentations for nonacademic audiences, support rather than challenge dominant narratives.

Instead of focusing solely on the political and ideological implications of providing multiple interpretations, two contributors to this volume (Chapman and Wallace) chose to provide an alternative interpretation to archaeological topics of importance in their respective regions, and situate these new interpretations within the sociopolitical milieus of their research areas. Focusing on the study of state formation in Bronze Age Spain, Bob Chapman (Chapter 10) describes historical materialist approaches adopted by Spanish archaeologists, and contrasts these approaches with Anglo-American conceptualizations of the state. Rather than viewing such alternative interpretations as hindrances to a proper understanding of the past, Chapman argues that these interpretations are beneficial, regardless of whether one accepts them or not. In the case of the study of state formation in Bronze Age Spain, such alternative perspectives challenge widely held assumptions regarding social evolutionary categories, and push archaeologists to analyze critically the theories and concepts that they employ and often take for granted. In dealing with the Viking Age Irish materials, Pat Wallace (Chapter 11) highlights the complexity of identifying ethnicity through archaeological analysis, and discusses the implications of his study in the context of contemporary debates on Irish and European nationalism. These contributions clearly indicate that interpretations of archaeological data and the examination of their sociopolitical contexts are not two separate research topics, but that they should be conducted simultaneously.

These five case studies demonstrate how political, ideological, and historical conditions, as well as the actions of individual archaeologists and other stakeholders, influence the creation of alternative narratives in different parts of the world. Together, they provide an excellent set of materials to consider the complementary nature of universalism and contextualism discussed by Trigger (Chapter 12) and Hodder (Chapter 13).

Junko Habu
Clare Fawcett
John M. Matsunaga

Chapter 7
Science or Narratives? Multiple Interpretations of the Sannai Maruyama Site, Japan

Junko Habu and Clare Fawcett

This paper examines the dynamic interaction between scholars, local residents and the mass media at the Sannai Maruyama site, Japan. Sannai Maruyama is an Early and Middle Jomon period site in Aomori Prefecture in northern Japan, dating to approximately 5900 to 4400 cal. B.P. The site was originally excavated as a salvage project by the prefectural board of education prior to the construction of a baseball stadium. This excavation unexpectedly revealed an extraordinarily large Jomon settlement: by the summer of 1994, more than 500 pit-dwellings had been recovered along with numerous other types of features. Following these discoveries, local residents formed a dedicated and effective preservation movement. As a result, in August 1994, the prefectural governor halted the construction of the stadium, and declared that the site should be preserved. Since then, it has been a major tourist attraction in Aomori Prefecture (Habu & Fawcett 1999).

In this paper, we first outline our theoretical concerns and give a historical background of the sociopolitical context of archaeology in modern Japan. We then provide an overview of the Sannai Maruyama site excavation and preservation movement, and analyze research strategies adopted by local archaeologists as well as their outreach efforts. In particular, we emphasize the importance of the actions of local archaeologists and residents in encouraging multiple interpretations of the site. Our analysis also highlights the complex historical, political, and social contexts in which these multiple interpretations have been formed, presented, and evaluated. We conclude by analyzing the significance of this case study in relation to the current dialog about multivocality in contemporary Anglo-American archaeology.

Theoretical Framework: Multivocality and the Sociopolitics of Archaeology

The Sociopolitics of Archaeology

Underlying our research is the recognition that archaeological practice in each country is shaped by its social, political, and economic contexts both domestically and internationally. One of the first studies to analyze this point was Bruce

J. Habu, C. Fawcett, and J. M. Matsunaga (eds.), *Evaluating Multiple Narratives: Beyond Nationalist, Colonialist, Imperialist Archaeologies.*
© Springer 2008

Trigger's 1984 article, "Alternative Archaeologies: Nationalist, Colonialist, Imperialist." In this paper, Trigger argued that most archaeological traditions have had some nationalist elements. Consequently, archaeological research in many parts of the world has been used to create patriotic sentiments, often with substantial government patronage (Trigger 1984:358). Trigger stressed that nationalist archaeology "is probably strongest among people who feel politically threatened, insecure or deprived of their collective rights by more powerful nations or in countries where appeals for national unity are being made to counteract serious divisions along class lines" (Trigger 1984:360).

Trigger (1984) also outlined two other common types of archaeological research, colonialist and imperialist. Colonialist archaeology, he said, "developed either in countries whose native population was wholly replaced or overwhelmed by European settlers or in ones where Europeans remained politically and economically dominant for a considerable period of time" (Trigger 1984:360). He argued that imperialist archaeological traditions are produced by states with global political, economic, and cultural power, such as the United Kingdom in the late nineteenth and early twentieth centuries, the Soviet Union during the mid-twentieth century, and the United States since the 1960s. These examples elegantly demonstrated how archaeologists working within each of these imperialist traditions had assumed global applicability of their theoretical and methodological approaches. Furthermore, these archaeologists had the financial and political means to organize archaeological projects in various parts of the world, were the teachers of students from a variety of other countries, and were able to publish widely.

While Trigger's (1984) work emphasized three distinctive types of archaeological research tradition that do not seem to be disappearing, Hodder (1999) has argued that in the late twentieth and early twenty-first century postindustrial, postmodern age of globalization, broad frameworks and general models that archaeologists previously used to interpret the past have been *both* homogenized into messages of universal human heritage *and* fragmented by the creation of local identities in an increasingly multivocal and pluralistic world. He suggests that this process of fragmentation will both enable and create resistance to the homogenizing effects of globalization. In contrast to the world systems framework adopted by Trigger, Hodder sees the relationship between archaeology and its sociopolitical context as a fluid process that is constantly in transition. "[T]he global," he tells us, "does not in any simple way win out over the local. There is rather a negotiated process in which the past serves a variety of interests" (Hodder 1999:176–177; see also Hodder 1997).

To operationalize this theoretical perspective in an archaeological context, Hodder (1999) introduced the concept of multivocality as a key methodological tool for his field research at the site of Çatalhöyük in Turkey. Anja Wolle and Ruth Tringham (2000) also adopt this concept in their work at Çatalhöyük with an emphasis on the use of multimedia. It is to this concept of multivocality that we now turn.

Multivocality: Theory and Practice

Hodder's discussion of multivocality stresses that, by accepting multiple interpretations of the past, archaeologists can facilitate perspectives of various groups or individuals, including perspectives of the socially or politically underrepresented. Put another way, multivocality not only provides a wider variety of interpretative options, but it also allows archaeologists to be socially and politically engaged. The latter is an integral part of this approach, and our paper welcomes such social and political commitment. Nevertheless, we agree with Trigger (this volume) that these interpretative options must be tested against multiple lines of archaeological evidence before they are accepted as valid. Interpretations cannot be accepted simply on the basis of their perceived political and moral integrity, or because they represent the perspective of either majority or marginalized groups (see also Trigger 1989a,b, 1995, 1998, 2003; Wylie 1989, 1992, 1995, cf. Fotiadis 1994; Little 1994). For us, multivocality is a process whereby archaeologists work with various groups of people to generate a wide variety of questions and novel interpretations. In this way, marginalized people have a voice, and the integrity of the archaeological data and research process is maintained at the same time. Examples of this kind of practice can be found in Leone et al. (1995) and Blakey (this volume).

Despite the progressive intent of empowering marginalized groups, however, the celebration of diversity might actually further the agenda of transnational capitalism (Trigger, this volume). Hall (1997:179) argues this when he points out that little of the cultural diversity that we associate with globalization represents indigenous difference and resistance to Western cultural hegemony. This is because, rather than obliterating non-Western cultural forms, global capital maintains hegemony by working through them and making them part of the larger global culture, the center of which always remains under the control of the West. In other words, Western political and commercial interests govern which cultural forms are tolerated and which are rejected. Hall argues that this is the view of globalization accepted by and emanating from the (Western) center. Hall, however, outlines another view of globalization. He points out that when globalization is analyzed from the perspective of the local rather than from that of the center, cultural representations can be seen to come from the margins in the voices of previously decentered or subaltern subjects. Here, global mass culture and the power of global capitalism are challenged and alternative voices maintain their independence and integrity (Hall 1997:186–187).

In archaeological terms, one could argue that when multivocality refers to situations in which Anglo-American archaeologists or other mainstream cultural interpreters act as gatekeepers controlling a variety of interpretations, diversity is not being celebrated; rather it is being co-opted. In such cases, archaeological interpretive diversity is often a means of marketing a site (see Silberman, this volume) or of providing a semblance of community involvement when powerful members of an archaeological hierarchy actually make key interpretive decisions. This parallels

Hall's first example of globalization as seen from the center. In contrast, multivocality could refer to situations where alternative archaeological interpretations created on the margins in traditions not based in or controlled by archaeological elites, including the Anglo-American archaeological center, challenge dominant disciplinary and interpretative paradigms. In such cases, marginalized people ask questions about the archaeological past on their own terms and in their own voices, and multivocality can be seen as a challenge to the dominant interpretative paradigms.

Historical Context: Japanese Archaeology and Nationalism from the Late Nineteenth Century to the Present

When examining the place of any particular archaeological tradition within the global power structure outlined above, we must consider not only the contemporary political and social context, but also the historical context of the region, nation, or community in which specific archaeological interpretations have been formed and presented (see e.g., Joyce, this volume). In the case of Japan, the development of emperor-centered ultra-nationalist ideology (hereafter imperial nationalism) before and during World War II (see e.g., Fujitani 1993) and the postwar rejection of imperial nationalism have significantly influenced Japanese archaeological practice and the theoretical positions of Japanese archaeologists (see e.g., Habu & Fawcett 2006).

Japanese archaeological research began during the early Meiji Period as part of Japan's national policy of adopting European and American institutions – including governmental, economic, educational, and military among others – as a means of forestalling any possibility of colonization by Western powers. Japan's efforts paid off. The nation resisted subjugation to colonial rule, and was accepted by Euro-American powers as an equal political and trading partner. Soon after, Japan also became a colonizing nation when the Japanese military, followed by civilians, moved into and annexed or supported governments in other parts of Asia. Defeat in the Second World War ended Japan's colonial domination of much of Asia. It also resulted in a short period of Allied military occupation during which Japan once again set about rebuilding its institutions to satisfy demands of a major Western power, this time, the United States (Halliday 1975; Hane 2001).

During the late nineteenth and early twentieth centuries, Japan felt threatened by the powerful nations of the West. Japanese imperial nationalism crystallized around the Emperor, who was presented to the people of Japan and to the world as the sacred descendant of the Sun-goddess. This strong form of nationalism merged text-based history, myth, and religion and pushed aside archaeology – the study of the past through an empirical examination of material remains – as a means of understanding the origins of Japan, the Japanese people, and the Japanese state (Edwards 1997; Fawcett & Habu 1990; Ikawa-Smith 1982). Before and during World War II, Japanese archaeologists reacted to imperial nationalism in two ways. Some archaeologists participated in colonialist archaeology in Korea and other areas of Japanese influence in Asia, while other archaeologists moved their research foci away from discussions of the social meaning of the artifacts and sites they discovered and concentrated on studying and categorizing artifacts, particularly pottery, into detailed typologies (Habu 1989).

After Japan's defeat in 1945, scholars in various academic fields, including archaeology and history, worked to counter prewar imperial nationalism by insisting that the Japanese people needed to discover the reality of Japanese history through empirical research on material remains. This new intellectual movement was explicitly anti-elitist, anti-imperialist, and anti-nationalist. It was strongly influenced by the classical Marxist theoretical positions advocated by Wajima (1948, 1958) and others (for details, see Fawcett 1990; Habu 1989; Habu & Fawcett 2006). Archaeologists took up these ideas by rejecting interpretations of the past based on the analysis of texts and stories, and by focusing their attention on writing ancient Japanese history using scientifically derived and materially verifiable archaeological remains.

Outside archaeological studies, the rapid economic growth of Japan beginning in the late 1960s and 1970s resulted in the development of a broad-based culturalist or nationalist discourse focused on the uniqueness of the Japanese people, culture, and nation: *Nihonjin-ron* and *Nihon-bunka-ron*. *Nihonjin-ron* emphasizes the uniqueness, and often the superiority, of the Japanese people and nation, whereas *Nihon-bunka-ron* focuses specifically on the uniqueness of Japanese culture and the process of its development. Unlike prewar forms of Japanese nationalism, these discourses are not based on veneration of the emperor or the imperial house; neo-imperial nationalist movements that endorse emperor worship do exist in Japan, but they are relatively small in number and are rejected by most Japanese citizens. Rather, expositors of *Nihonjin-ron*, and the closely related *Nihon-bunka-ron*, typically see the Japanese people and culture as special and unique among world cultures and peoples. Several scholars have pointed out that the emphasis on Japanese uniqueness characteristic of *Nihonjin-ron* and *Nihon-bunka-ron* bolsters ideologies of Japanese homogeneity and mutes recognition of diversity in terms of class, gender, and ethnicity within the country (e.g., Befu 1993; for anthropological discussion of the differences between prewar and postwar discussions about the homogeneity of the Japanese people, see Oguma 2002). Supporters of *Nihonjin-ron* and *Nihon-bunka-ron* also typically assume that the categories of Japanese people, culture, and nation overlap, hence our use of the terms "nationalist" and "culturalist" to describe this phenomenon.

Parallel to the resurgence of this new form of nationalism was the de-politicization of archaeology during and after the 1970s. There were several reasons for this. First, archaeologists became de-politicized as the nature of their work changed. Beginning in the 1960s, a rapid increase in the number of rescue excavations in Japan resulted in the creation of the new rescue excavation system throughout the Japanese archipelago. Under this system, so-called cultural property centers (*Maizo Bunkazai Senta*) were created at all the prefectures and many municipal units, including cities, towns, and villages (Barnes 1993; Tanaka 1984; Tsude 1995). When cultural property centers were not instituted, boards of education of each prefectural or municipal unit took charge of rescue excavations. The apex of this system of "administrative excavation" (*gyosei hakkutsu*) was the Nara National Cultural Properties Institute, which had the authority to give instructions about how rescue excavations should be conducted. The number of rescue excavations conducted by these centers and boards of educations increased exponentially through the 1970s and 1980s. Archaeologists in charge of these excavations were local or national government officials who could not easily adopt a particular political stance. Furthermore, since most rescue excavations were conducted prior to large-scale land developments funded by the national government or large companies with close ties to Japan's political elites, archaeologists could not maintain explicit commitments to antinationalistic agendas.

The second reason for the de-politicization of archaeologists was generational change. Many of the archaeologists trained during the late 1970s and 1980s were part of the post-1960s academic generation which had not directly experienced World War II, the early postwar period, or the student movements of the 1960s.

A third reason for the de-politicization of archaeology was that archaeologists' emphasis on salvage work and the detailed, scientific analysis of data resulted in gradual narrowing of their research focus. Ironically, the more archaeologists tried to dismiss prewar imperial nationalist views of Japanese history through empirical research, the more they focused on the study of the origins and "formation process" of the ancient Japanese state. Gradually, most Japanese archaeologists lost contact and stopped interacting with archaeologists from other countries. Japanese archaeologists were outward-looking and interested in incorporating ideas from other archaeological traditions from the late nineteenth to the early twentieth centuries and immediately after World War II. By the 1960s and 1970s, however, they had become insular and disconnected from theoretical and methodological trends in other parts of the world. The increase in Cultural Resource Management excavations as described above also kept Japanese archaeologists from seeking active academic interaction with archaeologists from other countries (Habu 1989). Because of this insularity, the growing political concerns of archaeologists in many parts of the world, including Europe and North America, during the 1980s and 1990s, as well as the theoretical frameworks and methodologies they had developed, went largely unnoticed by Japanese archaeologists.

The de-politicization, insularity, and narrow focus on Japanese origins and early state formation all provided a context in which archaeologically derived knowledge about the Japanese past was gradually incorporated into the culturalist and nationalist discourses of *Nihon-bunka-ron* by authors writing for popular presses and the mass media. These authors, most of whom were not archaeologists, began to use archaeological data to sustain and develop a meta-narrative describing the origins of the Japanese people and culture. In contrast, many Japanese archaeologists continued to be antinationalist in orientation. Furthermore, archaeological practice, still underlain by a theoretical framework derived from classical Marxism (see Habu & Fawcett 2006), continued to foster a strong belief in archaeology as empirical science, an explicit focus on the reconstruction of commoners' lifeways, and an emphasis on outreach activities to educate the general public. In short, contemporary Japanese archaeology is situated between these two radically different orientations. With this in mind, the following section analyzes a case study from the Sannai Maruyama site.

Case Study of Sannai Maruyama

Salvage Excavation and the Decision to Preserve the Site

Located in Aomori Prefecture in northern Japan (Fig. 7.1), the Sannai Maruyama site (*circa* 3,900–2,300 B.C.) is currently the largest known Jomon Period settlement (Habu 2004; Habu et al. 2001; Kidder 1998). From 1992 to 1994, the site was excavated as a salvage project by the prefectural board of education prior to the construction of a baseball stadium. Results of this three-year, large-scale excavation revealed that the entire area planned for the stadium had been a prehistoric settlement (Fig. 7.2): in fact, the settlement extended outside the limits of the proposed stadium area. Features identified within the stadium area included more than 500 pit-dwellings,

Fig. 7.1 Map of Japan showing the location of the Sannai Maruyama site

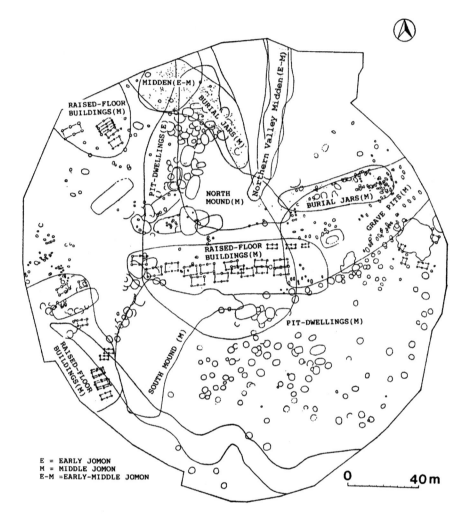

Fig. 7.2 Distribution of features at the Baseball Stadium Area of the Sannai Maruyama site (from Okada and Habu 1995)

long-houses, post-molds of raised-floor buildings, grave pits, burial jars, water-logged middens, and three mounds filled with potsherds and other refuse deposits. Among these was a feature associated with six extremely large posts.

Shortly after the discovery of this feature, in July 1994, the news of this excavation was reported on the front page of the local newspaper, *To'o Nippo*, as well as the front page of several other national newspapers. A site preservation movement supported by Aomori citizens quickly developed, resulting in the governor of Aomori Prefecture deciding to halt the construction of the baseball stadium and preserve the site. In 1997, the Japanese government designated Sannai Maruyama a national historic site (Fig. 7.3).

Fig. 7.3 The Sannai Maruyama National Historic Park

After the initial rush of visitors to the site, a phenomenon dubbed "Sannai Maruyama Fever" by the media, the number of people touring Sannai Maruyama continued to increase each year until Fiscal Year 1997 when approximately 560,000 people visited the site. Visitation rates declined in subsequent years. Nevertheless, in Fiscal Year 2004, over 156,000 people toured Sannai Maruyama, an unusually large number of visitors for a Japanese archaeological site (Preservation Office of the Sannai Maruyama Site 2006).

To facilitate further excavations, data analysis and outreach activities, *Sannai Maruyama Iseki Taisaku-shitsu* (the Preservation Office of the Sannai Maruyama Site; hereafter the Preservation Office) was established in January 1995 as a branch office of the Board of Education of Aomori Prefecture. The Preservation Office staff includes six full-time archaeologists (hereafter the site archaeologists), all of whom were prefectural government officials. All of them hold B.A. or M.A. degrees in either archaeology or related fields, such as history. From 1995 to the present, these archaeologists have conducted 30 test excavations and published over 20 volumes of excavation reports (Archaeological Center of Aomori Prefecture 1994a–b, 1995, Cultural Affairs Section of the Agency of Education of Aomori Prefecture 1996a–b, 1997a–b, 1998a–d, 1999, 2000a–d, 2001, 2002a–b, 2003a–b, 2004a–c, 2005a–c).

Site Archaeologists' Approaches

The theoretical and methodological approaches adopted by the site archaeologists were generally empirical, data-oriented, and inductive. Excavation reports published by these archaeologists include drawings and photographs of all the representative artifacts with three-dimensional measurements and information about provenience. As we have discussed above, the root of this empiricism can be found in the broad postwar archaeology movement that stressed the importance of "scientific" approaches as a means of ensuring that imperial nationalist ideology would not affect archaeological interpretation.

Based on the Sannai Maruyama excavation results, Yasuhiro Okada (1995a,b), currently the chair of the Preservation Office, who also directed the salvage excavation team from 1992 to 1994 and was the head archaeologist of the Preservation Office from 1995 to 2002, suggested that the site was a fully sedentary settlement continuously occupied for over 1500 years. He also supported the idea that the site population must have reached over 500 people at its peak. Furthermore, analyses of changes in feature distribution led Okada to propose gradually developing and declining patterns of site size (Okada 1998). More recently, Okada used results of his Sannai Maruyama study to infer long-term changes in the Jomon culture in the Tohoku region (Okada 2003).

While Okada and other Sannai Maruyama site archaeologists have adopted strict empiricist and culture historical approaches to excavation and data presentation, their research strategies, as well as their outreach efforts to promote the importance of the site and maintain the public interest, have involved several nonconventional approaches. First, they have collaborated with the media, especially TV directors and newspaper reporters, to advertise the spectacular nature of the site. Second, they have welcomed the participation of specialists of various disciplines in interpreting the nature and function of the site. Third, these archaeologists have chosen to work with local residents to disseminate the results of their excavation to site visitors and the general public. Fourth, they have actively sought ties and collaborations with international scholars and institutions.

Working Together with the Media

The site archaeologists' collaboration with the media began prior to the government's decision to preserve the site during the summer of 1994. According to Okada, the archaeological team excavating the Sannai Maruyama site took public outreach seriously even before the prefectural governor announced that the site was to be preserved. At that time, neither Okada nor the other site archaeologists expected the site to be preserved. Accordingly, they felt that the least they could do was to let the local people know the spectacular nature of Sannai Maruyama through public outreach such as site tours to visitors (Okada & Habu 1995).

After the prefectural governor declared that the site was to be preserved, Okada and the other archaeologists used the media consciously and strategically to explain the importance of the site clearly, simply, and comprehensibly to the public. Throughout the summer and the autumn of 1994, the mass media continued to report archaeological discoveries at Sannai Maruyama. A number of TV specials were aired, and "Sannai Maruyama Fever" swept Japan. In most of these TV specials, Okada played a prominent role, summarizing the excavation results and emphasizing the importance of the site for understanding Japanese prehistory (for a summary of Okada's interpretations, see e.g., Okada 2003).

Among the media, *To'o Nippo,* the Aomori-based newspaper, has played a particularly noteworthy role in maintaining public interest in Sannai Maruyama. As noted above, *To'o Nippo* was an important actor in developing the 1994 site preservation movement. Since then, the paper has continued to provide timely coverage of new excavation results and other everyday news related to the site, including outreach events and public symposia. It has also sponsored a number of archaeological exhibitions that featured archaeological remains unearthed from Sannai Maruyama.

Interdisciplinary Approaches

To interpret the function and nature of the Sannai Maruyama settlement, site archaeologists have actively collaborated with specialists from various disciplines. Archaeologists have formally collaborated with various specialists in the natural and physical sciences to conduct analyses of excavated artifacts and samples. Collaborative research has occurred with scholars in genetic biology (Ishikawa 2003, 2004; Kiyokawa 2001; Sato 1997a, b, 1998, 2000; Yamanaka et al. 1999), paleobotany (Suzuki 2004; Tsuji 1997, 1998, 2000, 2001, 2005; Toyama 1995), zooarchaeology (Nishimoto 1995, 1998), parasitology (Kanehara 1995), entomology (Mori 1995, 1998a–c, 1999), and geochemistry (Akanuma 2003, 2004; Matsumoto 2003, 2004, 2005; Nishida et al. 2005; Warashina 1998, 2000, 2005). Collaboration with the natural and physical sciences is common in Japanese archaeology, but the extent of the interdisciplinary collaboration at Sannai Maruyama has been more extensive than in most other Japanese archaeological projects. The research projects of the collaborating scientists have contributed significantly to understanding the lifeways of the site residents, as well as site chronology and the environmental setting of the site.

In addition to these natural and physical scientists, two additional groups of scholars have also participated in the interpretation of Sannai Maruyama: (1) high-profile archaeologists, including professors teaching at well-known universities or researchers at national institutions, and (2) social scientists who specialized in related fields, such as cultural anthropology, ethnography, folklore, and architecture. The participation of these scholars sometimes occurred in the context of public symposia. In other contexts, the producers of TV and radio programs and writers of newspaper and magazine articles actively sought out the opinions of these scholars. Together with the natural and physical scientists discussed above, these two groups of specialists provided their own views about and interpretations of the Sannai Maruyama site through newspapers, television, magazines, popular books, and the Internet. As a result, the general public has had access to multiple interpretations of the site.

Among these scholars was Shuzo Koyama, a professor (currently an emeritus professor) of the National Museum of Ethnology. As a specialist of Jomon subsistence studies and population estimates (Koyama 1978, 1984; see also Koyama & Thomas 1981), and as an ethnographer who worked on Australian Aborigines, Koyama (1995, 1997) suggested that the Sannai Maruyama residents should be seen as part of the "affluent" hunter–gatherer cultures of the North Pacific Rim. By emphasizing the contribution of the Sannai Maruyama data to the study of world archaeology and anthropology, Koyama extended the use of the site beyond the boundaries of Aomori Prefecture and Japan, and moved the discussion of its importance away from Japanese history to broader global issues. He also tried to move away from the dry, empirical study of artifacts toward the reconstruction of the life of the site's residents.

Another prominent actor in the public debate about the size and function of the Sannai Maruyama settlement was the late Makoto Sahara, a former vice-director of the National Museum of History. As a specialist in Japanese prehistoric archaeology, Sahara fully recognized the importance of the Sannai Maruyama data to Jomon archaeology. However, he was critical of the idea that the population of the Sannai Maruyama settlement was as large as 500 people (see e.g., his statements in Iizuka 1995). As a result, his interpretation regarding the size and function of the Sannai Maruyama settlement was quite different from that of Okada's (1995a).

Other scholars who have participated in the discussion of Sannai Maruyama include cultural anthropologist Tadao Umesao (Umesao et al. 1995), environmental archaeologist Yoshinori Yasuda (1995), and architectural historian Chojiro Miyamoto (1995). Umesao (Umesao et al. 1995) proposes that the feature associated with six large posts had a religious function, and discusses its importance in comparison to early civilizations in different parts of the world. His interpretation of Sannai Maruyama also emphasizes continuity from Jomon to later Japanese history. Yasuda (1995) identifies the Jomon culture of northeastern Japan, including Tohoku, as the mixture of the northern culture of the subfrigid, coniferous forest zone and the southern culture of the subtropical, evergreen forest zone, and interprets the prosperity of Sannai Maruyama and other Jomon sites in Eastern Japan as a result of their unique environmental conditions. Miyamoto (1995) suggested that the superstructure of the feature associated with the six large posts must have been a raised-floor building, thus questioning the interpretation of another architect Yuichiro Takashima, who proposed that the feature was a tower of over 15 m.

Collaboration with Local Residents

One unique feature of the Sannai Maruyama excavation project is the professional archaeologists' active collaboration with local residents. The history of this collaboration goes back to 1995. Throughout late 1994 and early 1995, as the mass media continued to report archaeological discoveries at Sannai Maruyama on almost a daily basis, the number of site visitors continued to increase dramatically. In this climate, *Sannai Maruyama Oentai* (the Sannai Maruyama Support Group; or the Support Group), a volunteer organization consisting primarily of local residents, was formed in May 1995. The primary goal of this group was "to help the prefecture preserve and utilize the Sannai Maruyama site from a perspective of local residents" (Sannai Maruyama Support Group 1997). Members of the Support Group received special lectures and training by archaeologists from the Preservation Office before they assumed their duties. The formation of this group resulted in the establishment of a "division of labor" between the site archaeologists and the Support Group (Koyama, Okada, & Ichikawa 1996). The Support Group took charge of providing site tours for visitors. The archaeologists who had previously been extremely busy providing site outreach to the public were able to spend more time on their research. The first president of the Support Group was Kanemaru Ichikawa, a prefectural archaeologist and a former president of the Aomori Archeological Association. Through various activities of the Support Group, Ichikawa encouraged the members of the group to actively imagine the lifeways of the Jomon people.

The site archaeologists' attempts to work with enthusiastic local residents also led to the creation of yet another voice in the interpretation of Sannai Maruyama when, in 1995, the *Sannai Maruyama Jomon Hasshin no Kai* (Sannai Maruyama Jomon Information Association) was formed. This Aomori-based nonprofit organization is administered by a local publisher, *Purizumu*, and many of the members of this association are Aomori citizens. The annual membership fees of the Sannai Maruyama Jomon Information Association cover subscription to the Association's monthly newsletter, *The Sannai Maruyama Jomon File*, published in both Japanese and English. This periodical carries updates of test-excavations, records of symposia, and lectures, as well as short essays by archaeologists and other scholars working at the Preservation Office. Importantly, the editors, who are employees of *Purizumu*, also add their own messages which stress how the discovery of the Sannai Maruyama site in their home town has helped them and other Aomori residents restore a sense of local pride.

The emphasis of the *Sannai Maruyama Jomon File* editors on the importance of Sannai Maruyama for building local pride must be understood in the context of the power and economic structures of contemporary Japan. Aomori and other rural prefectures in the Tohoku region are economically and politically disadvantaged compared to the large, central metropolitan areas of Tokyo and Osaka. Furthermore, many people living in central Honshu consider these rural prefectures to be less culturally important than other parts of central Japan. The use of Sannai Maruyama to create local awareness of and confidence in the importance of the region's cultural assets is a significant step towards the development of regional pride in the Tohoku region.

International Collaborations

Okada and other site archaeologists have actively sought opportunities to work with institutions and scholars from other parts of the world. One example of these international connections is the fostering of collaboration with Chinese archaeologists, several of whom have been invited to participate in public symposia on Sannai Maruyama (e.g., Wang 1998). These academic exchanges have resulted in several members of the Preservation Office taking part in the study of the Xinglonggou site in northeastern China (Sannai Maruyama Jomon Information Association 2001). Another example of active international exchange occurred during the autumn of 1998, when the National Museum of Ethnology, Osaka, hosted the Eighth International Conference on Hunting and Gathering Societies (CHAGS8) in Aomori (Habu, Savelle, Koyama, & Hongo 2003). Participants visited the Sannai Maruyama site, and a full-day public symposium was devoted to a discussion of the nature and function of the site from a comparative perspective. More recently, in autumn 2004, a museum exhibition of archaeological remains excavated from the Sannai Maruyama site was presented in Germany.

The site archaeologists' attempts to collaborate with non-Japanese institutions have also involved Habu, one of the authors of this chapter, and her students from the University of California at Berkeley. The idea of the collaboration between the Berkeley team and the Preservation Office was first raised in the summer of 1996, when Koyama, Okada, and Habu met at a workshop and discussed alternative interpretations of Sannai Maruyama (Koyama, Okada, & Habu 1996). Following this discussion, the Berkeley Sannai Maruyama project was initiated. From 1997 to 2006, the Berkeley team conducted 2–4 weeks of field/laboratory work every summer and collected data for several interrelated projects. These include studies of faunal and floral remains (Habu et al. 2001; Kim 2005), feature assemblages (Habu 2002, 2004), lithic tools and debitage (Habu 2006a), and regional settlement patterns. In addition, X-ray fluorescence analyses of pottery, clay figurines, and obsidian were conducted to examine artifact production and circulation (Habu 2005, 2006a; Habu, Hall, & Ogasawara 2003). A carbon and nitrogen isotope analysis was applied to a human skeletal sample excavated from an Early Jomon site near Sannai Maruyama (Chisholm & Habu 2003) and the result was used to examine dietary patterns in the Aomori area.

Based on the results of these projects, Habu (2002, 2004, 2006b) presented an alternative interpretation of the life history of the site, with an emphasis on changes over time in the size and function of the Sannai Maruyama settlement. In particular, these results indicate that the site may have been occupied only seasonally at least in one or more occupational phases. Despite the fact that this interpretation is markedly different from Okada's (1995a, b, 1998, 2003) interpretation, the Preservation Office and the site archaeologists welcomed the Berkeley team's research, and future collaborative plans are under way.

Positive and Negative Implications of the Local Archaeologists' Strategies

The above-described strategies adopted by the site archaeologists have helped break down the existing power structure and encourage multiple interpretations in several ways. First, by collaborating directly with scholars in other fields and institutions in Japan and overseas, the site archaeologists have been able to retain control over the analysis and interpretation of the Sannai Maruyama data. This is in sharp contrast with several other nationally known sites, where local archaeologists have submitted research initiatives to national government officials because of an academic hierarchy that governs Japanese archaeology. Through these collaborations, and by working with the media, interpretations of the site provided by a wide variety of scholars were publicized.

Equally importantly, site archaeologists have worked closely with local residents. The root of this practice comes at least partly from the classical Marxist tradition of postwar Japanese archaeology, in which participation of local residents was strongly encouraged (see e.g., Kondo 1998). The relationship between the site archaeologists and members of the Sannai Maruyama Support Group is an example of archaeologist–citizen collaboration. Working together, these professional archaeologists and members of the Support Group developed outreach activities (Fig. 7.4), for instance, pottery-making classes held at the site.

Unfortunately, the site archaeologists' efforts to collaborate with other scholars, the media, and local residents have also resulted in several problems. One problem, which arose as a direct result of allowing multiple interpretations in the public sphere, was the resurrection of unwelcome ties between archaeology and *Nihon-bunka-ron*. Several individuals have proposed that data from Sannai Maruyama shows that the Jomon can be considered the foundation of "Japanese" culture. According to these interpretations, core characteristics of the Jomon culture had been incorporated into, and became emblematic of, later Japanese culture. This was largely a new phenomenon, because, even though most archaeological outreach programs treated the Jomon people as part of the ancestors of the modern Japanese (or "us"), their hunting–gathering lifeways were not generally regarded as part of the distinct "Japanese" cultural tradition (Habu & Fawcett 1999). However, Sannai Maruyama provided the supporters of *Nihonjin-ron* and *Nihon-bunka-ron* with an opportunity to integrate the Jomon as part of their meta-narratives.

Fig. 7.4 Outreach activity at the Sannai Maruyama site: making clay figurines

One of the vocal proponents of this perspective is Takeshi Umehara (1995), a philosopher and an influential Japanese intellectual. He suggested that the "spirit" or "essence" of the Jomon people was fundamentally different from that of the rice-cultivators who inhabited the Japanese islands during the Yayoi period (*circa* 400 BC–AD 300). Umehara argued, furthermore, that aspects of this unique Jomon "spirit" could be found among modern Japanese people, and that they had formed the foundation of contemporary Japanese culture. Rather than focusing on the Jomon culture itself, such an argument uses the Sannai Maruyama data to understand the origins of the uniqueness of the modern Japanese people and culture. These ideas have much in common with *Nihonjinron*, which can feed into the meta-narrative of Japanese origins, and the construction of a new nationalist story for Japan (for a criticism of Umehara's work, see also Hudson 2003). In this regard, promoting multiple interpretations of Sannai Maruyama, especially through the media, is clearly a double-edged sword for the site archaeologists.

Another problem is a tendency, in some of the alternative interpretations, to overemphasize the complex and "advanced" nature of the site. Despite the fact that many scholars and individuals participated in the interpretations of Sannai Maruyama, many of the general images of the site presented through the media bear a strong resemblance to each other, with an emphasis on large settlement size, long duration of site occupation, and an abundance of sophisticated artifacts. This led to the criticism that some of the information presented about Sannai Maruyama in the media was inaccurate or overly simplistic. For example, Masaki Nishida (1996), a professor of anthropological archaeology at Tsukuba University, criticized the site archaeologists' emphasis on the large size of the "settlement." He argued that the "site's" large size could have been the result of the long-term occupation of a much smaller settlement.

Over the past several years, the site archaeologists have adjusted some of their approaches. This reflects their efforts to resist commercialism while still maintaining the interest and participation of the local people. For example, right after the site preservation was first announced by the prefectural governor and the site became extremely popular, Okada (e.g., 1995a,b) and publications of the Board of Education of Aomori Prefecture tended to emphasize the spectacular nature of the Sannai Maruyama site and its artifacts. Interpretations that cast doubt on this picture were not necessarily welcomed by the site archaeologists or by the media. Recently, however, the site archaeologists have become more careful about simply promoting Sannai Maruyama as "advanced." This change seems partly to have been a response to criticism by their archaeological colleagues (see above). In addition, local people have also questioned the validity of the stereotypical picture of Sannai Maruyama. For example, Seiji Wakayama (2002), one of the local residents who volunteered to work as a site tour guide, questions whether interpretations provided by the site archaeologists were accurate and reliable, and wants to present other interpretations together with those of the site archaeologists. In other words, the approaches adopted by archaeologists are constantly monitored by local residents and others, and archaeologists are flexible enough to adjust their research and interpretative strategies on the basis of this feedback. In this way, the site archaeologists encourage interpretative diversity at their site and practice a form of multivocal archaeology.

Discussion

From the above discussion, it becomes clear that the archaeology of Sannai Maruyama has been operationalized within a complex political and social milieu. In particular, when looking at the archaeological practice at Sannai Maruyama, at least three levels of power imbalance can be detected. On the world archaeology scene, archaeology practiced by Japanese scholars, including those working at Sannai Maruyama, has been significantly underrepresented due to the differences in language, and because of the theoretical and methodological frameworks employed (see also Habu 1989). Thus, the site archaeologists realize that collaborations with international scholars and institutions will be key in effectively disseminating the results of research from Sannai Maruyama. As archaeologists from non-Japanese institutions, we feel that it is our responsibility to facilitate these interactions, but without claiming the privileged status of North American archaeology over Japanese archaeology (see also Habu 2004: Chapter 1).

At the domestic level, Aomori archaeologists who have been in charge of the site excavation and data analysis have a less powerful standing within the academic hierarchy than professors at major universities and scholars at national institutions. As discussed by several scholars (e.g., Barnes 1993:36–37; Tanaka 1984), contemporary Japanese archaeology is highly centralized. In the tightly structured CRM system that has developed in postwar Japan, national government officials and scholars from major national and private universities have power over local archaeologists. This academic and bureaucratic hierarchy is paralleled by social and economic inequities between large metropolitan areas, such as Tokyo and Osaka, and rural areas, including Aomori Prefecture, where the Sannai Maruyama site is located. The significance of Sannai Maruyama is that interpretations presented by the Japanese archaeological centers – the professional archaeologists and thinkers working in elite academic institutions and national government agencies – are resisted by less powerful Aomori Prefectural archaeologists and citizens of Aomori Prefecture.

Finally, from the perspective of academic authority, both groups of Japanese archaeologists exercise a certain level of authority over nonarchaeologists on the basis of their academic and professional training. However, the case study described above demonstrates the archaeologists' sincere attempts to break down this power structure by seeking collaboration with the local residents. Furthermore, the last level of power imbalance is counteracted, at least to some extent, by the fact that the majority of the funding for archaeological research in Japan comes from tax money from various levels of government. In other words, the relevance of archaeologists' interpretations to the local community is constantly monitored by the citizens.

It should be emphasized that the power structure outlined above is constantly being affected by a number of social, political, and economic factors at the local (i.e., within Aomori Prefecture), domestic (within Japan), and international levels. Thus, we can say that the practice of archaeology at Sannai Maruyama is framed in a complex political and social milieu in which the power balance between the center and periphery, as well as between professional archaeologists and nonarchaeologists, are constantly changing.

Sannai Maruyama is also noteworthy when analyzing the concept of multivocality because it illustrates how archaeologists support multiple interpretations within a specific historical and sociopolitical context. One thing that is crucial and positive about the dynamic interaction between archaeologists, the media, and the local residents is that the different groups of people presenting the various interpretations of the site worked together to ensure that the site was preserved, and to present as much information about the site as possible to the public. Archaeologists, furthermore, were willing to engage in or allow the development of new and varied narratives and accept interpretative pluralism. They did this because they knew the site would be preserved and research funding maintained only if Sannai Maruyama remained popular locally and nationally. In addition, the site archaeologists, such as Okada, and other Aomori archaeologists, such as Ichikawa, wanted to move away from the dry descriptions of archaeological materials and pottery chronologies that had dominated empirically based Jomon archaeological research (Koyama, Okada, & Ichikawa 1996). They felt that it was time archaeologists talked about Jomon society and people using vivid stories, which could bring reconstructions of the Jomon people's life-ways into existence. Finally, Sannai Maruyama demonstrates the key role of the media in site interpretation and presentation, since prefectural archaeologists collaborated with the media to make sure that Sannai Maruyama excited the public imagination.

Do multiple interpretations promoted by the site archaeologists at Sannai Maruyama differ from multivocality espoused by Anglo-American archaeologists? We suggest that multiple interpretations of Sannai Maruyama arose because of the specific social, political, and historical contexts described in this chapter. The idea of embracing multiple interpretations, however, was not borrowed from other archaeological traditions; it is an indigenous Japanese development. Japanese archaeology, with its tradition of inductive reasoning and amateur involvement in excavation and interpretation of sites, has allowed for the acceptance of multiple interpretations as possible hypotheses. Furthermore, archaeologists working in Japan during the postwar period have been conscious of the importance of educating the public about archaeology so that when an important site needs to be preserved or a salvage excavation must be done in a neighborhood, they can count on public support. This education has often involved story-telling at sites, in local festivals, through museums and in articles written for and by the mass media. Thus, Japanese archaeology has had the foundation to facilitate multivocal interpretations, although this multivocality has not been theorized.

Thinking about this case study in relation to the current dialog in North American and British archaeology, we suggest that the adoption of multiple interpretations of the Sannai Maruyama site is not an example of Japanese archaeology's incorporation into a burgeoning Anglo-American archaeological tradition of multivocality. Rather, the site's interpretative diversity is an example of the nascent yet independent development of a multivocal interpretative framework. Without understanding the historical contexts of Japanese archaeology over the past half a century, in which antinationalism, collaboration with the local residents, large-scale rescue excavations, and wide press coverage all played key roles, it is impossible to evaluate the roots and implications of multiple interpretations of Sannai Maruyama.

To date, theoretical discussions of multivocality have been developed primarily in the context of Anglo-American archaeology. Presenting theoretical discussions of the relevance of multivocality solely from the perspective of Anglo-American archaeology could lead to the development of a form of imperialist archaeology as defined by Trigger (1984). Non-Anglo-American perspectives should not be underrepresented in the very field that aims to dismantle dominant structures of power. Certainly, at the international level, East Asian archaeology, including Japanese archaeology, has been underrepresented and sometimes even marginalized. Japanese archaeologists have studied Anglo-American archaeological methods and theory and have incorporated some of these interpretative frameworks and practices into their own work. Over the years, however, they have maintained a distinctive set of interpretative frameworks and practices and have resisted incorporation into a global archaeological system. They have done this by accepting and adapting only those Anglo-American contributions *they* considered relevant to archaeology within a Japanese social, political, and historical context. In this regard, the multivocal approach developed at Sannai Maruyama can be seen to be the result of resistance to global archaeological trends rather than as the outcome of incorporation into these trends.

As discussed above, elements of a nationalist (or at least Japan-oriented) perspective can be seen in some interpretations of the Sannai Maruyama site. However, the way these elements are embedded in each interpretation varies, and labeling individual interpretations as nationalist does not do justice to the multifaceted nature of these interpretations. This is partly due to the historically specific definition of "nationalism" understood by the Japanese people, including archaeologists. In this regard, we conclude that although the application of general theories, such as world systems theory, do provide a broad framework for understanding the relationship between archaeological traditions and their social and political milieux, we must also take into account the specific historical context of each local archaeological tradition. In the case of Sannai Maruyama, Japan's historical and present-day position as a state in a world political and economic system has influenced archaeological practice and interpretation by making both empirical research and questions of Japanese identity and origins core features of research and interpretation.

Conclusions

In this chapter, we argued that, by encouraging multiple interpretations of the site of Sannai Maruyama, and by working together with local residents, Aomori archaeologists have independently developed strategies that can question and break down the intellectual power structures of their discipline. This is significant given the fact that their intellectual traditions and theoretical perspectives are based outside Western postmodern social theory. Our chapter also highlighted the complex historical, political, and social contexts in which these multiple interpretations have been formed, presented, and evaluated.

The case study presented here also demonstrates that local agency is important. The Sannai Maruyama case exemplifies the interplay between structural constraints imposed on interpretations by global economic and political systems and the ability of individual people and small groups at the local level to resist the homogenization of the global marketplace by using archaeology imaginatively to create local identities. The local movement at Sannai Maruyama is kept from slipping into commercialism or neo-nationalism by the deep-seated belief of Aomori archaeologists, such as Ichikawa (Koyama, Okada, & Ichikawa 1996), that the core of the local movement should be grass-roots and noncommercial. This is the main reason that, despite the possible resurgence of neo-nationalism and the creation of a neo-nationalist meta-narrative, we feel optimistic about the future of the archaeology of Sannai Maruyama. Whether archaeological practice at Sannai Maruyama will be able to keep itself away from neo-nationalism, and/ or resist global economic forces to create a commercial heritage site, will be dependent on the extent to which archaeologists working on the site's material, including ourselves, can continue to mold the image and meaning of this site in politically strategic ways.

Acknowledgments We would like to express our gratitude to the members of the Preservation Office of the Sannai Maruyama Site and the Sannai Maruyama Support Group for providing us with useful information regarding the archaeology of Sannai Maruyama and its sociopolitical contexts. We also thank Mark Hall, John Matsunaga and a unanimous reviewer for their valuable comments. Responsibility for all the interpretations and errors in this chapter, of course, are ours.

References

Akanuma, H. (2003). A study of the production and use of pigments at the Sannai Maruyama site [Sannai Maruyama iseki ni okeru iro-zairyo no seisaku to shiyo ni kansuru kenkyu]. *Annual Bulletin of the Sannai Maruyama National Historic Site [Tokubetsu Shiseki Sannai Maruyama Iseki Nenpo]*, 6, 43–49 (in Japanese).

Akanuma, H. (2004). Surface treatment techniques of stone tools and pottery excavated from Ento Culture sites [Ento Doki Bunka-ken ni okeru sekki narabi ni doki hyomen kako gijutsu ni kansuru kenkyu]. *Annual Bulletin of the Sannai Maruyama National Historic Site [Tokubetsu Shiseki Sannai Maruyama Iseki Nenpo]*, 7, 65–71 (in Japanese).

Archaeological Center of Aomori Prefecture [Aomori-ken Maizo Bunkazai Chosa Center], (Ed.). (1994a–b). *The Sannai Maruyama (2) Site, Vols. II–III [Sannai Maruyama (2) Iseki II–III]*. Aomori: Board of Education of Aomori Prefecture [Aomori-ken Kyoiku Iinkai] (in Japanese).

Archaeological Center of Aomori Prefecture [Aomori-ken Maizo Bunkazai Chosa Center], (Ed.). (1995). *The Sannai Maruyama (2) Site, Vol. IV [Sannai Maruyama (2) Iseki IV]*. Aomori: Board of Education of Aomori Prefecture [Aomori-ken Kyoiku Iinkai] (in Japanese).

Barnes, G. L. (1993). *China, Korea and Japan*. London: Thames & Hudson.

Befu, H. (1993). Nationalism and Nihonjin-ron. In Harumi Befu (Ed.), *Cultural Nationalism in East Asia* (pp. 108–135). Berkeley: Institute of East Asian Studies, University of California.

Chisholm, B. S., & Habu, J. (2003). Stable isotope analysis of prehistoric human bone from the Furuyashiki site, Kamikita Town, Aomori, Japan. In J. Habu, J. M. Savelle, S. Koyama, & H. Hongo (Eds.). *Hunter-Gatherers of the North Pacific Rim* (pp. 221–233). Senri Ethnological Studies, No. 63 Osaka: National Museum of Ethnology.

Cultural Affairs Section of the Agency of Education of Aomori Prefecture [Aomori-ken Kyoiku-cho Bunka-ka] (Ed.). (1996a–b). *The Sannai Maruyama Iseki, Vols. V–VI [Sannai Maruyama Iseki, V–VI]*. Aomori: Board of Education of Aomori Prefecture [Aomori-ken Kyoiku Iinkai] (in Japanese).

Cultural Affairs Section of the Agency of Education of Aomori Prefecture, (Ed.). (1997a–b). *The Sannai Maruyama Site, Vols. VII–VIII [Sannai Maruyama Iseki, VII–VIII]*. Aomori: Board of Education of Aomori Prefecture [Aomori-ken Kyoiku Iinkai] (in Japanese).

Cultural Affairs Section of the Agency of Education of Aomori Prefecture (Ed.). (1998a–d). *The Sannai Maruyama Site, Vols. IX–XII [Sannai Maruyama Iseki, IX–XII]*. Aomori: Board of Education of Aomori Prefecture [Aomori-ken Kyoiku Iinkai] (in Japanese).

Cultural Affairs Section of the Agency of Education of Aomori Prefecture (Ed.). (1999). *The Sannai Maruyama Site, Vol. XIII [Sannai Maruyama Iseki, XIII]*. Aomori: Board of Education of Aomori Prefecture [Aomori-ken Kyoiku Iinkai] (in Japanese).

Cultural Affairs Section of the Agency of Education of Aomori Prefecture (Ed.). (2000a–d). *The Sannai Maruyama Site, Vols. XIV–XVII [Sannai Maruyama Iseki, XIV–XVII]*. Aomori: Board of Education of Aomori Prefecture [Aomori-ken Kyoiku Iinkai] (in Japanese).

Cultural Affairs Section of the Agency of Education of Aomori Prefecture (Ed.). (2001). *The Sannai Maruyama Site, Vol. XVIII [Sannai Maruyama Iseki, XVIII]*. Aomori: Board of Education of Aomori Prefecture [Aomori-ken Kyoiku Iinkai] (in Japanese).

Cultural Affairs Section of the Agency of Education of Aomori Prefecture (Ed.). (2002a–b). *The Sannai Maruyama Site, Vols. XIX–XX [Sannai Maruyama Iseki, XIX–XX]*. Aomori: Board of Education of Aomori Prefecture [Aomori-ken Kyoiku Iinkai] (in Japanese).

Cultural Affairs Section of the Agency of Education of Aomori Prefecture (Ed.). (2003a–b). *The Sannai Maruyama Site, Vols. 21–22 [Sannai Maruyama Iseki, 21–22]*. Aomori: Board of Education of Aomori Prefecture [Aomori-ken Kyoiku Iinkai] (in Japanese).

Cultural Affairs Section of the Agency of Education of Aomori Prefecture (Ed.). (2004a–c). *The Sannai Maruyama Site, Vols. 23–25 [Sannai Maruyama Iseki, 23–25]*. Aomori: Board of Education of Aomori Prefecture [Aomori-ken Kyoiku Iinkai] (in Japanese).

Cultural Affairs Section of the Agency of Education of Aomori Prefecture (Ed.). (2005a–c). *The Sannai Maruyama Site, Vols. 26–28 [Sannai Maruyama Iseki, 26–28]*. Aomori: Board of Education of Aomori Prefecture [Aomori-ken Kyoiku Iinkai] (in Japanese).

Edwards, W. (1997). Japan's new past: how a century of archaeology helped dispel a nation's mythic origins. *Archaeology*, 50(2), 32–42.

Fawcett, C. (1990). A study of the socio-political context of Japanese archaeology. Doctoral Dissertation, Department of Anthropology, McGill University, Montreal.

Fawcett, C., & Habu, J. (1990). Education and archaeology in Japan. In P. Stone & R. MacKenzie (Eds.), *The Excluded Past: Archaeology in Education* (pp. 217–232). London: Unwin Hyman.

Fotiadis, M., 1994. What is archaeology's "mitigated objectivism" mitigated by? Comments on Wylie. *American Antiquity*, 59(3), 545–555.

Fujitani, T. (1993). Inventing, forgetting, remembering: toward a historical ethnography of the nation-state. In H. Befu (Ed.), *Cultural Nationalism in East Asia* (pp. 77–106). Berkeley: Institute of East Asian Studies, University of California.

Habu, J. (1989). Contemporary Japanese archaeology and society. *Archaeological Review from Cambridge*, 8(1), 36–45.

Habu, J. (2002). A life-history of the Sannai Maruyama site [Sannai Maruyama iseki no life-history]. In S. Sasaki (Ed.), *New Perspectives on the Study of Prehistoric Hunter-Gatherer Cultures* [Senshi Shuryo-Saishu Bunka Kenkyu no Atarashii Shiya] (pp. 161–183). Senri Ethnological Report 33. Osaka: National Museum of Ethnology, Osaka (in Japanese).

Habu, J. (2004). *Ancient Jomon of Japan*. Cambridge: Cambridge University Press.

Habu, J. (2005). Jomon cultural landscapes, clay figurines and gender archaeology [Jenda kokogaku kara mita Jomon dogu to bunka-teki keikan]. *Annual Bulletin of the Sannai Maruyama National Historic Site [Tokubetsu Shiseki Sannai Maruyama Iseki Nenpo]*, 8, 92–96 (in Japanese).

Habu, J. (2006a). The archaeology of Sannai Maruyama in the context of world hunter-gatherer archeology: mechanisms of long-term change in cultural landscapes [Sekai no shuryo saishumin kenkyu kara mita Sannai Maruyama: bunka keikan no choki-teki henka to sono mekanizumu]. *Annual Bulletin of the Sannai Maruyama National Historic Site [Tokubetsu Shiseki Sannai Maruyama Iseki Nenpo]*, 9, 48–55 (in Japanese).

Habu, J. (2006b). Settlement growth and decline in complex hunter-gatherer societies: A case study from the Jomon period Sannai Maruyama site. Paper presented at the Department of Anthropology and the Council for East Asian Studies Colloquium, Yale University, October 5.

Habu, J., & Fawcett, C. (1999). Jomon archaeology and the representation of Japanese origins. *Antiquity*, 73, 587–593.

Habu, J., & Fawcett, C. (2006). Marxist theories and settlement studies in Japanese archaeology: direct and indirect influences of V. Gordon Childe. In R. F. Williamson & M. S. Bisson (Eds.), *The Archaeology of Bruce G. Trigger: Theoretical Empiricism* (pp. 80–91). Montreal: McGill-Queens University Press.

Habu, J., Kim, M., Katayama, M., & Komiya, H. (2001). Jomon subsistence-settlement systems at the Sannai Maruyama site. *Bulletin of the Indo-Pacific Prehistory Association*, 21, 9–21.

Habu, J., Savelle, J. M., Koyama, S., & Hongo, H. (Eds.). (2003). *Hunter-Gatherers of the North Pacific Rim*. Senri Ethnological Studies, No. 63. Osaka: National Museum of Ethnology.

Habu, J., Hall, M., & Ogasawara, T. (2003). Pottery production and circulation at the Sannai Maruyama site, northern Japan. In J. Habu, J. M. Savelle, S. Koyama, & H. Hongo (Eds.), *Hunter-Gatherers of the North Pacific Rim* (pp. 199–220). Senri Ethnological Studies, No. 63. Osaka: National Museum of Ethnology.

Hall, S. (1997). The local and the global. In A. McClintock, A. Mufti, & E. Shohat (Eds.), *Dangerous Liasons* (pp. 173–187). Minneapolis: University of Minnesota Press.

Halliday, J. (1975). *A Political History of Japanese Capitalism*. New York: Pantheon Books.

Hane, M. (2001). *Modern Japan: A Historical Survey*. Third Edition. Boulder: Westview Press.

Hodder, I. (1997). 'Always momentary, fluid and flexible': towards a reflexive excavation methodology. *Antiquity*, 71(273), 691–700.

Hodder, I. (1999). *The Archaeological Process*. Oxford: Blackwell.

Hudson, M. (2003). Foragers as fetish in modern Japan. In J. Habu, J. M. Savelle, S. Koyama, & H. Hongo (Eds.), *Hunter–Gatherers of the North Pacific Rim* (pp. 263–274). Senri Ethnological Studies, No. 63. Osaka: National Museum of Ethnology.

Ikawa-Smith, F. (1982). Co-traditions in Japanese Archaeology. *World Archaeology*, 13(3), 296–309.

Iizuka, T. (1995). Video: *Kingdom of Wood and Earth: The Sannai Maruyama Site, 1994 [Ki to Mori no Okoku: Aomori-ken Sannai Maruyama Iseki'94]*. Aomori: Jomon Eiga Seisaku Iinkai (in Japanese).

Ishikawa, R. (2003). Examination of the Jomon plant cultivation hypothesis at the Sannai Maruyama site using DNA analysis [DNA Kokogaku ni yoru Sannai Maruyama Jomon nokoron no kensho]. *Annual Bulletin of the Sannai Maruyama National Historic Site [Tokubetsu Shiseki Sannai Maruyama Iseki Nenpo]*, 6, 50–54 (in Japanese).

Ishikawa, R. (2004). Reconstruction of Jomon vegetation using results from DNA archaeology [DNA Kokogaku ni yoru Jomon shokusei no saisei]. *Annual Bulletin of the Sannai Maruyama National Historic Site [Tokubetsu Shiseki Sannai Maruyama Iseki Nenpo]*, 7, 78–82 (in Japanese).

Kanehara, M. (1995). Jomon people and their parasite problems [Hitobito wa kiseichu ni nayamasarete ita]. In T. Umehara & Y. Yasuda (Eds.), *Discovery of the Jomon Civilization [Jomon Bunmei no Hakken]* (pp. 199–206). Tokyo: PHP Kenkyu-jo (in Japanese).

Kidder, J. E. (1998). The Sannai Maruyama site: New views on the Jomon period. *Southeast Review of Asian Studies*, XX, 29–52.

Kim, M. (2005). Making sense of small seeds: cultural complexity of Jomon hunter–gatherers and changes in plant exploitation at Sannai Maruyama. (Doctoral dissertation, Department of Anthropology, University of California at Berkeley).

Kiyokawa, S. (2001). A genetic engineering study of walnuts excavated from the Sannai Maruyama site [Sannai Maruyama Iseki kara shutodo shita kurumi no idenshi-kogaku-teki kenkyu]. *Annual Bulletin of the Sannai Maruyama National Historic Site [Tokubetsu Shiseki Sannai Maruyama Iseki Nenpo]*, 4, 50–54 (in Japanese).

Kondo, Y. (1998). *The Tsukinowa Tumulus [Tsukinowa Kofun]*. Okayama: Kibi-jin Shuppan (in Japanese).

Koyama, S. (1978). Jomon subsistence and population. *Senri Ethnological Studies, 2*, 1–65.

Koyama, S. (1984). *The Jomon Period [Jomon Jidai]*. Tokyo: Chuo Koron-sha (in Japanese).

Koyama, S. (1995). The flourishing of a sophisticated northern culture [Hanayaka narishi "kita no taikoku"]. In T. Umehara & Y. Yasuda (Eds.), *Discovery of the Jomon Civilization: New Findings at the Sannai Maruyama Site [Jomon Bunmei no Hakken: Kyoi no Sannai Maruyama Iseki]* (pp. 50–77). Tokyo: PHP Kenkyu-jo (in Japanese).

Koyama, S. (1997). Jomon society reconstructed from a perspective of ethnoarchaeology [Minzoku kokogaku ga fukugen suru Jomon shakai]. In Y. Okada & NHK Aomori (Eds.), *Excavating a Jomon City [Jomon Toshi o Horu]* (pp. 149–162). Tokyo: NHK (in Japanese).

Koyama, S., & Thomas, D. H. (Eds.). (1981). *Affluent Foragers*. Senri Ethnological Studies No. 9. Osaka: National Museum of Ethnology.

Koyama, S., Okada, Y., & Habu, J. (1996). International studies of the Jomon Period [Joumon ga Jomon ni naru hi: Nihon kokogaku no kokusaika]. In Y. Okada and S. Koyama (Eds.), *Discussion on the Jomon Period: The World of the Sannai Maruyama [Jomon Teidan: Sannai Maruyama no Sekai]* (pp. 165–180). Tokyo: Yamakawa Shuppan (in Japanese).

Koyama, S., Okada, Y., & Ichikawa, K. (1996). Local people's support of Jomon cultural studies [Shimin ga sasaeru Jomon bunka]. In Y. Okada and S. Koyama (Eds.), *Discussion about the Jomon Period: The World of Sannai Maruyama [Jomon Teidan: Sannai Maruyama no Sekai]* (pp. 199–216). Tokyo: Yamakawa Shinbun-sha (in Japanese).

Leone, M., Mullins, P. R., Creveling, M. C., Hurst, L., Jackson-Nash, B., Jones, L. D., Kaiser, H. J., Logan, G. C., & Warner, M. S. (1995). Can an African-American historical archaeology be an alternative voice? In I. Hodder, M. Shanks, A. Alexandri, V. Buchli, J. Carman, J. Last, & G. Lucas (Eds.), *Interpreting Archaeology: Finding Meaning in the Past* (pp. 110–124). London: Routledge.

Little, B. J. (1994). Consider the hermaphrodic mind: comment on "The interplay of evidential constraints and political interests: recent archaeological research on gender." *American Antiquity*, 59(3), 539–544.

Matsumoto, K. (2003). Chemical analysis of clay and pottery samples from the Sannai Maruyama site [Sannai Maruyama Iseki nendo saikutsu-ko nendo to iseki shutodo doki no seibun bunseki]. *Annual Bulletin of the Sannai Maruyama National Historic Site [Tokubetsu Shiseki Sannai Maruyama Iseki Nenpo]*, 6, 59–64 (in Japanese).

Matsumoto, K. (2004). Movement of pottery and clay figurines in the distribution area of the Ento Pottery Culture [Ento Doki Bunka-ken ni okeru doki, dogu no ido ni kansuru kenkyu]. *Annual Bulletin of the Sannai Maruyama National Historic Site [Tokubetsu Shiseki Sannai Maruyama Iseki Nenpo]*, 7, 65–71 (in Japanese).

Matsumoto, K. (2005). Changes in the chemical composition of clay fabric of pottery excavated from Sannai Maruyama [Sannai Maruyama iseki shutodo doki taido seibun no jikanteki henka ni kansuru kenkyu]. *Annual Bulletin of the Sannai Maruyama National Historic Site [Tokubetsu Shiseki Sannai Maruyama Iseki Nenpo]*, 8, 76–80 (in Japanese).

Miyamoto, C. (1995). The true identity of the feature associated with large posts [Kyobokuchu iko no shotai]. In T. Umehara & Y. Yasuda (Eds.), *Discovery of the Jomon Civilization [Jomon Bunmei no Hakken]* (pp. 214–222). Tokyo: PHP Kenkyu-jo (in Japanese).

Mori, Y. (1995). Evidence of artificial forests demonstrated by insects characteristic of human-disturbed environments [Hitozato konchu ga kataru jinko no hayashi]. In T. Umehara & Y. Yasuda (Eds.), *Discovery of the Jomon Civilization [Jomon Bunmei no Hakken]* (pp. 154–181). Tokyo: PHP Kenkyu-jo (in Japanese).

Mori, Y. (1998a). Insect remains recovered from the standard column of the Sixth Transmission Tower Area of the Sannai Maruyama site [Sannai Maruyama iseki dai 6 tetto standard column kara sanshutsu shita konchu kaseki]. In Cultural Affairs Section of the Agency of Education of Aomori Prefecture [Aomori-ken Kyoiku-cho Bunka-ka] (Ed.), *The Sannai Maruyama Site, Vol. IX, Part 2 [Sannai Maruyama Iseki, IX, dai 2 bunsatsu]* (pp. 19–25). Aomori: Board of Education of Aomori Prefecture [Aomori-ken Kyoiku Iinkai] (in Japanese).

Mori, Y. (1998b). Insect remains recovered from Layers VIa and VIb of the Sixth Transmission Tower Area of the Sannai Maruyama site [Sannai Maruyama iseki dai 6 tetto chiku dai VIa, VIb so kara erareta konchu kaseki]. In Cultural Affairs Section of the Agency of Education of Aomori Prefecture [Aomori-ken Kyoiku-cho Bunka-ka] (Ed.), *The Sannai Maruyama Site, Vol. IX, Part 2 [Sannai Maruyama Iseki, IX, dai 2 bunsatsu]* (pp. 151–162). Aomori: Board of Education Aomori Prefecture [Aomori-ken Kyoiku Iinkai] (in Japanese).

Mori, Y. (1998c). Dipterous chrysalises recovered from layers of elderberry seed concentrations [Niwatoko no shushi shuseki-so kara sanshutu shita soshi-moku no sanagi ni tsuite]. *Annual Bulletin of the Sannai Maruyama National Historic Site [Tokubetsu Shiseki Sannai Maruyama Iseki Nenpo]*, 2, 17–25 (in Japanese).

Mori, Y. (1999). Examining the large settlement through the analysis of insect remains [Konchu kaiseki de daishuraku o saguru]. *Science [Kagaku]*, 54(9), 34–38 (in Japanese).

Nishida, M. (1996). Overheated media coverage on archaeological discoveries [Kanetsu suru koko journalism]. *Shukan Kin'yobi*, 4(32), 17–19 (in Japanese).

Nishida, Y., Miyao, T., Yoshida, K., & Nakamura, O. (2005). A study of information obtained from scientific analyses of Jomon pottery and clay artifacts [Jomon doki, doseihin no bunseki kagaku ni motozuku joho no kaimei]. *Annual Bulletin of the Sannai Maruyama National Historic Site [Tokubetsu Shiseki Sannai Maruyama Iseki Nenpo]*, 8, 97–102 (in Japanese).

Nishimoto, T. (1995). Fish and birds as primary protein sources: animal food of the residents of Sannai Maruyama [Sakana to tori no nikushoku seikatsu: Sannai Maruyama iseki no dobutsu-shitsu shokuryo no mondai]. In T. Umehara & Y. Yasuda (Eds.), *Discovery of the Jomon Civilization: New Findings at the Sannai Maruyama Site [Jomon Bunmei no Hakken: Kyoi no Sannai Maruyama Iseki]* (pp. 207–213). Tokyo: PHP Kenkyu-jo (in Japanese).

Nishimoto, T. (1998). Bird and mammal remains recovered from the Sixth Transmission Tower Area of the Sannai Maruyama site [Sannai Maruyama iseki dai 6 tetto chiku shutsudo no cho-rui, honyu-rui itai]. In Cultural Affairs Section of the Agency of Education of Aomori Prefecture [Aomori-ken Kyoiku-cho Bunka-ka] (Ed.), *The Sannai Maruyama Site, Vol. IX, Part 2 [Sannai Maruyama Iseki, IX, dai 2 bunsatsu]* (pp. 53–60). Aomori: Board of Education of Aomori Prefecture [Aomori-ken Kyoiku Iinkai] (in Japanese).

Oguma, E. (2002). *A Geneology of 'Japanese' Self-images*. Melbourne: Trans Pacific Press (Translated by David Askew).

Okada, Y. (1995a). A large settlement from the Ento Pottery culture: the Sannai Maruyama site in Aomori Prefecture [Ento Doki bunka no kyodai shuraku]. *Archaeology Quarterly [Kikan Kokogaku]*, 50, 25–30 (in Japanese).

Okada, Y. (1995b). The largest Jomon site in Japan, "the Sannai Maruyama site" [Nihon saidai no Jomon shuraku "Sannai Maruyama iseki"]. In T. Umehara & Y. Yasuda (Eds.), *Discovery of the Jomon Civilization [Jomon Bunmei no Hakken]* (pp. 12–30). Tokyo: PHP Kenkyu-jo (in Japanese).

Okada, Y. (1998). Long-term change in the Sannai Maruyama settlement [Sannai Maruyama iseki no shuraku hensen]. In *International Conference on Hunting and Gathering Societies (CHAGS): Aomori Symposium [Kokusai Shuryo-saishu-min Kaigi Aomori Symposium]* (pp. 10–12, 29–31). Aomori: Committee for CHAGS Aomori Symposium (in Japanese).

Okada, Y. (2003). Jomon culture of northeastern Japan and the Sannai Maruyama site. In J. Habu, J. M. Savelle, S. Koyama, & H. Hongo (Eds.), *Hunter-Gatherers of the North Pacific Rim* (pp. 173–186). Senri Ethnological Studies 63. Osaka: National Museum of Ethnology.

Okada, Y., & Habu, J. (1995). Public presentation and archaeological research: a case study from the Jomon period Sannai Maruyama site. Paper presented at the 1995 Chacmool Conference, November 11, Calgary.

Preservation Office of the Sannai Maruyama Site [Sannai Maruyama Iseki Taisaku-shitsu]. (2006). Site attendance during the Heisei 16 (2004) fiscal year [Heisei 16-nen-do no Kengaku-sha Doko ni tsuite]. *Annual Bulletin of the Sannai Maruyama National Historic Site [Tokubetsu Shiseki Sannai Maruyama Iseki Nenpo]*, 9, 17–19 (in Japanese).

Sannai Maruyama Support Group [Sannai Maruyama Oentai]. (1997). *Story-Tellers of a Northern Capital: Record of Volunteers at the Sannai Maruyama Site* [Kita no Mahoroba no Kataribe: Iseki Borantia no Katsudo Kiroku]. Aomori: Sannai Maruyama Support Group (in Japanese).

Sato, Y. (1997a). DNA analysis of chestnuts excavated from the Sannai Maruyama site [Sannai Maruyama Iseki shutudo no kuri no DNA bunseki nit suite]. *Annual Bulletin of the Sannai Maruyama National Historic Site [Tokubetsu Shiseki Sannai Maruyama Iseki Nenpo]*, 2, 13–16 (in Japanese).

Sato, Y. (1997b). Civilization of the forest: the Jomon world [Mori no bunmei, Jomon no sekai]. In Y. Okada, & NHK Aomori (Ed.), *Excavating a Jomon City [Jomon Toshi o Horu]* (pp. 163–178). Tokyo: NHK (in Japanese).

Sato, Y. (1998). DNA analysis of chestnuts recovered from the Sixth Transmission Tower Area of the Sannai Maruyama site [Sannai Maruyama iseki dai 6 tetto chiku shutsudo no kuri no DNA bunseki]. In Cultural Affairs Section of the Agency of Education of Aomori Prefecture [Aomori-ken Kyoiku-cho Bunka-ka] (Ed.), *The Sannai Maruyama Site, Vol. IX, Part 2 [Sannai Maruyama Iseki, IX, dai 2 bunsatsu]* (pp. 141–146). Aomori: Board of Education of Aomori Prefecture [Aomori-ken Kyoiku Iinkai] (in Japanese).

Sato, Y. (2000). Origins of the lacquer tree (sumac) using DNA analysis [DNA bunseki ni yoru urushi no kigen]. *Annual Bulletin of the Sannai Maruyama National Historic Site [Tokubetsu Shiseki Sannai Maruyama Iseki Nenpo]*, 3, 68–72 (in Japanese).

Suzuki, M. (2004). An interdisciplinary study of the use and conservation of chestnut resources, Part 2 [Jomon jidai ni okeru kuri shigen riyo to shigen saisei ni kansuru sogo kenkyu (2)]. *Annual Bulletin of the Sannai Maruyama National Historic Site [Tokubetsu Shiseki Sannai Maruyama Iseki Nenpo]*, 7, 40–43 (in Japanese).

Tanaka, M. (1984). Japan. In H. Cleere (Ed.), *Approaches to the Archaeological Heritage* (pp. 82–88). Cambridge: Cambridge University Press.

Toyama, S. (1995). Interaction between people and the natural environment [Hitobito no seikatsu to shizen to no kakawari]. In T. Umehara & Y. Yasuda (Eds.), *Discovery of the Jomon Civilization [Jomon Bunmei no Hakken]* (pp. 182–198). Tokyo: PHP Kenkyu-jo (in Japanese).

Trigger, B. G. (1984). Alternative archaeologies: nationalist, colonialist, imperialist. *Man*, 19, 355–370.

Trigger, B. G. (1989a). *A History of Archaeological Thought*. Cambridge: Cambridge University Press.

Trigger, B. G. (1989b). Hyperrelativism, responsibility, and the social sciences. *Canadian Review of Sociology and Anthropology*, 26, 776–797.

Trigger, B. G. (1995). Romanticism, nationalism and archaeology. In P. L. Kohl & C. Fawcett (Eds.), *Nationalism, Politics, and the Practice of Archaeology* (pp. 263–279). Cambridge: Cambridge University Press.

Trigger, B. G. (1998). Archaeology and epistemology: dialoguing across the Darwinian chasm. *American Journal of Archaeology*, 102, 1–34.

Trigger, B. G. (2003). Introduction: understanding the material remains of the past. In B. G. Trigger, *Artifacts & Ideas: Essays in Archaeology* (pp. 1–30). New Brunswick: Transaction Publishers.

Tsude, H. (1995). Archaeological theory in Japan. In P. J. Ucko (Ed.), *Theory in Archaeology: A World Perspective* (pp. 298–311). London: Routledge.

Tsuji, S. (1997). The ecosystems that supported Sannai Maruyama [Sannai Maruyama o sasaeta seitaikei]. In Y. Okada, & NHK Aomori (Eds.), *Excavating a Jomon City [Jomon Toshi o Horu]* (pp. 174–188). Tokyo: NHK (in Japanese).

Tsuji, S. (1998). The Sannai Maruyama site: contents of early Jomon sediments and environmental reconstruction [Sannai Maruyama iseki: Jomon jidai zenki no taiseki butsu no naiyo to kankyo fukugen]. In Cultural Affairs Section of the Agency of Education of Aomori Prefecture [Aomori-ken Kyoiku-cho Bunka-ka] (Ed.), *The Sannai Maruyama Site, Vol. IX, Part 2 [Sannai Maruyama Iseki, IX, dai 2 Bunsatsu]*, (pp. 27–28). Aomori: Board of Education of Aomori Prefecture [Aomori-ken Kyoiku Iinkai] (in Japanese with English title and summary).

Tsuji, S. (2000). Human-nature interaction at the Sannai Maruyama site, Part I [Sannai Maruyama iseki ni okeru hito to shizen no kosho-shi I]. *Annual Bulletin of the Sannai Maruyama National Historic Site [Tokubetsu Shiseki Sannai Maruyama Iseki Nenpo]*, 3, 53–57 (in Japanese).

Tsuji, S. (2001). Human-nature interaction at the Sannai Maruyama site, Part II [Sannai Maruyama iseki ni okeru hito to shizen no kosho-shi II]. *Annual Bulletin of the Sannai Maruyama National Historic Site [Tokubetsu Shiseki Sannai Maruyama Iseki Nenpo]*, 4, 33–39 (in Japanese).

Tsuji, S. (2005). Ecological history of Sannai Maruyama, with special references to the origin, change and decline of the Ento Pottery Culture [Sannai Maruyama iseki no seitaikei-shi kenkyu: toku ni Ento Doki Bunka no keisei to henyo, shuen]. *Annual Bulletin of the Sannai Maruyama National Historic Site [Tokubetsu Shiseki Sannai Maruyama Iseki Nenpo]*, 8, 60–70 (in Japanese).

Umehara, T. (1995). The ancestral home of the spirit of the Japanese people [Nihonjin no seishin no kokyo]. In T. Umehara & Y. Yasuda (Eds.), *Discovery of the Jomon Civilization: Amazing Discoveries at the Sannai Maruyama site* [Jomon Bunmei no Hakken: Kyoi no Sannai Maruyama Iseki] (pp. 12–30). Tokyo: PHP Kenkyujo.

Umesao, T., Koyama, S., & Okada, Y. (1995). Image of a city–Sannai Maruyama [Nihon no rekishi wa Sannai Maruyama kara hajimaru]. *Sannai Maruyama Jomon Era File*, 3, 3–8 (in English and Japanese).

Wajima, S. (1948). The organization and composition of prehistoric settlements [Genshi shuraku no kosei]. In Historical Association of the University of Tokyo [Tokyo Daigaku Rekishigaku Kenkyu-kai] (Eds.), *Lectures in Japanese History [Nihon Rekishi-gaku Koza]* (pp. 1–32). Tokyo: University of Tokyo Press [Tokyo Daigaku Shuppan-kai] (in Japanese).

Wajima, S. (1958). The Nanbori shell-midden and settlements of the prehistoric period [Nanbori kaizuka to genshi shuraku]. In *History of Yokohama City*, Vol.1 [*Yokohama Shi-shi, 1*] (pp. 29–46). Yokohama: Yokohama City (in Japanese).

Wakayama, S. (2002). Problems and future Prospective of the Sannai Maruyama Support Group [Sannai Maruyama Oentai no mondai-ten to shorai no tenbo ni tsuite]. In T. Fukuda, S. Narita, & F. Shiratori (Eds.), *The Archaeology of the Ocean [Umi to Kokogaku to Roman]* (pp. 33–46). Aomori: Group for the Celebration of the 70th Birthday of Mr. Kanemaru Ichikawa [Ichikawa Kanemaru sensei Koki o Iwau Kai].

Wang, W. (1998). Similarities between prehistoric cultures in Northeast Asia [Hokuto Asia no senshi jidai bunka no ruijisei]. In *Sannai Maruyama Iseki Jomon Forum '98* (p. 8). Aomori: Committee for the 1998 Sannai Maruyama Jomon Forum [Sannai Maruyama Iseki Jomon Forum Jikko Iinkai, 1998] (in Japanese).

Warashina, T. (1998). Provenience studies of obsidian artifacts [kokuyoseki-sei ibutsu no genzai sanchi bunseki]. In Cultural Affairs Section of the Agency of Education of Aomori Prefecture [Aomori-ken Kyoiku-cho Bunka-ka] (Ed.), *The Sannai Maruyama Site, Vol. IX, Part 2 [Sannai Maruyama Iseki, IX, dai 2 Bunsatsu]* (pp. 163–185). Aomori: Board of Education of Aomori Prefecture [Aomori-ken Kyoiku Iinkai] (in Japanese with English title and summary).

Warashina, T. (2000). Provenience studies of obsidian artifacts excavated from the Baseball Stadium area and its vicinity [Sannai Maruyama iseki Yakyujo chiku oyobi shuhen chiku shutudo no kokuyoseki-sei ibutsu no genzai sanchi bunseki]. *Annual Bulletin of the Sannai Maruyama National Historic Site [Tokubetsu Shiseki Sannai Maruyama Iseki Nenpo]*, 3, 26–44 (in Japanese).

Warashina, T. (2005). Provenience studies of obsidian artifacts and flakes excavated from the Sannai Maruyama site [Sannai Maruyama iseki shutudo no kokuyoseki-sei sekki, hakuhen no genzai sanchi bunseki]. *Annual Bulletin of the Sannai Maruyama National Historic Site [Tokubetsu Shiseki Sannai Maruyama Iseki Nenpo]*, 8, 13–52 (in Japanese).

Wolle, A. & Tringham, R. (2000). Multiple Çatalhöyüks on the worldwide web. In I. Hodder (Ed.), *Towards Reflexive Method in Archaeology: The Example at Çatalhöyük by Members of the Çatalhöyük Teams* (pp. 207–218). Cambridge: McDonald Institute for Archaeological Research.

Wylie, A. (1989). Archaeological cables and tacking: the implications of practice for Bernstein's "Options beyond objectivism and relativism." *Philosophy of the Social Sciences*, 19, 1–18.

Wylie, A. (1992). The interplay of evidential constraints and political interests: recent archaeological research on gender. *American Antiquity*, 57(1), 15–35.

Wylie, A. (1995). Epistemic disunity and political integrity. In P. R. Schmidt & T. C. Patterson (Eds.), *Making Alternative Histories* (pp. 255–272). Santa Fe: School of American Research Press.

Yamanaka, S., Okada, Y., Nakamura, I., & Sato, Y. (1999). Evidence for ancient plant domestication based on DNA analysis of plant remains: Chestnut domestication in Sannai Maruyama sites [Shokubutsu itai no DNA takei kaiseki shuho no kakuritsu ni yoru Jomon jidai zenki Sannai Maruyama iseki no kuri saibai no kanosei]. *Archaeology and Natural Science [Kokogaku to Shizen Kagaku]*, 38, 13–28 (in Japanese with English title).

Yasuda, Y. (1995). A cultural center of the Circum Pacific Rim where civilizations meet [Kan-Taiheiyo no bunmei yugo senta]. In T. Umehara & Y. Yasuda (Eds.), *Discovery of the Jomon Civilization [Jomon Bunmei no Hakken]* (pp.78–95). Tokyo: PHP Kenkyu-jo (in Japanese).

Chapter 8
Multivocality, Multifaceted Voices, and Korean Archaeology

Minkoo Kim

Introduction

This chapter reflects on current discussions regarding multivocality with reference to archaeological narratives in Korean archaeology. The basis of this chapter stems from a recognition that the validity of multivocality has been commonly discussed in research traditions that were once (or are still) classified as colonialist or imperialist archaeology. In other words, the concept of multivocality is mostly introduced to and propagated in the regions where "Europeans remained politically and economically dominant for a considerable period of time" (Trigger 1984:360) and/or regions where general theories and evolutionary schemes developed in Anglo-American archaeology have been vigorously applied and tested. This implies that the debate on multivocality, despite its strong emphasis on globalization, transcontinental networks, and breakdowns of national boundaries, is still contained largely within a particular tradition of archaeological research. Many research traditions that were once categorized as nationalist archaeology by Trigger (1984) rarely appear in these discussions, and the implications of multivocality in these research settings have seldom been considered.

Using Korean archaeology as a point of reference, I argue that the process of multivocality in nationalist research settings may raise as much controversy as it resolves. Problems appear partly because differentiating dominant voices from marginalized "other" voices is not necessarily as straightforward as is often implied. In a country such as Korea, where people have a collective memory of colonization, oppression, and exploitation throughout the twentieth century, archaeology creates powerful narratives that vest the entire country with a new identity and provide the people with a reason and the means to resist foreign colonizers and oppressors. Being essentially nationalistic, however, such narratives may also express the superiority of previously oppressed groups in relation to foreigners. It is not difficult to find cases in which alleged marginalized voices readily transform into ultra-nationalistic or colonialist narratives when these voices successfully find a niche in archaeology. By presenting a brief history of Korean archaeology and introducing readers to the controversy over the purported "world's oldest rice" discovered in Korea, I intend to show that empowering "marginalized" voices and/or small groups does not necessarily imply

J. Habu, C. Fawcett, and J. M. Matsunaga (eds.), *Evaluating Multiple Narratives:*
Beyond Nationalist, Colonialist, Imperialist Archaeologies.
© Springer 2008

disempowering dominant ones. In reality, they are inextricably mixed and may simply feed off each other. This study highlights that, where nationalist archaeology prevails, archaeologists have a double-loaded ethical responsibility to empower small interest groups and marginalized voices while continuously trying to disempower (ultra)nationalistic agendas, which archaeologists themselves may have once benefited from.

Multivocality: Prospect and Problems

The debate about multivocality is, to a large extent, prompted by discussions about globalization. Citing Featherstone (1991) and Castells (1996), Hodder (1997, 1999) presents globalization as a dual process of homogenization and fragmentation. He notes that, on the one hand, the world is becoming increasingly homogenized as it shrinks into a "global village." This process of homogenization is particularly noticeable in the global economy, information technology, and concern about the environment: more commodities are produced and circulated on global scales; trans-global networks facilitate the easy transmission of information over long distances; and more people in different nations and continents share common interests in environmental issues. Homogenization gives more weight to supranational organizations such as the EU (European Union), the WTO (World Trade Organization), or the WHO (World Health Organization) (see also Castells 2000). The process of globalization, however, is also seen as a means of fragmentation. Over the last century, the world has witnessed the burgeoning of diverse small-scale interest groups. The same information technologies and communication networks that have stimulated homogenization have also enabled these small groups to become empowered, and to educate themselves and others. Being either real or virtual (existing only on the Web), these groups proliferate and challenge the formation and spread of dominant discourses. These small groups, equipped with computer networks and a willingness to participate in the interpretation and dissemination of information, have changed the nature of knowledge by making it possible to create and distribute many varied messages from multiple sectors (Castells 2000).

Hodder finds in archaeology the same processes of homogenization and fragmentation that characterize other domains impacted by globalization. On the one hand, archaeologists in various parts of the world share techniques and terminology. For example, radiocarbon dating, which was first developed by scientists working in the West, is now used routinely by archaeologists around the world. Many cultural remains are considered the common property of humankind, and supranational organizations such as UNESCO (United Nations Educational, Scientific, and Cultural Organization) play an increasingly important role in their protection and display (Hodder 1999:162). On the other hand, as Hodder argues, cultural heritage can play a pivotal role in creating and reinforcing local identities and supporting small-scale communities. Local communities that are marginalized or whose people are often subjugated are empowered through engagement with their heritage (Hodder 1999:163). Hodder expects digital technology and network-connected computers to play a decisive role in this empowerment. Unlike the centrally dispatched communication systems of the previous era, communication in the twenty-first century is multimodal, decentralized, and fast. Therefore, it can easily motivate special groups to develop, to create their identities, and to disseminate local meanings. With this in mind, Hodder suggests that the undermining of dominant discourses and the empowering of marginalized voices are central themes of multivocality.

Hodder notes that the ability to participate in the process of global cultural production may vary depending on region and country. Many parts of the world, especially those where poverty prevails, are not yet integrated into the computer-networked global society (Hodder 1999:151). Although the Internet is an important constituent in the fight against marginalization, access to the Internet depends on income, education, and physical location. For this reason, the Internet tends to reflect existing forms of dominance and marginalization. Furthermore, because the Internet is increasingly dominated by English and English-speaking people, language-related inequalities are exacerbated. Hodder (1999:151) expects that these problems will discourage many small groups in developing countries, particularly those in Africa, from voicing their ideas and empowering themselves.

Aside from a brief consideration of how differential access to the Internet may affect people in various regions, archaeologists have not discussed the implications of multivocality in a wide variety of settings around the world. This may be because most of the discussions on multivocality have been written by Anglo-American archaeologists regarding projects with which they are directly involved. For example, Anglo-American archaeologists have written about the validity and implications of multivocality in relation to Native American and African American communities (Leone et al. 1995; Swidler 1997; Vizenor 1996; Zimmerman 2001; see also Anawak 1996; Condori 1996). At Çatalhöyük, a site located in Turkey, Anglo-American archaeologists have considered multivocality when working in close collaboration with local people and communities (Hodder 2000). The current debate on multivocality, therefore, seems to be in reaction to the grand narratives and universal schemes characteristic of colonialist or imperialist archaeologies as defined by Trigger (1984). In these settings, a common agreement seems to have been reached among the public about what constitutes the dominant discourses (usually those of the colonial power or empire) and the marginalized voices (usually those of the colonized or imperially dominated), and who belongs to the dominant or subjugated groups. I suspect that such settings are not representative of archaeology around the world. In fact, I believe that archaeologies categorized by Trigger (1984) as nationalist actually prevail, and that the unique archaeological traditions of specific regions may elude easy demarcation into dominant versus marginalized voices or dominant versus subjugated groups. For a deeper insight into multivocality, we must analyze how archaeological discourses are organized in these "other," non-Anglo-American, settings.

Nationalist Archaeology: Definition and Characteristics

The definition of nationalist archaeology varies widely. For example, Kohl (1998:226) defines nationalist archaeology both as "archaeological records compiled within given states" and "policies adopted by the state that make use of archaeologists and their data for nation-building purposes." According to his argument, nationalist archaeology is most influential within a nation-state, but it can also extend its influence beyond the borders of the state (Kohl 1998:226). This rather broad definition leads to the conclusion that archaeology, no matter where it is practiced, is fundamentally nationalistic in orientation. While recognizing the nationalistic orientation of most archaeological research, Trigger (1984) effectively separates nationalist archaeology from two other kinds of archaeologies: colonialist archaeology and imperialist archaeology. Trigger argues that the purpose of nationalist archaeology is "to bolster the pride and morale of nations or ethnic groups" (Trigger 1984:360). He further notes that nationalist archaeology is strong among "peoples who feel politically threatened, insecure or deprived of their collective rights by more powerful nations or in countries where appeals for national unity are being made to counteract serious divisions along class lines" (Trigger 1984:360).

The term "nationalism" may have either a positive or a negative connotation depending on the context. This is also true of the term "nationalist archaeology." Nationalist archaeology is often closely affiliated with the so-called culture historical approach that systematically traces temporal and spatial variations in the archaeological record. As Trigger (1995:277) notes, this approach sometimes provides people with collective pride, which helps them resist imperial discourses (see also Kohl 1998). Nationalist archaeology, therefore, has helped various groups of people construct their own collective identities and, in doing so, has been a form of resistance, particularly in the nations that suffer or have suffered from colonization and exploitation. The connection between the nation and archaeology may be beneficial even from the perspective of archaeologists. The emergence of nationalism stimulated the creation of archaeology as a scientific discipline beyond the status of a pastime (Trigger 1989). Furthermore, during nation building, museums are created, archaeology appears in higher educational curricula, archaeologists find permanent positions in universities and museums, and legislation to protect ancient remains is put into place (Díaz-Andreu & Champion 1996; Trigger 1989).

Problems in nationalist archaeology are also apparent and can overshadow the positive elements mentioned above. Ethnicity is often considered fixed and securely traceable, rather than malleable and constantly in the process of evolving. A common nationalist understanding of the past is to equate particular archaeological cultures with a specific national or ethnic group. When taken to the extreme, this approach assumes a perfect correlation among material remains, ethnicity, and a nation, and the roots of a present nation-state are extended back to time immemorial (Kohl 1998:228). Ethnic groups are thought to be more or less securely differentiated on the basis of durable and fixed material criteria, such as house forms, food items, and tools. These assumptions are not only misleading but may also be dangerous:

contentious territorial and proprietary claims are often based on such identifications, and the immigration of people and diffusion of cultural traits are frequently interpreted as evidence of one group's ethnic superiority over another. In these cases, nationalist archaeologies support entitlement, privilege, and the supremacy of certain groups at the expense of others, and easily generate ultranationalistic or imperialistic interpretations (Kohl 1998:231).

I suggest that, particularly in the nation-states that have freed themselves from colonial rule and emulated other countries' earlier experiences of nation building during the second half of the twentieth century, these positive and negative aspects of nationalist archaeology will be inextricably interwoven. In reference to the basic tenets of multivocality, how then can we understand nationalist interpretations of the past? Do these nationalist interpretations represent oppressed, neglected, and marginalized voices that are finally being articulated? Or are they simply new forms of domination that must eventually be disempowered? In the following section, I turn to Korean archaeology to answer these questions.

Korean Archaeology and Nation Building

Discourses about the past on the Korean peninsula have rarely been free of foreign influences. Yi (2001), for instance, shows that people during the Chosun (or Joseon) period (1392–1910) made sense of prehistoric remains by relating them directly to ideologies adopted from mainland China that were widely followed by the ruling class of the Chosun dynasty. For example, stone tools were called "thunder axes," and this term was directly adopted from China (Yi 2001:160). Furthermore, the existence of stone tools was explained with reference to the Principle of Yin/Yang and the Five Primary Substances (metal, wood, water, fire, and earth) (Yi 2001:185). The origin of thunder axes was explained according to the circulation of *gi*, a form of energy that is present in the five primary substances. According to the Principle of Yin/Yang and the Five Primary Substances, the *gi* of fire, at its extremity, becomes the *gi* of earth. A stone is simply a solidified form of earth. This framework explained why it might be "natural" to find strange stones where lightning, an extreme and peculiar form of fire, was present. This kind of explanation was considered rational and logical throughout the Chosun period and overshadowed other folk narratives by criticizing them as irrational, mystical, or subjective.

Over the course of the twentieth century, Korea has undergone a series of dramatic political upheavals. These political changes began with the Japanese annexation of the country in 1910. The liberation of the Korean peninsula in 1945 after the end of World War II was followed by the Korean War (1950–1953) and the subsequent establishment of two competing nations, the Republic of Korea and the Democratic People's Republic of Korea (commonly referred to as South Korea and North Korea, respectively). A series of upheavals in the political framework of Korea shaped a particular and unique social milieu, within which current archaeological narratives are situated.

The modern practice of archaeology in Korea started with Japan's growing political influence over the Korean peninsula and northeastern regions of China at the end of the nineteenth and beginning of the twentieth centuries. The first Japanese archaeologist to conduct archaeological site surveys on the peninsula was Shozaburo Yagi who entered Korea in 1893. He was followed by Japanese scholars such as Tadashi Sekino, Ryuzo Torii, and Ryu Imanishi. The Japanese colonial era (1910 1945) witnessed systematic archaeological surveys and excavations, the promulgation of a body of legislation regulating the protection and registration of cultural properties, and the display of archaeological collections in museums (Pai 1998). This was also the time when a rudimentary chronological framework was established for Korea and various prehistoric "cultures" on the Korean peninsula were identified. Throughout the colonial period, however, archaeological excavations and site surveys were exclusively carried out by Japanese scholars. No Koreans were adequately trained in excavation and analytic skills to conduct this work, and consequently, Korean voices that might have interpreted their own past were silenced. Until the liberation of the peninsula in 1945, Koreans only held nonacademic positions in national museums (Arimitsu 1996).

The colonial era is remembered by Koreans as the time when their past was "fabricated" and "distorted" by the Japanese colonizers. Scholars who have examined the history of Korean archaeological and historical work during this period of time argue that archaeological interpretations were predetermined by the agenda set by the Government General of Korea, which was the principal organ of governance during the Japanese colonial rule from 1910 to 1945. Pai (1994:39), for instance, points out that four research themes were emphasized during the colonial period: (1) the common ancestral origins of the Korean and Japanese peoples; (2) the existence of Japanese colonies on the Korean peninsula in the past; (3) the overwhelming impact of Chinese cultures on the Korean peninsula; and (4) the backwardness and stagnation of Korean cultures (see also Pai 2000). Archaeological remains, which are intrinsically subject to a variety of interpretations, were easily exploited to justify the Japanese colonization of Korea. This use of the past to justify Japanese colonization was systematic and beyond the control of individual researchers. Finally, the colonial period witnessed racist assertions partly justified by interpretations of archaeological evidence, which claimed that the Korean people were characterized by "a lack of independence" and "a servile attitude towards bigger nations." The argument was made, furthermore, that Koreans could become subjects of the Japanese emperor by overcoming their bad characteristics (Pai 1994:40).

The Korean War (1950–1953), which swept the country 5 years after the 1945 liberation of Korea from Japan, killed approximately 2.5 million military personnel and civilians, devastated the economy, and completely destroyed the country's infrastructure. In the two nations that were established as a result of the war (North Korea and South Korea), archaeology was considered a legitimate scientific discipline, and archaeology has served similar purposes during nation building. Its main role has been to denounce colonial interpretations that emphasized the racial and cultural inferiority of the Korean people. As in many postcolonial states, Korean archaeology after liberation has taken a central role in refashioning national identity and restoring national pride. Given the scarcity of early historical documents and the opinion of scholars and officials that archaeological materials could provide "objective material evidence" for the effective deconstruction of colonialist claims, the role of archaeology in nation building was emphasized over that of other disciplines. Archaeology, however, was also expected to produce interpretations of the past that were compatible with the political ideology of each nation and, implicitly or explicitly, to serve each regime. Consequently, the theoretical perspectives and methodological practices that archaeologists employed were not politically neutral. This ultimately contributed to significantly different versions of the same history.

In both North Korea and South Korea, as in many other countries where nationalist archaeology dominates, a nation is conceived of as the natural unit of a people. Each unit has the right to constitute a natural political entity. This political entity is considered to have a past that can be studied and objectively described. In North Korea, a Marxist-oriented framework was used to understand the past of the Korean people. A Marxist framework was readily accepted because Marxism blended well with the communist ideology of North Korea, and because many Korean students, educated during the Japanese colonial period, considered the Marxist movement a powerful tool in the battle against imperialism. North Korean scholars described Korea's past as a history of continuous struggles between different classes of people, particularly the struggles of the common people against members of the bourgeois class, imperialists, and other oppressors. The perspective adopted in North Korea has generally presented the unilineal development of Korean culture as passing through various historical stages beginning with the Paleolithic and culminating with the current North Korean regime (Academy of Social Science 1977, 1991). In this model, present-day Korean people are considered a homogeneous population untainted by foreign lineages since the Paleolithic period. Interestingly, such claims about the "unilinearity" of Korean culture and the "homogeneity" of the Korean people were not overt in the writings of Yuho Do, a prominent archaeologist working in North Korea between 1946 and 1966. Rather, Do focused on describing artifacts discovered on the Korean peninsula and comparing them with similar artifacts found in neighboring countries (Do 1960 (reprinted in 1994)). Books and articles published after the early 1970s, however, have strongly and openly advocated unilinearity and homogeneity in Korean history (Yi 1992). Discussions of foreign artifacts, furthermore, have emphasized their differences from those of Korea.

The capitalist ideology of South Korea and the international politics of the Cold War period made most South Korean scholars deliberately avoid Marxist-oriented interpretive frameworks. On one level, archaeology in South Korea has been carried out in an ideological vacuum because it is heavily biased towards empirical studies of the temporal and spatial variations of archaeological remains. Inductive research and descriptive studies of archaeological materials are emphasized and are seen as important steps toward understanding the unique historical trajectory of the Korean people and their culture. In this sense, South Korean archaeologists have effectively dissociated themselves from any particular political ideology. On another level, however, selected artifacts and cultural traits are interpreted as evidence of migration and cultural diffusion throughout the Eurasian continent. Modern Korean culture is often described as the final product of a series of cultural interactions that occurred across this vast geographical region from the Paleolithic period onward. Such interpretations are common in South Korean archaeology. For example, the Chulmun period (ca. 8,000 (Im 1996) to 1,300 BC) is characterized by extensive migration and cultural contacts that encompassed the current regions of northeast China, Siberia, and Japan (see Han 1996 and Pai 2000:77–81 for a critical review). The drastic cultural changes in the subsequent Mumun period (ca. 1,300 to 300 BC) are thought to be the result of immigration from the north (W. Kim 1986:65; see Pai 2000:82–87 and Roh 1996 for a critical review). Highlighting harmonious blending of different cultural traits and emphasizing cultural interactions over a vast region may appear to contradict claims in nationalist narratives that assume ethnic superiority. However, it should be noted that such interpretations implicitly describe ancient Koreans as people with a grandiose geographical scope whose lives were not confined to the small peninsula. Furthermore, describing cultural achievements that occurred in the Korean peninsula and their transmission to other regions often intentionally aims at suggesting creativity and superiority of the Korean people over others.

In both North Korea and South Korea, archaeology is considered a legitimate academic discipline that has become an integral part of nation building. In contrast with European countries where such developments occurred over centuries, the relationship between archaeology and nationalism in Korea has developed over only a few decades. The history of Korean archaeology during the twentieth century shows that the Korean people played an increasingly dominant role in archaeological research and interpretation. Korean archaeology is no longer organized around the colonialist/imperialist agendas of other powers, and the dominant narratives of previous periods have become less powerful. This demonstrates, using Hodder's phrase, that the "subaltern can speak back" (Hodder 2004:4). This allows for "alternative agendas to be set and alternative perspectives to be explored" (Hodder 2004:4). In a country where people have constructed nations in the face of a strong colonialist legacy, however, the place of archaeology is paradoxical. As Nelson (1995:223) notes, "Koreans have not been interested in world prehistory, nor in the comparative history of humankind, but in unearthing and validating their own past." While local heritage and archaeological remains continue to be the sources of people's pride and identity, nationalist archaeology inevitably intervenes and manipulates or reshapes archaeological interpretations around the nationalist agenda. In both North and South Korea, these two processes seem to have happened over a relatively short period of time or even simultaneously. They are intrinsically intermixed and will be extremely difficult to disentangle.

Articulating Multifaceted Voices

As I have indicated above, the development of archaeology in North Korea and South Korea is related to both resistance and dominance. Archaeology in the post-war period has been legitimized as an academic discipline through the refutation of interpretations of the past associated with Japanese colonialist and imperialist agendas. At the same time, however, archaeology has played an important role in the process of nation building and the production of dominant nationalist discourses. Following this observation, it will be logical to ask how small interest groups that increasingly play an active role in nation-states such as North Korea and South Korea interact with grand nationalist discourses, provide alternative perspectives, and disempower dominant voices.

In delving into this issue, we suffer from differential access to information. North Korea is currently known as one of the world's most oppressive and reclusive regimes (U.S.D.S. 2006). It is extremely difficult to know how archaeological narratives are produced and dispersed in this country, and how locals interact with the dominant archaeological interpretations. Having one of the most isolated economies in the world, North Korea is also known for its destitute economic conditions and chronic food shortages. The food shortages have been exacerbated by recurring natural disasters and continued shortages of fertilizer and fuel since 1995, leaving a significant portion of the nation's population in a state of prolonged malnutrition and starvation. We can easily imagine that this country's economic destitution, along with its restricted political freedom and its isolation from the rest of the world, will militate against the formation of small interest groups. People's involvement in interpreting their own past will be restrained in North Korea, and it will be difficult to assume the dual process of homogenization and fragmentation.

South Korea, in contrast, has gone through dramatic economic growth after the Korean War, especially over the past 30 years. Economic reformation and development proceeded according to the government-directed industrial plans during the 1970s and 1980s. Although the rapid economic growth steered by the central government came at high costs such as autocratic leadership, restricted political freedom, and lack of interest in human rights, transition towards a more democratic and open society steadily took place after the mid 1980s. Because it was greatly dependent on international trade, South Korea was quickly integrated into the global community. In South Korea, there are multiple small groups classified according to gender, age, social status, physical location, and other features. Accordingly, we can expect that "at various scales and levels, marginal, subordinate or disadvantaged groups" will claim "an interpretation of the past which is their own" (Hodder 1999:15). In relation to this issue, it is worth noting that South Korea currently has one of the highest ratios of high-speed Internet users. It has been reported that South Korea has approximately 60 Internet users per every 100 people and about 70% of them use high-speed Internet (U.N.S.D. 2005). Many small groups actively use the Internet to shape their identities, share information, express opinions, and participate in the political decision-making process. Does the growth of the Internet and the circulation of unregulated information give these small groups voices? If so, does a variety of small groups in South Korea actually disempower the nationalist discourses that are imposed upon them?

To understand the relationship between small groups and dominant nationalist narratives, I turn to the Sorori site, an Upper Paleolithic site in Korea that has evoked enormous controversy. The current debate about this site is an interesting case of how small interest groups may be empowered by creating their local heritage while simultaneously dominant voices presenting nationalist agendas remain powerful. The Sorori site derives its name from a nearby town, Soro-ri in Cheongwon County, South Korea (Fig. 8.1). The site was discovered in 1994 by a site survey team of the Chungbuk National University Museum (Lee & Woo 2000). This archaeological site survey was conducted before the construction of an industrial complex planned by the local government of North Chungcheong Province. The site survey revealed that the entire region is rich in Paleolithic remains. In adjacent regions, Paleolithic stone tools were discovered from at least three other localities. The Sorori site is divided into three areas (Areas A, B, and C) and three research organizations participated in the site excavation: Chungbuk National University Museum (Area A), Dankook University Museum (Area B), and the University of Seoul (Area C). The total excavation area measured up to approximately 3.4 ha (Lee & Woo 2000). In 1997, the excavation that followed the site survey and small-scale test excavations led to the discovery of Paleolithic stone tools such as choppers, scrapers, flakes, and cores. Until the completion of the first excavation in early 1998, the Sorori site was nothing more than an ordinary archaeological site dated to the Upper Paleolithic period with an estimated date of approximately 30,000–20,000 years ago (Han & Son 2000).

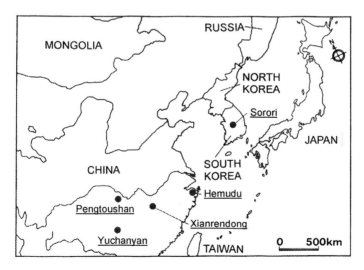

Fig. 8.1 The location of sites mentioned in the text

Fig. 8.2 A rice grain excavated from the Sorori site (Courtesy of the Chungbuk National University Museum)

In 2000, Yung-jo Lee, director of the Chungbuk National University Museum and Sorori site (Area A) excavation supervisor, claimed that his excavation team had recovered the husks of rice grains (Fig. 8.2). He further claimed that the layer from which these remains had been found dated back to 13,000 years ago, and that the rice remains should logically be as old as the layer (Lee & Woo 2000:608). He provided "scientific" data that supported this claim. According to an unofficial site excavation report of 2002, the radiocarbon (AMS) dates of charcoal fragments associated with the rice remains ranged from 14,820 to 12,500 uncalibrated bp (Lee & Woo 2002). A total of 13 charcoal samples were within this range. The dates were obtained by two independent research organizations: Geochron Lab in the U.S. and AMS Lab of Seoul National University. Allegedly, a sample of rice remain(s) was/were AMS-dated and found to be 12,500±200 (SNU 01–293) uncalibrated bp (Lee & Woo 2002:22). Lee compared the Sorori rice samples with rice remains from the Xianrendong site and the Yuchanyan cave site in China. These two Chinese sites had purportedly yielded the oldest evidence of rice yet discovered (cf. Higham & Lu 1998). He argued that because the Sorori rice pre-dated these remains by 3,000 years, it should now be considered the oldest rice in the world (Lee & Woo 2002:18). He further argued that the recovered rice remains were in the early stage of domestication (Lee & Woo 2002:18).

Most scholars were highly skeptical of Lee's report and, in general, the influence of the report on Korean archaeology was minimal at best. Most specialists agree that rice is not indigenous to the Korean peninsula. The conventional perspective in East Asian archaeology is that rice cultivation started along the banks of the Yangtze River in southern China and subsequently moved northward (Ahn 1993; Barnes

1993; Chang 1986; Smith 1998). The earliest evidence of rice that is agreed upon among researchers comes from the Pengtoushan site, Hunan Province of China. The AMS dates for rice grains from this site are 7775±90 (OxA2210) and 7259±140 (OxA2214) uncalibrated bp (Crawford & Shen 1998). Although the rice from Pengtoushan represents some of the oldest evidence for rice, it is not clear whether the rice from this site was cultivated (Higham 1995). Rich data sets of rice come from excavations of the Hemudu site, a waterlogged settlement with remarkably good preservation of organic materials in the lower Yangtze valley. The Hemudu site has produced more rice grains than any other early East Asian agricultural settlement. Two AMS dates obtained from rice grains are 6240±100 bp (1σ: 7270–7000 cal. bp) (BK78114) and 6085±100 bp (1σ: 7160–7120 [6.5%], 7100–7070 [2.9%], 7030–6790 [57.3%], 6770–6760 [1.5%] cal. bp) (ZK-0263(2)) (Crawford & Shen 1998). The rice grain assemblages from Hemudu are reported to represent two different subspecies of domesticated rice, long grained rice (*Oryza sativa* ssp. *indica*), and short grained rice (*Oryza sativa* ssp. *japonica*) (Smith 1998:127). Archaeologists agree that the rice from Hemudu was cultivated (Higham 1995). In the case of the Korean peninsula, the oldest date for rice yet known does not predate 4,000 years ago, and even this date remains controversial among scholars (Ahn 1993:321, 1998:33). The use of rice as a staple food on the Korean peninsula is believed to have started at the beginning of the Mumun period in approximately 3,250 bp. Clearly, finding rice dating back to 13,000 years ago or earlier at the Sorori site on the Korean peninsula would be both surprising and groundbreaking.

Despite strong skepticism in academia, the story of the oldest rice in the world spread widely and rapidly. The Sorori site excavation team's findings were published in several major South Korean newspapers, although the story was not featured as a headline (Lee 2000; Shin 1998). By the end of 2003, most major South Korean newspapers had covered this story, generally as a short article in the culture or society section of the papers. The story was eventually covered by the BBC's Internet news site in an article entitled "World's 'oldest' rice found" (Whitehouse 2003). The coverage of the story by a foreign media outlet gave weight to the authenticity of the finding among some Koreans (see also Discovery Channel 2003).

The Sorori site successfully attracted the interests of people living in the region and became a source of local identity. In January 2004, the government of Cheongwon County, where the site is located, launched a virtual museum to introduce the findings of the Sorori site to the public. The Web site is officially entitled "Cyber Museum of Sorori Rice" (http://www.sorori.com). It presents the location of the site; a brief history of the excavation; pictures of excavated stone tools; the results of pollen analysis; photographs and description of organic remains such as wood and insect fragments; as well as dating results and photographs of the rice remains that were recovered from the site. The Web site also has special sections that introduce the Paleolithic period of the Korean peninsula and explain the social and ecological implications of agriculture in general. This Web site is intended to be interactive: it is linked to video clips, and visitors to the site can post questions and make comments about the findings. To attract a wider range of

Internet surfers, the Web site is presented in English, Japanese, and Chinese in addition to Korean. In June 2004, the "Cyber Museum of Sorori Rice" Web site was selected by the Ministry of Information and Communication of the South Korean government as a recommended Web site for teenagers and, soon after, it was ranked among the top 6 of the 120 recommended sites (Y. Kim 2004).

Around the same time in early 2004, the Sorori site moved to the center of debates that involved archaeologists, local people, and the general public. The Korea Land Corporation (KLC), the owner of the land where the Sorori site is located, decided to sell the property to a private company. This company planned to construct the industrial complex that had originally prompted the site survey and subsequent excavations of the Sorori site. The company's construction plans were opposed by many local people and organizations that thought the site should be preserved. They sent letters to government officials, contributed articles to newspapers and magazines, and made public statements. The various organizations and activist groups that publicly opposed the decision included the National Trust (NT) of Korea, a nongovernmental organization that protects historical relics and the natural environment (http://www.nationaltrust.or.kr); Citizen's Solidarity for Participation and Self-Government of Chungbuk (http://www.citizen.or.kr); the Hoseo Archaeological Society; the Korean Paleolithic Society (http://www. kolithic.or.kr); professors of the Chungbuk National University affiliated with the Collaborative Agricultural Research Group; and the local government of Cheongwon county (http://www.puru.net), to name just a few. Eventually, the local government of Cheongwon County filed a petition for the preservation of the site.

In November 2004, the Cultural Heritage Administration (CHA), a branch of the Ministry of Culture and Tourism (MCT) of the South Korean government, convened their Cultural Properties Committee to discuss the preservation of the site. The committee rejected the petition from Cheongwon County to register the Sorori site as a national cultural property and to preserve it permanently. The reason for this decision was not made public. The evaluation simply stated that "the preservation of the layers associated with rice remains is not supportable, and additional preservation of the site seems unnecessary" (Yoo 2004). The members of the Cultural Properties Committee were likely unconvinced of the validity of the early date or the authenticity of the rice remains. In a domino effect, the Cultural Properties Committee of Chungcheong Province, where Cheongwon County is located, also rejected a petition from the county to register the site as a provincial cultural property (Chungcheong Province 2004). These decisions frustrated and disappointed some people, but local residents had no further reactions.

A review of controversies surrounding the interpretation and preservation of the Sorori site reveals that the voices of both small local groups and activists, and the voices of dominant decision makers, specifically the Cultural Properties Committee (especially of the central government), were articulated. The Cultural Properties Committee (*Munhwajae Wiwonhoe*) is a consultation branch associated with the Cultural Heritage Administration (CHA) of the South Korean government. The committee is composed of approximately 120 scholars who have knowledge and experience in the academic fields related to cultural properties. The committee members have a 2-year term and are selected primarily at the request of the director of the Cultural Heritage Administration. The members typically have doctoral degrees and hold academic positions in universities or museums. On the other hand, many small activist groups that claim that the site should be preserved virtually have no professional archeologists as their members. Nevertheless, the views of these groups' members were expressed regardless of whether or not their opinions were accepted by professional archaeologists.

The site has also been used by those who are not particularly interested in its preservation. In May 2004, 17 local households adjacent to the Sorori site launched a research society. Motivated partly by the possible early date of rice found in the region, members of this society decided to try to produce high-quality organic rice that retains the taste of traditional rice (J. Kim 2004). The Sorori rice has also been featured in an advertisement for a commercially available brand of local rice (H. Kim 2005). Both the advertisement and the research society emphasize the high quality of rice from this area, and the Sorori rice adds temporal dimension to their claims.

The commercialization of local rice in this manner closely relates to the situation South Korean farmers are facing: global free trade and the opening of Korean rice markets. Under the global trading regulations of the World Trade Organization (WTO), South Korea is facing the difficult challenge of sustaining its farming sector, especially rice farming. Opening the national rice market to imported rice, which can be sold at much lower prices than domestic rice, will devastate Korean farmers and agricultural markets. As agricultural producers, farmers understand that a drastic opening of the market is inevitable. The claim that Sorori rice is the world's oldest bolsters their efforts to market their local products, because they can present the region as the place where rice agriculture started. The commercial interests of these local farmers and rice distributors may be served by this claim regardless of the scientific credibility of the archaeological findings.

The process described above cannot be described simply as the articulation of marginalized voices. Sorori rice is also featured in nationalist discourses which assume that the Korean people have fixed and securely traceable cultural traits. Such discourses are often implicitly or explicitly related to the claims of ethnic superiority. For example, Hyojin Oh, the district governor of Cheongwon County where the Sorori site is located, says that the purpose of the Sorori Web site is "to let the world know that Cheongwon is the origin of the rice." In a greeting message to the Web site's visitors, he reiterates that the Sorori rice is 3,000 years older than any rice found in China. The importance of the findings is emphasized by implicitly attributing them with the supposed superiority of Koreans over Chinese.

Numerous examples can be found where Sorori rice is featured in nationalist statements. Byung-chan Kwak, an editorial writer for Hankyoreh Newspaper, a major newspaper in South Korea, reflects on the implications of the Sorori rice findings by stating, "Rice was the basis of life in the Korea peninsula over 15,000 years. Sedentary agricultural societies started and became the root of culture that is based on communities. It is hardly deniable that rice is the protoplasm of our bodies and spirit of our culture" (Kwak 2005). Suil Jeong, professor of Dankook

University, traces the origin of the Korean culture from time immemorial and argues that the Sorori rice proves that Korea was the original place of so-called Rice Culture in East Asia (Jeong 2005). Sunghun Kim, processor at Chungang University and a representative of the National Trust (NT) of Korea, argues that the Sorori site should be preserved saying, "this is a way, as a suzerain state of rice culture and industry, to announce that rice is indeed Korean people's blood, flesh, and spirit" (S. Kim 2004). If statements in personal blogs may also be included, we see that many marginalized individuals also raise their voices to relate the Sorori site findings to nationalist discourses. The process described above, therefore, seems to be double-edged: while we witness the burgeoning of small groups that articulate their marginalized voices and benefit from their engagement with the past to challenge the nation-state's message, we also witness nationalist discourses being propagated through the same mechanisms by both powerful societal leaders and individuals, and presumably marginalized citizens. Furthermore, these two processes seem to feed off each other.

Finally, an obvious question is whether the rice remains found at the Sorori site are authentic and whether the projected dates are reliable. Despite assertions of their importance, the reports of rice remains from the Sorori site have not appeared in any international journals, nor do analyses of these remains appear in key Korean archaeological journals. While preparing this chapter, I examined the Sorori site excavation report (Lee & Woo 2000). I was also able to acquire miscellaneous documents about the site, which were mostly proceedings from local conferences. Finally, I downloaded some gray literature that was available at the Sorori website (http://www.sorori.com). As many people have already noted, these documents are full of contradictory information. Most importantly, these documents reveal that the actual rice remains discovered from the site's crucial layers were never radiocarbon-dated. Instead, the samples sent to the AMS labs were considered to be "quasi-rice" (Lee & Woo 2002:18). "Quasi-rice" is a category that the site excavators invented during the process of identification. Although remains classified as quasi-rice are generally shaped like a rice grain, they do not have the palea/lemma structures and checkerboard cell arrangements on the husks that are distinctive of rice (Heu et al. 2002). The controversies over the Sorori rice will not be easily resolved unless archaeologists and the general public are offered more convincing evidence.

Discussion and Conclusion

In Korea, both nationalism and archaeology were something alien before the twentieth century. Palais (1998), for instance, points out that nationalistic sentiment was extremely weak for most of the Chosun period (1392–1910). The population was strictly divided by a variety of factors that include hereditary social hierarchy. Such social structure must have obstructed the development of nationalistic consciousness among people. Furthermore, social elites of the Chosun dynasty, by committing themselves to Neo-Confucianism which had originated from ancient China, pursued ultimate moral excellence and general models for human existence that were taught by the sages of antiquity. From the perspective of Chosun's elites, it was not the Chineseness or Koreanness that mattered. Rather, the teachings of ancient sages should supersede any local beliefs and customs, and the civilization that was once achieved by the ancient sages should be restored in Chosun. Such social atmosphere played its part in alienating archaeological practice. Concepts such as material culture, excavation, and protection of cultural properties simply did not harmonize well with people who sought after moral perfection codified in ancient classics. Presumably it was not until imperialist threats materialized at the end of the nineteenth century that nationalist consciousness developed and led to a sense of political solidarity and national unity. Archaeology as a scientific discipline was transplanted only during the colonial period in the early twentieth century.

The appearance of nationalism and its rendezvous with archaeology, which finally took place after Korea gained independence in 1945, should be seen as a fruit containing both sweetness and poison. For those who share a common language, customs, and historical memories, and who have suffered political and economic oppression, the emergence of nationalist archaeology provides a means to reintroduce self-confidence and cultural pride. On the positive side, postcolonial Korean archaeology has restored the Korean people's past: Koreans now understand their history as their own and archaeologists ask questions about Korean history that matter to the public. Voices of Koreans that had been considered marginalized during the colonial period have become dominant in the postwar era of nation building. On the negative side, however, these new dominant voices have legitimized the politics of nation building in both North and South Koreas and have prompted some limited views of the past, such as rigid Marxist-oriented interpretations in the North and essentialist constructions of the modern Korean people and culture in the South. Archaeology that was once rejuvenating is now also dominating. Furthermore, nationalism that is liberating for one minority can be easily used to justify hostility towards neighbors and domestic minorities. I argue that the history of Korean archaeology does not fit in with the one-sided characterization of empowering marginalized voices and groups. The positive and negative sides happen simultaneously and may not be easily divisible.

It is against this general background that we should try to understand how voices of marginalized groups are articulated. Specifically, we can ask the following question: do alternative interpretations pursued by local people always disempower grand narratives set by nationalist archaeology? In South Korea, the number of archaeological excavations has dramatically increased over the past decades, and thanks to the burgeoning provincial archaeological teams, museums, and journals, a large number of excavations are carried out by local sectors. The local and autonomous nature of archaeological research has had many positive effects. One of them has been the improved academic status of archaeologists hired by local institutions. These archaeologists collaborate and compete with researchers from other regions and specialties, and this promotes professionalism and solidarity among the local archaeologists. This new emphasis in archaeological research, in a sense, empowers outlying regions and local archaeologists. However, as in the case of the archaeological narratives on the Sorori site, this paradigmatic shift may also pave the way for the emergence of a new supremacy. Interpretations of archaeological materials can be tailored to support the claims of regional supremacy and, moreover, they bolster the nationalist discourses produced by various social sectors. In other words, the weakening of a centrally based nationalist archaeology may simply lead to a series of ethnocentric nationalist archaeologies (see also Falkenhausen 1995).

In addition, the role that new developments in communication technology can play in the process of disempowering dominant nationalist narratives should not be overestimated. It is true that archaeological information on the past is increasingly brought to the public's attention through easily accessible media such as newspapers, magazines, books, and television. It is also clear that the proliferation of Internet technologies in recent years has increased the public's awareness of and engagement with archaeological information. This can eventually result in the creation of multiple versions of the past by different groups who have different interests in the past. While I agree that these technological developments have contributed to the demise of centrally distributed archaeological interpretations and can lead to the empowerment of marginalized voices, I also believe that this very process may easily empower dominant voices. The case study discussed in this chapter suggests that decentralization in archaeological interpretations does not necessarily lead to the demise of nationalist interpretations of the past. Nationalist interpretations of the past may simply find new niches that were not available in the archaeological practice of previous eras. This process cannot be simply conceptualized in terms of disempowering dominant voices versus empowering subalterns.

One question that arises from the above discussion is: what roles should archaeologists play in the new global era with the proliferation of multiple voices and interpretations? Hodder argues that it will be increasingly difficult for archaeologists to defend their status against "fringe" groups, such as "antiquarians, looters, Creationists, metal detector users, reburial movements, goddess worshippers," and that "the rigid maintenance of disciplinary boundaries, while effective in some circumstances, constrains the reaching of dialogue and compromise in others" (Hodder 1999:195). In my opinion, archaeologists in the global era simply have increased responsibilities to distinguish themselves from the "fringes." Archaeologists, more than anyone else, understand the devastating consequences of irrelevant and incorrect interpretations of archaeological remains. The interpretation of the archaeological record is hardly straightforward and reconstructions of the past are always ambiguous. It should be pointed out that even though evidence is continuously being accumulated, there is always room for disagreement over the interpretations of the evidence. Many of the questions that the state and the people of South Korea have asked archaeologists during the period of postwar nation building may not be easily answerable using archaeological materials. It becomes imperative, therefore, for archaeologists to recognize their ethical responsibility in order to highlight the strengths and limitations of the archaeological record, to discuss the implications of their research, and to work with the public to restructure their questions so that they can be better addressed using archaeological materials. In this sense, debates about multivocality proposed by Hodder (1997, 1999) are still relevant in the contexts of nationalist archaeologies, but the emphasis of these debates may need to be repositioned.

References

Academy of Social Science. (1977). *Chosun Gogohak Gaeyo [Introduction to Chosun Archaeology]*. Pyongyang: Gwahak Baekgwasajeon Chulpansa [Science Encyclopedia Press] (In Korean).

Academy of Social Science. (1991).*Chosun Jeonsa [A History of Chosun]*. Pyongyang: Gwahak Baekgwasajeon Chulpansa [Science Encyclopedia Press] (In Korean).

Ahn, S. (1993). *Origin and Differentiation of Domesticated Rice in Asia* (Doctoral dissertation, Institute of Archaeology, University of London).

Ahn, S. (1998). *Dong asia seonsa-ui nonggyeong-gwa saengeop [Prehistoric Agriculture and Subsistence in East Asia]*. Seoul: Hakyeon Munhwasa (In Korean).

Anawak, J. (1996). Inuit perceptions of the past. In R.W. Preucel & I. Hodder (Eds.), *Contemporary Archaeology in Theory: A Reader* (pp. 646–651). Oxford: Blackwell.

Arimitsu, K. (1996). 1945–46 nyeon-e iteotdeon na-ui gyeongheomdam [Archaeology and museum in Korea between 1945–1946: a personal account]. *Hanguk gogohakbo [Journal of Korean Archaeological Society]*, 34, 7–27 (In Korean).

Barnes, G. L. (1993). *China, Korea and Japan: the rise of civilization in East Asia*. London: Thames and Hudson.

Castells, M. (1996). *The Rise of the Network Society*. Oxford: Blackwell Publishers.

Castells, M. (2000). Toward a sociology of the network society. *Contemporary Sociology*, 29(5), 693–699.

Chang, K. (1986). *The Archaeology of Ancient China*. New Haven: Yale University Press.

Chungcheong Province. (2004). *Bodojaryo: Chungbukdo jijeongmunhwajae simui gyeolgwa [News report summary: The selection of provincial cultural properties]*: Munhwa yesulgwa, Munhwajae damdang [The Office of Culture and Arts, Department of Cultural Resource Management] (November 16, 2004) (In Korean).

Condori, C. M. (1996). History and prehistory in Bolivia: what about the Indians? In R.W. Preucel & I. Hodder (Eds.), *Contemporary Archaeology in Theory: A Reader* (pp. 632–645). Oxford: Blackwell.

Crawford, G. W., & Shen, C. (1998). The origins of rice agriculture: recent progress in East Asia. *Antiquity*, 72, 858–866.

Díaz-Andreu, M., & Champion, T. (1996). Nationalism and archaeology in Europe: an introduction. In M. Díaz-Andreu & T. Champion (Eds.), *Nationalism and Archaeology in Europe* (pp. 1–24). London: UCL Press.

Discovery Channel. (2003). World's 'Oldest' Rice Found in South Korea (October 22, 2003); http://dsc.discovery.com/news/afp/20031020/rice.html.

Do, Y. (1960) [1994]. *Chosun wonsi gogohak [Prehistoric Archaeology of Chosun]*. Pyongyang (Seoul): Gwahakwon chulpansa (reprinted by Balsan) (In Korean).

Falkenhausen, L. V. (1995). The regionalist paradigm in Chinese archaeology. In P.L. Kohl & C.P. Fawcett (Eds.), *Nationalism, Politics, and the Practice of Archaeology* (pp. 198–217). Cambridge: Cambridge University Press.

Featherstone, M. (1991). *Consumer Culture and Postmodernism*. London: Sage.

Han, Y. H. (1996). The origin of Korean ethnicity. In *Hanguk minjok-ui giwon-gwa hyeongseong [The origin of Korean ethnicity and its formation]* (pp. 73–117). Seoul: Sohwa (In Korean).

Han, C. G., & Son, G. E. (2000). Cheongwon sorori guseokgi yujeok (B jigu)-ui jicheung-gwa chulto yumul [The layers and artifacts of the Sorori Paleolithic site (Area B) in Cheongwon]. *Silhak Sasang Yeongu*, 14, 635–653 (In Korean).

Heu, M. H., Lee, Y. J., & Woo, J. Y. (2002). Morphological observations of carbonized rice remains excavated from the Sorori Paleolithic site. *First International Conference of Cheongwon County – Prehistoric Agriculture in Asia and Sorori Rice* (pp. 31–39). Cheongju: Chungbuk National University Museum and Korea Land Corporation.

Higham, C. (1995). The transition to rice cultivation in Southeast Asia. In T. D. Price & A. B. Gebauer (Eds.), *Last Hunters, First Farmers: New Perspectives on the Prehistoric Transition to Agriculture* (pp. 127–155). Santa Fe: School of American Research Press.

Higham, C., & Lu, T. (1998). The origins and dispersal of rice cultivation. *Antiquity*, 72, 867–877.

Hodder, I. (1997). 'Always momentary, fluid and flexible': towards a self-reflexive excavation methodology. *Antiquity*, 71(273), 691–700.

Hodder, I. (1999). *The Archaeological Process: An Introduction*. Oxford: Blackwell.

Hodder, I. (Ed.). (2000). *Towards Reflexive Method in Archaeology: The Example at Çatalhöyük*. Cambridge: McDonald Institute for Archaeological Research and British Institute of Archaeology at Ankara.

Hodder, I. (2004). *Archaeology Beyond Dialogue*. Salt Lake City: University of Utah Press.

Im, H. (1996). New discoveries in the Korean Neolithic archaeology. In K. Omoto (Ed.), *Interdisciplinary Perspectives on the Origins of the Japanese* (pp. 155–168). Tokyo: International Research Center for Japanese Studies.

Jeong, S. I. (2005). Munmyeong gyoryu gihaeng (47) [Traveler's journal of cultural interactions (47)]. *Hankyoreh Sinmun* (May 10, 2005), p. 16 (In Korean).

Kim, W. Y. (1986). *Hanguk gogohak gaeseol [Introduction to Korean Archaeology]*. Seoul: Iljisa (In Korean).

Kim, J. H. (2004). Segye choego byeopssi chulto-doen cheongwon sorori jumin choego ssal saengsan-wihae yeonguhoe baljok [People at Sorori, where the oldest rice was found, launched a research society]. (May 15, 2004); http://news.naver.com/news/read.php? mode=LSD &office_id=003&article_id=0000058441&section_id=102&menu_id=102.

Kim, S. H. (2004). Ssal-eun minjok-ui hon [Rice is ethnic sprit]. *Segye Ilbo* (June 7, 2004), p. 27 (In Korean).

Kim, Y. E. (2004). Sorori byeopssi bakmulgwan 6wol-ui gwonjang site [The Sorori rice museum: the recommended site for June]. *Kyunghyang Sinmun* (June 24, 2004) (In Korean).

Kim, H. M. (2005). 'Cheongwon saengmyeong ssal' Internet shopping mall gaejang ['Cheongwon organic rice' Internet shopping mall open]. *Daejon Ilbo* (April 26, 2005), p. 13 (In Korean).

Kohl, P. L. (1998). Nationalism and archaeology: on the constructions of nations and the reconstructions of the remote past. *Annual Review of Anthropology*, 27, 223–246.

Kwak, B. C. (2005). Sorori byeopssi [Sorori rice]. *Hankyoreh Sinmun* (December 9, 2005), p. 26 (In Korean).

Lee. K. P. (2000). Segye choego byeopssi guknae balgul hwakin [The world's oldest rice excavated in Korea]. *Donga Ilbo* (August 2, 2000) (In Korean).

Lee, Y. J., & Woo, J. Y. (2000). *Cheongwon sorori guseokgi yujeok [The Sorori Paleolithic Site in Cheongwon County]*. Cheongju: Chungbuk National University Museum and Korea Land Corporation (In Korean).

Lee, Y. J., & Woo, J. Y. (2002). Sorori byeopssi-ui balgul-gwa gwaje [The excavation of the Paleolithic Sorori rice and its important problems]. *First International Conference of Cheongwon County – Prehistoric Agriculture in Asia and Sorori Rice* (pp. 17–24). Cheongju: Chungbuk National University Museum and Korea Land Corporation (In Korean).

Leone, M., Mullins, P., Creveling, M., Hurst, L., Jackson-Nash, B., Jones, L., Kaiser, H., Logan, G., & Warner, M. (1995). Can an African-American historical archaeology be an alternative voice? In I. Hodder, M. Shanks, A. Alexandri, V. Buchli, J. Carman, J. Last, & G. Lucas (Eds.), *Interpreting Archaeology: Finding Meaning in the Past* (pp. 110–124). London: Routledge.

Nelson, S. M. (1995). The politics of ethnicity in prehistoric Korea. In P. L. Kohl & C. P. Fawcett (Eds.), *Nationalism, Politics, and the Practice of Archaeology* (pp. 218–231). Cambridge: Cambridge University Press.

Pai, H. I. (1994). The politics of Korea's past: the legacy of Japanese colonial archaeology in the Korean peninsula. *East Asian History*, 7, 25–48.

Pai, H. I. (1998). The colonial origins of Korea's collected past. In H. I. Pai & T. R. Tangherlini (Eds.), *Nationalism and the Construction of Korean Identity* (pp. 13–32). Berkeley: Institute of East Asian Studies, University of California.

Pai, H. I. (2000). *Constructing "Korean" Origins: A Critical Review of Archaeology, Historiography, and Racial Myth in Korean State-formation Theories*. Cambridge: Harvard University Press.

Palais, J. (1998). Nationalism: good or bad? In H. I. Pai & T. R. Tangherlini (Eds.), *Nationalism and the Construction of Korean Identity* (pp. 214–228). Berkeley: Institute of East Asian Studies, University of California.

Roh, H. J. (1996). The Bronze Age. *Hanguk minjok-ui giwon-gwa hyeongseong [The origin of Korean ethnicity and its formation]* (pp. 119–183). Seoul: Sohwa (In Korean).

Shin, H. (1998). 10 mannyeonjeon byeo balgul [Rice 100,000 years old excavated]. *Chosun Ilbo* (March 17, 1998), p. 17 (In Korean).

Smith, B. D. (1998). *The Emergence of Agriculture*. New York: Scientific American Library.

Swidler, N. (Ed.). (1997). *Native Americans and Archaeologists: Stepping Stones to Common Ground*. Walnut Creek: AltaMira Press.

Trigger, B. G. (1984). Alternative archaeologies: nationalist, colonialist, imperialist. *Man*, 19, 355–370.

Trigger, B. G. (1989). *A History of Archaeological Thought*. Cambridge: Cambridge University Press.

Trigger, B. G. (1995). Romanticism, nationalism, and archaeology. In P. L. Kohl and C. P. Fawcett (Eds.), *Nationalism, Politics, and the Practice of Archaeology* (pp. 263–279). Cambridge: Cambridge University Press.

U.N.S.D (United Nations Statistical Divisions). (2005). Internet users per 100 population (ITU estimates) [code 29969]. (March 10, 2005); http://unstats.un.org/unsd/cdb/cdb_series_xrxx. asp?series_code=29969.

U.S.D.S (United States Department of State). (2006). Democratic People's Republic of Korea: Country Reports on Human Rights Practices – 2005. (March 8, 2006). The Bureau of Democracy, Human Rights, and Labor; http://www.state.gov/g/drl/rls/hrrpt/2005/61612.htm.

Vizenor, G. (1996). Bone courts: the rights and narrative representation of tribal bones. In R. W. Preucel & I. Hodder (Eds.), *Contemporary Archaeology in Theory: A Reader* (pp. 652–663). Oxford: Blackwell.

Whitehouse, D. (2003). World's 'oldest' rice found. *BBC News Online* (October 21, 2003); http:// news.bbc.co.uk/2/hi/science/nature/3207552.stm.

Yi, S. (1992). Bukhan gogohaksa siron [A preliminary discussion on North Korean archaeology]. *Dongbanghakji*, 74, 1–74 (In Korean).

Yi, S. (2001). Noebugo [On the thunder-axe]. *Hanguk gogohakbo [Journal of Korean Archaeological Society]*, 44, 151–188 (In Korean).

Yoo, T. J. (2004). Sorori byeopssi chultoji gukga munhwajae jijeong musan [Proposal to register the Sorori site as a national cultural property rejected]. *Chosun Ilbo* (November 3, 2004), p. Chungcheong A14 (In Korean).

Zimmerman, L. J. (2001). Usurping Native American Voice. In T. L. Bray (Ed.) *The Future of the Past: Archaeologists, Native Americans, and Repatriation*, (pp. 169–184). New York: Garland Publishing.

Chapter 9
Virtual Viewpoints: Multivocality in the Marketed Past?

Neil Asher Silberman

You don't have to read Neil Postman's scathing jeremiad *Amusing Ourselves to Death* (1986) to know that we live in an age of flashing, shallow, and ideologically-loaded TV images. As the virtual pieces of a fluid, postmodern mosaic, they embody and articulate a breathless public narrative of change, conquest, and consumption that often controls and reinforces – rather than passively reflects – the shape of contemporary society. And you don't have to open Dean MacCannell's *The Tourist* (1976), or such later studies as those of Kirshenblatt-Gimblett (1998) or Young and Riley (2002), among many other works, to understand that the emotional appeal of theme parks, studio tours, and heritage visits is based on a search by work-weary vacationers for "authentic experience."

What do these elements – the TV image and the virtual heritage experience – have in common? And what is their relevance to a volume on archaeological concepts of multivocality? Put simply, I would like to argue that the use of slickly produced multimedia representations of alternative voices from the past that have become increasingly popular at elaborate heritage site presentations in recent years should *not* be confused with the concept of multivocality, as it is discussed by other contributors to this volume – and indeed as it is generally understood in the scholarly literature of postmodernism. For I believe that an emerging form – one might even say "genre" – of site presentation now widely adopted in the United States and Europe and at major archaeological and historical sites throughout the Mediterranean effectively utilizes the *appearance* of many voices and multiple stories, while subtly undermining the presumed power of multivocality to contest dominant narratives. It does this, I would argue, by incorporating a mosaic of conflicting or contrasting voices into a single, embodied experience of "heritage tourism," whose primary motivation is the marketing of leisure entertainment and the stimulation of subsidiary economic activities such as service employment in hotels and restaurants, and the sale of souvenirs and subsidiary merchandise.

From the perspective of Brussels, administrative capital of the European Union – and the site of nearly endless planning meetings, press conferences, and funding announcements by international cultural organizations; national, regional, and municipal governments; the European Commission; UNESCO; and the Council of

J. Habu, C. Fawcett, and J. M. Matsunaga (eds.), *Evaluating Multiple Narratives:*
Beyond Nationalist, Colonialist, Imperialist Archaeologies.
© Springer 2008

Europe – the scope and influence of the twenty-first century "heritage industry" can be seen in high relief. Billions of euros are budgeted annually to promote the preservation and public presentation of archaeological and historical sites as sources of what is longingly called "sustainable development." Quite unconnected to ongoing academic discussions and research agendas, European cultural planners are continually reviewing and assessing the potential of a wide range of archaeological and historical sites throughout the European Union and neighboring associated regions with the goal of transforming them into engines of local economic activity.

What began in the 1980s in the United States and the United Kingdom as a project of piecemeal substitution of private for public funding in the field of culture (e.g. Corner & Harvey 1991; Walsh 1992: 41–52) has now become a matter of general cultural strategy. Within the European Union, structural funding mechanisms like the various Interreg programs seek to bind together economically depressed areas – often through the development of regional cultural heritage sites, in hopes of creating local employment opportunities, and stimulating interregional tourism and trade (European Commission 2002). More general funding programs like those of the European Commission's Culture 2000 (DG Education and Culture 2003) and the World Bank's "Framework for Action in Cultural Heritage and Development in the Middle East and North Africa" (World Bank 2001) have set standards – and offer substantial economic incentives – for governmental investment in the form, structure, and even presentational genre of major archaeological sites. With such considerable funding available for cultural heritage projects, an already extensive professional network of tourist consultants, designers, preservation experts, and cultural IT specialists are busy at work on dozens of major projects. Their task is to reconfigure the physical, visual, and spatial environment in which large numbers of visitors will be attracted to archaeological and other cultural heritage sites to enjoyably and profitably "experience" the past.

The use of an archaeological or historical site as a locus for leisure time entertainment is nothing very revolutionary. The growth of the nineteenth-century tourist industry in Europe and the Mediterranean regulated and channeled visitors to specially selected and presented cultural sites as an essential part of the ritual of the increasingly democratized Grand Tour. But today, a much more complex constellation of technologies and facilities forms the core of many important new heritage sites. Traditional didactic, museum-type text displays are now utilized mostly when budgetary constraints mandate only the cheapest, no-frills presentation. More creative and energetic interpretive solutions, such as special-interest or thematic guided tours, costumed or character-based interpreters, special educational activities, and interactive applications and virtual reality experiences are almost always utilized when the project budget permits (Addison 2001). For we live in an age that has shifted from the book and the museum to the virtual image and personal experience, in which the sought-after visitor (sought after in terms of potential economic benefit to the community's hotels, restaurants) can be persuaded to choose the heritage site over alternative forms of recreation. And since the quality of the tourist experience is the main product, great efforts have been taken to create stunning historical environments, interactive interpretive installations, and a wide enough range of vivid images and impressions to satisfy almost every visitor's taste (Lowenthal 2002).

In recent years, a particular emphasis has been placed on utilizing New Technologies to recreate a wide range of visitor experiences that offer a sense of involvement and interactivity. To position an archaeological or historical site, effectively on the market, visits must be designed to appeal to personal involvement and promise a memorable experience, even if it is virtual. Thus beyond computer-based games or databases, there are now elaborate – and sometimes immersive – virtual reconstructions of landscapes and structures (Barceló et al. 2000) and the opportunity to interact with simulated ancient characters (e.g. Wojciechowski et al. 2004). Of course, this element of public interpretation also has a history that stretches far back before the Digital Age. The costumed guides at World's Fairs and early twentieth-century open air-museums first challenged the omniscient voice of guide books and text panels. The first-person reenactors at Colonial Williamsburg and Plimoth Plantation integrated extensive research and historical study to their public performances. But today, the characters are often presented within sophisticated multimedia presentations and their speeches are carefully planned, scripted, and presented – often by filmmakers and multimedia design firms that also provide services to industrial exhibitions, theme parks, and factory tours.

Interactive screens can summon up a colorful range of historical perspectives portrayed by videotaped actors or virtual humans, chosen with the click of a mouse or the touch of a button, for visitors to experience a particular gender, profession, or lifestyle associated with the ancient site. The use of character-based interpretation, first extensively adopted at the Jorvik Viking Center and elaborated in other forms at the United States Holocaust Museum in Washington, the "In Flanders Fields" Museum in Belgium, and the Mashantucket Pequot Museum in Connecticut, has been further elaborated and adopted in a wide range of worldwide heritage locales.

At a site I am associated with, Ename in East-Flanders, Belgium, an extraordinary flow of government support over the past 20 years has led to the development of several prototype interactive installations, moving from simple computer reconstructions to self-guided interactive tours and databases, to an elaborate 23-character virtual performance piece called "The Feast of a Thousand Years" (Pletinckx et al. 2002). It links selected archaeological artifacts with 23 personal historical viewpoints, portrayed by prominent modern Flemish actors in period dress, on a large wall-mounted video display. The selection of characters is determined by the visitors in pressing a button beside an appropriate artifact. The characters span time, social rank, gender, age, and personal background – from the tenth-century Lord of Ename to an eleventh-century peasant woman; from an invalid monk of the fifteenth century to the monastery's abbot of the seventeenth century; from a turn-of-the-century Scheldt ferryman to a traveling Romany woman of the 1930s; and to an archaeologist of the present day. Written as dramatic monologues, these "voices" are based on detailed archaeological, historical, or archival evidence. They considerably widen the appeal of an otherwise didactic or univocal presentation, and offer visitors a range of personal perspectives to relate to and sympathize with. But does this technology of virtual perspectives and the growing number of elaborate heritage sites that use it have anything to do with the concept of multivocality?

The concept of multivocality, as I understand it, is meant to challenge dominant interpretive narratives and to create spaces and structures at heritage sites that will promote the co-existence of potentially conflicting approaches and perceptions of the site's significance. Its aim is to build and sustain the kind of interlocked multivocality as utilized at Çatalhöyük (Hodder 1998); hoped for at archaeological sites in Palestine and Israel (Killebrew 2004), and potentially invaluable as a focus for historical reflection in places of ethnic or communal conflict all over the world. But these remain relatively isolated experiments, far outweighed in sheer numbers and almost always in public visibility by World Heritage Sites or European-funded projects where visitor enjoyment and edification – rather than political discourse and dynamic social interaction – are the keys to the vaunted goal of economic development.

The work of Handler and Gable (1997) at Colonial Williamsburg has examined how the many character-based voices that greet and converse with the visitors are expressions of a fairly coherent narrative that closely follows corporate culture and philosophy. I would like to stress a more down-to-earth element. The use of a wide range of images and voices is part of a total visitor experience. And it is part of a carefully scripted narrative inscribed in walking paths and circulation routes through ruins and exhibit spaces. It is a unilinear narrative meant to be read with the feet.

For the archaeological or historical site is a bounded physical space whose design and layout create a distinctive kind of narrative-in-motion. Especially in the cases of elaborate site development with extensive facilities, a visit consists of passage through a series of Goffman-esque "frames": from the parking lot, through the ticket booth, into the main reception and information area, along the marked or suggested paths of public interpretation, then out to the shop and cafeteria, and then out to the parking lot again. The visit is itself a kind of narrative journey into the past that is perceived (or intended) as an enjoyable personal experience with a beginning, middle, and end. And the interactive installations and virtual viewpoints, however they may individually expand the boundaries of historical diversity, are physically arranged as a mosaic of sound bytes and video bytes incorporated into a seamless experience that defines the visitor's perception of the overall significance of the site.

The gap between compelling historical representation and entertainment is steadily narrowing as heritage has become increasingly tied to substantial investment and economic concerns. Finances and balance sheets are the real tyrants in this age of increasingly self-supporting culture. And although they do not determine the contents of the narrative in its *specifics*, they demand that it be coherent, easy to follow, and capable of holding the attention of the *widest* possible audience. That is precisely what true multivocality cannot and should not provide. In its provocative, uneasy coexistence of alternative interpretations and significances, multivocality should embody a stimulating interweaving of crossed, contradicted, and interrupted conversations – the kind of fascinating and often maddening confusion and crossed-purposes characteristic of Robert Altman's films. But Altman is for art houses. The new wave of lavishly funded, multimedia-enhanced heritage sites have a great deal more in common with multiplex cinemas.

So, what roles do or should archaeologists play in this process? Over the past generation, a significant part of the discipline has become sensitive to the danger of dominating narratives. The emergence of the concept of multivocality has been one of the most influential results. Yet in the field of site presentation – arguably the arena that reaches the widest audience with tangible representations of the past, archaeologists and historians are often primarily content consultants; the bulk of the investment goes into the infrastructure and presentation technologies.

If archaeologists – as individuals and as a discipline – are going to have a positive influence on the development of public interpretation of archaeological sites and landscapes, they have to start thinking not only of ideology and epistemology, but also of the changing physical structures, spatial characteristics, communications media, and, above all, the socioeconomic context of the twenty-first-century heritage site. Flows of international and government funding subtly yet pervasively shape the fields on which today's visions of the past are experienced. And archaeology will only advance beyond theoretical, small-scale, or privately funded experiments with multivocality when they more carefully examine the deeper material structures of major heritage sites across the world. The many voices of modern high-tech heritage sites may no longer be read from the same hymnal. But they often sing together in an entertaining choir in service of tourist consumption and regional economic development that is hardly multivocal at all.

References

Addison, L. (2001). Virtual heritage: Technology in the service of culture. In S. N. Spenser (Ed.), *VAST 2001: Virtual Reality, Archaeology and Cultural Heritage* (pp. 343–354). New York: Association for Computing Machinery.

Barceló, J. A., Forte, M., & Sanders, D. H., (Eds.). (2000). *Virtual Reality in Archaeology*. Oxford: British Archaeological Report International Series 843.

Corner, J. & Harvey, S. (Eds.). (1991). *Enterprise and Heritage*. London: Routledge.

DG Education and Culture, European Commission. (2003). *Report on the State of Cultural Cooperation in Europe*. Brussels: European Commission.

European Commission. (2002). *Structural Policies and European Territory: Cooperation Without Frontiers*. Luxembourg: Office for Official Publications of the European Communities.

Handler, R., & Gable, E. (1997). *The New History in an Old Museum: Creating the Past at Colonial Williamsburg*. Durham, NC: Duke University Press.

Hodder, I. (1998). The past as passion and play: Çatalhöyük as a site of conflict in the construction of multiple pasts. In Lynn Meskell (Ed.), *Archaeology Under Fire* (pp. 124–139). London: Routledge.

Killebrew, A. (2004). Archaeology and the public in the 21st century: The view from Israel. In D. Callebaut & A. Killebrew (Eds.), *Interpreting the Past* (pp. 41–48). Brussels: Institute for Archaeological Patrimony.

Kirshenblatt-Gimblett, B. (1998). *Destination Culture*. Berkeley: University of California Press.

Lowenthal, D. (2002). The past as a theme park. In T. Young & R. Riley (Eds.), *Theme Park Landscapes: Antecedents and Variations* (pp. 11–23). Washington: Dumbarton Oaks.

MacCannell, D. (1976). *The Tourist: A New Theory of the Leisure Class*. New York: Schocken Books.

Pletinckx, D., Silberman, N. A., & Callebaut, D. (2002). Why multimedia matter in cultural heritage: The use of new technologies in the Ename 974 Project. In F. Niccolucci & S. Hermon

(Eds.), *Multimedia Communication for Cultural Heritage* (pp. 65–72). Budapest: Archaeolingua.

Postman, N. (1986). *Amusing Ourselves to Death: Public Discourse in the Age of Show Business.* New York: Viking Press.

Walsh, K. (1992). *The Representation of the Past.* London: Routledge.

Wojciechowski, K., Smolka, B., Palus, H., Kozera, R.S., Skarbek, W., & Noakes, L. (2004). Empathic Avatars in VRML For Cultural Heritage. *Computer Vision and Graphics* 32, 1049–1055.

World Bank. (2001). *Cultural Heritage and Development: A Framework for Action in the Middle East and North Africa.* Washington: The World Bank.

Young, T., & Riley, R. (Eds.). (2002). *Theme Park Landscapes: Antecedents and Variations.* Washington: Dumbarton Oaks.

Chapter 10
Alternative States

Robert Chapman

Introduction

Debate on different archaeologies and interpretations of the past takes place on varying scales, from the local to the regional and the international. It might be argued that factors such as the expansion of the means of communication (e.g., the use of English as the international language, international educational exchanges, the development of organizations such as the World Archaeological Congress and the European Association of Archaeologists, the availability of more publication outputs, the expansion in the use of digital technologies and the Internet) have enabled debate to the point that we can make claims for a "global" archaeology. In other words, we are now partners in a twenty-first century profession rather than members of different, unequal, regional traditions (for the latter concept, see Trigger & Glover 1981).

Recent observations and criticisms suggest that this global view is idealistic and does not conform to current reality. Access to information technology is markedly unequal (Chapman 2003:4; Hodder 1999:151–152), as is access to library resources and the infrastructure for both scientific analyses and fieldwork. Collections of essays on archaeological theory in Europe (Hodder 1991) and the world (Ucko 1995) show the different intellectual traditions, institutional structures and political contexts, and the selective, uneven, or marginal impact of the main Anglo-American "schools" of thought, as well as the linguistic barriers to communication. The last point is evident in the unequal opportunities for the publication of translated research between English and non-English speaking countries, and the problems posed for comprehension by the subtleties of meaning, concepts, and expression in different languages. We think through language.

There is also fierce criticism of Anglo-American "hegemony" in theoretical debate (e.g., Holtorf & Karlsson 2000; Olivier 1999; Olsen 1991) and the assertion of intellectual independence coupled with the need to understand archaeological thought within its regional context (e.g., Vázquez Varela & Risch 1991:46). The criticism of the interest of North American archaeologists in the data, but not the theoretical approaches of Latin America (Politis 2003:261), is an example of perceived inequality and an assertion of local independence.

J. Habu, C. Fawcett, and J. M. Matsunaga (eds.), *Evaluating Multiple Narratives:*
Beyond Nationalist, Colonialist, Imperialist Archaeologies.
© Springer 2008

A pluralistic rather than a global archaeology requires more balanced interaction with non-English speaking traditions and engagement with their intellectual frameworks and interpretations. It also requires a recognition that there are variations within regional traditions as well as historical and current networks of interaction and engagement (e.g., between the Spanish speaking countries), which make this a more complex issue than just one of the polarized relationships between a dominant Anglo-American world and individual, isolated, regional traditions.

In this chapter, I explore an example of this engagement as it relates to a different conception of the early state used by Spanish archaeologists. How do they define the state? How do they work with this definition to study Bronze Age social formations in southern Spain? What are, or might be, the reactions to this "alternative" state within the Anglo-American world? I examine four possible reactions: rejection, criticism of the dominant Anglo-American model of the early state, abandonment of the concept of the state, and the evaluation of the "alternative" state model and its application according to standard criteria. As a whole, the case study is also important because of the issues it raises about the state as the pinnacle of social development in the progressive history of the West. But first we need to explore the standard definition of the state that has been employed in the Anglo-American world during the last four decades.

Cultural Evolutionism, Decision-Making, and the State

The concept of the state has an intellectual history stretching back to Plato, but recent interest by archaeologists, as with other social types, stems from the seminal publications of anthropologists Elman Service (1962) and Morton Fried (1967). I want to begin with Flannery's (1972:412) much-cited argument that "the most striking difference between states and simpler societies lies in the realm of decision-making and its hierarchical organization, rather than in matter and energy exchanges." Central to this decision-making was the need for greater information processing in more complex social structures, which were both more centralized and more segregated. The earliest examples of these complex structures were found in civilization, defined as "that complex of cultural phenomena which tends to occur with the particular form of socio-political organization known as the state" (Flannery 1972:400). Among the characteristics possessed by the early civilizations/states of the Old and New Worlds were centralized governments, ruling classes with a monopoly of force, economic stratification, craft specialization, bureaucracy and specialist bureaucrats, and large-scale population densities. The definition of these early civilizations as state societies provided a set of readily recognizable characteristics that set them apart from "simpler" societies, while their study as complex systems (as defined in cultural ecology) provided a theoretical basis for the analysis of their evolution and collapse.

Flannery's argument was developed by Wright and Johnson, who defined the state as "a society with specialized administrative activities" by which control was exercised (Wright & Johnson 1975:267). They proposed that chiefdoms had one level of decision-makers above the primary producers, while states had two or more levels of such decision-makers. Chiefdoms lacked the internal administrative specialization or bureaucracy of state societies, as well as their ability to exercise control through coercion (see Wright 1977). Horizontal and vertical specialization in decision-making in states were viewed as responses to the needs of societies seeking to process more information sources and coordinate larger numbers of activities (see Johnson 1978, 1982). The number of levels in site size in a settlement hierarchy was argued to be the best measure of such decision-making hierarchies, and therefore of the difference between chiefdom and state: this inference was based on the arguments that (1) thresholds in the needs for information processing were related to the scale of the social system, (2) the population size of organizational units was one measure of this scale, and (3) settlement size was a measure of population size. Wright and Johnson (1975) used the archaeological record of state development in southwest Iran in the fourth millennium BC to exemplify their argument. In a later paper, Wright (1986) proposed that there were up to five levels in the settlement hierarchies of early Mesopotamian and Andean states.

This theoretical framework has set the agenda for the archaeological analysis of the state in the Anglo-American world during the last three decades. The focus has been on the development of administrative hierarchies rather than political control and economic exploitation, on the development and needs of information processing rather than the exchange of matter and energy. The use of extensive surface surveys in both the Old and New Worlds has enabled archaeologists to identify the number of levels in settlement hierarchies and thereby distinguish between chiefdoms and states. In contrast to areas such as Mesopotamia and Egypt in the Near East, European societies from the fourth to the second millennia BC had minimal levels of settlement hierarchy and were argued to find their best analogies in tribal and chiefdom societies (e.g., Renfrew 1973). During the second millennium BC, the early state in Europe was restricted to Crete (e.g., Manning 1994) and mainland Greece (e.g., Shelmerdine 2001) and only appeared further to the west, in central Italy, in the early first millennium BC (Barker & Rasmussen 1998).

Alternative States

In contrast to this view of later prehistoric societies in Europe, two papers published in 1986 proposed the existence of state society in southeast Spain at the beginning of the second millennium BC, the period of the Argaric Bronze Age. At the end of an analysis of Argaric burials, Lull and Estévez (1986:451–452) put forward the hypothesis that this period was that of a state rather than a chiefdom society: this hypothesis was based principally on the evidence for a "dominant class" associated with "idiotechnic items of power/prestige," including weapons that gave witness to the presence of institutionalized force or coercion. Other evidence (e.g., differences in access to instruments of production between occupation structures) supported the inference of the Marxist conception of the state as repressive, formed to maintain the politico-economic interests of the dominant class. In the same volume, Schubart and Arteaga (1986:305) also preferred the inference of a state rather than chiefdom society for the Argaric, although they defined neither term and principally referred to evidence for hierarchy in the burials and regional organization of agricultural and metallurgical production. The same lack of definition, whether of the state or of classes, was seen in a later publication by Arteaga, although a definition of the state could be inferred from his reference to the "new development of productive forces...(which) were centralized by the apparatus of the state, which was endowed with sovereignty, power and coercive force" (Arteaga 1992:198). Much of the argument also focused on the pre-state productive systems and socio-economic structures of the third millennium BC in southeast Spain.

Both definition and situation within a theoretical context had to wait until Lull and Risch (1995) used a classical Marxist approach to propose that the key characteristic of state societies is that they are based on relations of class. It is the institutions of the state that guarantee the interests of the dominant class: in other words, "the class which is economically dominant also becomes the class which is politically dominant" (Lull & Risch 1995:99, my translation). Such dominance is based on coercion, whether physical or ideological, or both. Lull and Risch follow Gramsci's argument that the state also is hegemony protected by coercion (Lull & Risch 1995:100): in other words, the state develops the apparatus of hegemony, formed by different ideological and cultural institutions, through which social coercion is practiced.

Lull and Risch (1995) proceed to argue that private property is the main interest of the dominant class that the state guarantees. This is defined as "the most direct expression of the unequal appropriation of human labor and its resulting product, and therefore the cause of the existence of workers and non-workers, or put another way, the cause of the development of a class society" (Lull & Risch 1995:100, my translation). Such property takes different forms, including land, labor, the means of production, and products. Lull and Risch propose that property relations are best studied by archaeologists through analysis of differential production and the generation of surplus: the latter is defined, not simply as an increase in production (whether the result of intentional action or interannual fluctuations), but as the appropriation of wealth by those not involved in its production (i.e., an unequal distribution of material and energetic costs and benefits in a society). In this sense, surplus is defined as the product of exploitation. Although exploitation also occurs in nonstate societies (e.g., the exploitation of women by men), "it is only when surplus ceases to be a good of direct consumption and is transformed into a value that can be managed, stored and transformed in the form of different material goods and services which ultimately benefit a certain social group, that there emerges the need for institutional control of private property" (Lull & Risch 1995:101).

Finally, Lull and Risch (1995) distinguish between the structural relations and material form of the state: "a state structure does not consist of the visible forms of power, pomp and circumstance (e.g., palaces, writing and exotic wealth items), but the systems of exploitation, extortion and physical and ideological coercion which

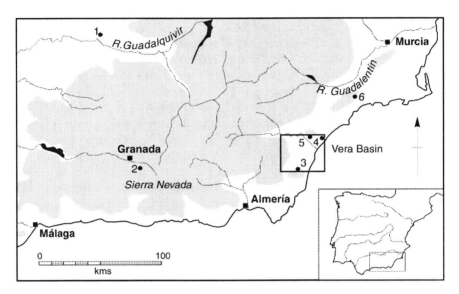

Fig. 10.1 Southeast Spain and the Vera Basin. 1. Peñalosa; 2. Cerro de la Encina, Monachil; 3. Gatas; 4. El Oficio; 5. Fuente Álamo; 6. Cabezo Negro

in each case can take distinct forms, given the possibilities of social development which are dialectically related to the needs of the dominant class" (Lull & Risch 1995:108, my translation).

Lull and Risch (1995; see also Castro et al. 1998, 2002; Chapman 2003; Risch 2002) use the case study of the Argaric Bronze Age in southeast Spain to argue that an early state, as they define it, developed here during the period ca. 2250–1550 BC, and particularly during the last two hundred years of this period (see Fig. 10.1 for location and sites mentioned in text). At the beginning of the Argaric there was a marked discontinuity in material culture, settlement patterns and architecture, and the disposal of the dead. In the Vera basin, the major low-lying third millennium Copper Age settlements were abandoned and most of the major Argaric settlements such as Gatas, El Oficio, and Fuente Álamo were located on intervisible, artificially terraced foothills around the basin, with more rectilinear buildings replacing individual circular structures. Greater population nucleation seems to have occurred in settlements up to 4 ha in size. Intramural, mostly individual, burial in artificial caves, stone cists, pottery urns, and pits replaced extramural, kin-based communal interment in free-standing megalithic tombs.

The bases of Lull and Risch's (1995) inference of a state society derive from evidence of exploitation, property, and surplus production. Agricultural production is seen to intensify in the Vera Basin, as measured, for example, in: (1) the markedly increasing frequency of cereals and grinding stones per volume of excavated deposit through the three periods of Argaric occupation at Gatas and Fuente Álamo (Risch 2002:230–232), and (2) the development of extensive barley monoculture by the last of these periods ca. 1700–1550 BC at both Gatas and Fuente

Álamo (Castro et al. 1999a:849–851). However access to this production was unequal. First, there was an inverse relationship between site size and the extent of available dry and wet farming land, which was in the low-lying areas of the basin, away from the foothill settlements: in other words, the sites with the greater needs for such production were located further away from its source (Castro et al. 1999a:851–852; Lull & Risch 1995:105), and there was unequal access to agricultural production between the primary producers on the valley bottom and the consumers on the hilltop settlements that surrounded the Vera basin. Secondly, there is evidence from settlements such as Fuente Álamo and Gatas of the storage of grain and instruments of production such as grinding stones and flint sickle blades (although the latter occur in small numbers and may have been more frequent in lower-lying settlements or simply deposited in the fields when broken in use – see Gibaja 2002). The placement of grinding stones in an active state of use in some structures at Fuente Álamo, Gatas and Cabezo Negro shows that more than ten people could have worked alongside each other. In occupation level B of trench 39 at Fuente Álamo (tentatively dated to ca. 1925–1775 BC), there were 25 such grinding stones placed in piles in three main clusters over an area of 10.5 m^2 (Risch 2002:211–216). The numbers of grinding stones per site were far in excess of those needed to support the needs of domestic production and even the entire populations living in these settlements: for Fuente Álamo, Risch (2002:234–235) calculates that the use of the grinding stones could have produced sufficient flour to support more than 1,400 people in phase III and 1,800 people in phase IV, as compared to the estimated population of ca. 300–400 for the site. This is all the more surprising, given that these stones came from secondary sources in the riverbeds of the basin, close to low-lying settlements (where they were rare) and areas of primary agricultural production.

What is inferred for the Vera basin in the Argaric is a regional, political system in which the processing of cereals into food, as well as possibly textile production (for which the raw material, flax, must have been cultivated along low-lying water courses, given its water requirements during germination and growth, while the frequency of loom weights on hill-top settlements indicates textile production away from these areas) was centralized and under the control of those living in the foot-hill settlements. Given both increased population size and the focus on extensive cultivation, human labor is argued to have been increased to support the appropriation of surplus (Castro et al. 1999a:851). Risch (1998:148) refers to the Argaric as a "system of vertical production" in which surplus production, as defined in terms of appropriation of the production of others, is channeled into local political and economic activities, rather than into the kinds of more extensive exchange networks that characterized the local Copper Age immediately prior to the Argaric.

Differences of both wealth and gender are visible in the disposal of the dead, as well as changes in the marking out of such differences in successive periods of the Argaric (Castro et al. 1993–1994; Chapman 2003:144–146; Lull 2000; Lull & Risch 1995:106). Differences of wealth (along with the production evidence cited above) are argued to signal the existence of classes: for example, the weapon associations with a small number of adult males are proposed to have symbolized the coercive power of a dominant class, the females of which are marked out by deposition with silver diadems. There is evidence for change in some symbols of such coercion through time (e.g., halberds being replaced by swords for males of the wealthiest social group – see Lull 2000:581). Analyses of child burials at El Argar show that differences in wealth consumption are fully marked out from 6 years of age, although members of the "dominant class" are distinguished from only a few months and there is evidence of increases in consumption with age, especially in adulthood (e.g., the deposition of halberds, swords and, diadems) (Lull et al. 2005).

The inequalities in deposition of metal objects, coupled with (debated) evidence for their raw materials being nonlocal (Montero 1999; Stos-Gale 2000), and the low frequencies of worked flint and observation of cut marks on animal bone and shells (e.g., Clemente et al. 1999; Sanz & Morales 2000), which use wear analysis show were not made by flint tools, support the inference that metal items were socially restricted tools, and were not purely of symbolic value. Within the most extensively excavated settlement at Fuente Álamo, Risch (2002:267–274) observes that there is a correlation between the deposition of the greatest weight of metalwork in intra-mural tombs and their location on the summit and eastern slopes, which have the main productive areas (e.g., metalworking on the east slope), as well as evidence for storage (the famous water cistern, possible grain stores, large pottery vessels) and consumption (the concentration of pottery forms, such as the "chalice," for the consumption of drink and food). In contrast, the southern slope specialized in cereal processing and had little evidence for habitation, burial and storage, and the western slope was intensively occupied but had few productive activities. In other words, wealth deposition with the dead was concentrated in an area of production, storage, and consumption. Two tombs out of just over one hundred contained 53% of the weight of metal deposited with the dead, while the areas of the summit and the eastern slope had 92% of the metal by weight: metal production and consumption, let alone food production and storage, were under the control of the dominant class. Risch (2002:275) also notes that during the period of maximum development of the Argaric state, deposition of the dead with the greatest concentrations of wealth (i. e., the dominant class), only happened in the hill-top settlements and not in those on the valley bottoms and plains.

Within Spain, Lull and Risch are not alone in their proposal of the existence of early prehistoric states. For example, Arteaga (2000, 2001) has also made the same proposal for the Argaric, while Eiroa (2004:413) refers to Argaric "states" rather than a single state system, given the area over which Argaric sites and materials were distributed, and Jover and López Padilla (2004:298) infer the existence of class society in the Vinalopó basin, to the north of the Argaric "frontier" ca. 1600–1200 BC (i.e., at the end of, and after, the Argaric). Cámara et al. (1996) argue for a strongly hierarchical, class society in the same period in the Upper Guadalquivir valley of southern Spain (see also Cámara 2001). Cruz-Auñon and Arteaga (1995) and Nocete (2001) have suggested that "initial class societies" existed in this region during the third millennium BC: this interpretation depends on evidence for the control of agricultural production and for visual and physical control of political territory, among other things, by the use of fortifications and frontiers (e.g., Nocete 1989; 1994).

Alternative Reactions: Rejection

What are we to make of this inference of early state societies in Spain, in an area for which many prefer the use of concepts such as "chiefdoms," "ranked," or even "stratified" societies, given prevailing models in use in the Anglo-American world? Let us consider four possible reactions, the first of which is to reject it out of hand.

From the decision-making perspective, the Argaric has at best a two-level settlement hierarchy, the settlements only had populations in the hundreds, and there were no palaces, temples or bureaucracies (Chapman 1990, 2003). How can this possibly compare with the "power, pomp and circumstance" of the early states of Mesopotamia or Mesoamerica, with their cities, ceremonial centers and monuments, writing, bureaucracies, and populations in their hundreds of thousands? Eleventh century AD Cahokia, in the American Midwest, with its settlement and social hierarchies, centralized economic control, regional trade, impressive monumental architecture, labor appropriation, and coercive force, is only classified as a complex/paramount chiefdom "perhaps on the verge of becoming a state" (Emerson 1997:251). Opinion on the first millennium BC culture of the Olmec, on the Gulf coast of Mexico, with its ceremonial centers, monuments, carved stone heads, craftsmen, and labor appropriation, is sharply divided between those who title it Mesoamerica's first state (e.g., Clark 1993, 1997; Grove 1997) and those who classify it within the range of known chiefdom societies (Flannery & Marcus 2000). How could Bronze Age society in southeast Spain gain entry into the early states club when these notable examples are excluded?

Outside the Near East, the earliest states in the Mediterranean are restricted to Crete and Mainland Greece in the second millennium BC, and it is not until the first millennium BC that the Etruscan state is recognized in central Italy. Elsewhere in the West Mediterranean the assumption is made that later prehistoric, rural societies were traditional, conservative or static, somehow lacking the dynamism to develop towards stratification and the state, except in a few areas. Some even deny the local development of stratification (Mathers & Stoddart 1994). In this context, the claims for early state societies in southern Spain in the third and second millennia BC may appear wildly optimistic. However, I would argue against assumptions about static Mediterranean societies. We need to focus more on the dynamic nature and potential of all such societies, each of them in flux, containing the seeds of their own transformation and marked by divisions of interest, contradictions between everyday practices and prevailing ideologies and by non linear change. Labeling regions or societies as inherently "traditional" or "conservative" assumes what we should be trying to evaluate, as well as devaluing their potential for change and their own histories.

The clearest rejection of the Argaric state, both in its own terms and by comparison with other early Old World states, comes from a Marxist archaeologist interested in class divisions and exploitation in prehistoric societies. Gilman (1991) compared the Bronze Age sequences of southeast Spain and the Aegean, noting striking differences in the second millennium BC in population nucleation and settlement size, specialization, the scale of production and storage, and the scale of trade networks: "the Aegean world has taken off into a higher, more unstable order of complexity; southeast Spain stagnates in a continuation of earlier patterns" (Gilman 1991:164). More recently, Gilman (2001) argues against inferences of a tribute system, ideological coercion and classes in the Argaric, preferring a model of "descent into internecine strife" (Gilman 2001:81) as competing lineages failed to establish themselves in an institutionalized social order.

There are both empirical and logical reasons to counter important parts of Gilman's argument. First, his proposal that there is no evidence of "elite intervention in agricultural production" (Gilman 1991:160) in southeast Spain, coupled with his rejection of a tribute system (Gilman 2001:77), has to rule out diverse lines of evidence (e.g., production, the instruments of production and wealth differences seen in the disposal of the dead) in support of a class system in the Vera basin. Given the presence of these lines of evidence together within individual settlements (for example, see the discussion of Fuente Álamo above), the case for a regional political system seems stronger than that against it. Secondly, the biological evidence in support of the inference of classes, or at least stratification, is still admittedly weak and based on paleopathologies from nineteenth-century excavations and from small samples from modern excavations. But to point out that only 63 out of 793 individuals studied from the earlier excavations exhibited pathologies associated with disease or dietary stress (Gilman 2001:79) fails to relate those individuals to wealth differences between them and, given the nature of the contextual evidence, cannot relate them to differences in production and consumption within many of the settlements. Isotopic evidence is, as Gilman points out, going to be of importance in developing the inference of social classes. Thirdly, the argument that "stylistic uniformity of Argaric ceramics, metalwork and burial practices suggests that the inhabitants of Argaric sites had mental templates in common, but not that these templates were imposed by ideological institutions" (Gilman 2001:77) fails to explain why such uniformity developed over seven hundred years and some 50,000 km^2 in the later third and early second millennium BC and not in the preceding millennium.

Of course, summary rejection of early Spanish states depends on acceptance of definitions (which Gilman consistently follows) of chiefdoms and early states within Anglo-American archaeology, coupled with the material indicators of these kinds of societies, and the equation of early states with early civilizations. It is a "top down" (from monuments) or "center out" (from cities) approach in which size (of settlements, production, storage, trade networks, etc.) is everything. Pristine early states are argued to have developed in a restricted number of regions of the world. Given this argument, it might be proposed that the definition of the state is being changed in order to extend the area over which early states appeared. Looking at the sociopolitics of archaeology in Europe, a case might be made for postdictatorship, intellectually and politically liberated Spanish archaeologists asserting their comparatively recent freedom by claiming an earlier development of the state, that most complex form of society, than anywhere in the Mediterranean apart from the Aegean. This would be the ultimate response to the *ex Oriente lux* diffusionism that dominated the first 60 years of the twentieth century, as Spanish archaeology now becomes intellectually central and legitimated as an area of activity. This would be a cynical and unjustified reaction, especially given that the same definition of the early state can be developed in other areas and it is not tailored specifically to Spanish contexts. Such a rejection would also fail to do justice to the distinction made between structural form and material representation, a distinction which has been part of Anglo-American theoretical debate over at least two decades (e.g., Hodder 1982).

It is also important to point out that Lull and Risch's definition of the state fits within a wider intellectual tradition of Marxist studies in archaeology, both in and outside of the Anglo-American world (e.g., McGuire 1992:145–177). The distinction made in this tradition between the processes of social and biological evolution has led, among other things, to a focus on the problems posed by states rather than exclusively on the problems which they solve through organizational adaptation (as in the development of decision-making hierarchies as responses to the needs for information processing in larger-scale societies). Drawing on thought since Engels (1884–1972 edition) and Lenin (1917–1969 edition), emphasis is placed on a more negative valuation of the state (e.g., exploitation, oppression, coercion) than seen in some anthropological and archaeological thought (for discussion, see Patterson 2003:70), and on a more historical study of the processes of state formation (including resistance to class domination) and their relation to the specific forms taken by such a state.

The contrast between kinship- and class-based societies is the structural change which is central to Marxist thought on pre-state and state societies. For Lull and Risch (1995), the emergence of classes signifies the formation of the state, rather than preceding it by "centuries" (as argued by Wright 1984:69) for Mesopotamia and Mesoamerica. But this is not necessarily a smooth or irreversible change and states have built-in instabilities, given the dialectical relationship between the domination, hegemony, and coercion of the nonproducers and the physical or ideological resistance of the producers. The outcome of these tensions is what has been called "heterogenous mosaics of societies, rather than polities with the same socio-political structure" (Patterson 2003:99–100), with shifting relations of domination and resistance and different trajectories of social, economic, and political change: these trajectories include state collapse, state expansion and the development of different forms of states (e.g., tributary, mercantile, and military). "States are like lids on pressure cookers. They attempt to control volatile, often explosive mixtures by keeping class antagonisms and contradictions in check: they often fail. States are fragile and unstable, because the contradictions that exist in the economic structure, especially those between different factions of the dominant class, are typically reproduced in the legal and political superstructure" (Patterson 2003:23).

Historical materialism is, of course, a diverse and evolving tradition of thought and there is no space here to discuss, for example, debates on class relations between classical and neo- or structural Marxists. My point is that Lull and Risch's (1995) definition of the state has a wider intellectual context both in the social sciences and in archaeology in general: as examples of the latter, we may cite the work of Gailey and Patterson (1987, 1988) on tribute-based states, Patterson (1991) on pre-Inca states and the Inka Empire, Bate (1984, 1998) on "initial class societies," and Kristiansen (1991, 1998) on the difference between tribal societies and archaic states (which included complex chiefdoms and stratified societies) in temperate Europe from the late second millennium BC. One could, of course, simply reject this intellectual context for theoretical reasons, but not only would that rule out intellectual engagement with a large segment of professional archaeologists across the world, it would also prove difficult to do, given what has been called "the disembedded and free-floating nature of Marxist ideas in Western society" (Trigger 1993:174). Rejection on the grounds that it is difficult to operationalize key concepts of historical materialism (Wenke 1981:117) is weakened by the observation that the definition and use of concepts such as exploitation, surplus, and property is one of the strengths of the Spanish case study (see below).

Alternative Reactions: Self-Criticism

A second reaction would be to take a self-critical look at the decision-making model of the state. Are there aspects of this model that are open to question? Two decades ago it was noted that decision-making hierarchies were not always expressed in settlement hierarchies, as seen in Polynesia, with its dispersed settlement patterns (Cordy 1981:35). The concept of centralized political and economic activities, pursued through a single, regional, decision-making and settlement hierarchy, has been criticized through use of the concept of heterarchy (Crumley 1979). Wailes (1995) cites the existence of multiple hierarchies (e.g., lay, Church, craft) within early medieval Irish societies. Potter and King (1995) argue that the lowland Maya had a stratified, political system, with hierarchical settlement and ceremonial centers, but economic and craft production was not universally centralized (e.g., mass-produced pottery and lithics were the subject of local, community specialization). The early states of southeast Asia have evidence for decentralized craft-specialization, long-distance exchange, rice production, and irrigation systems (White 1995). There is also now evidence that the earliest state societies in Minoan Crete were decentralized: Schoep (2002:117) argues that the town of Malia contained multiple elite groups, rather than a centralized palace authority, and that it had a "heterarchical social landscape," while Knappett (1999:631) uses the evidence of noncentralized pottery production in the Malia territory to argue that there were "low levels of administrative intervention in the day-to-day economic affairs of dependent populations."

These examples help us to see how the single, regional hierarchy is one model of a state society and not necessarily the most appropriate one for early state societies. For these societies, it is argued that the degree of centralization was an outcome of the interests and political strategies of the ruling elites or dominant class(es) and the interests and resistance of the dominated groups. Instead of having uncontested control, these early states were "organizations operating within a social environment that, for a variety of reasons, they only partially controlled" (Stein 1994:13). In Mesopotamia the population was nucleated in large urban centers such as Uruk (for reasons that included defense against raiding and labor control), but there was still considerable everyday autonomy for the sizeable rural population (Stein 1994:15).

This view of centralization in the early state allows us to argue that it is not inflexible and that decentralization is not some kind of "adaptive failure" (Blanton 1998:139). Instead of these polar opposites in state societies, we now see a "fuzzy model, grounded in culturally unique configurations of conflict and contingency, rather than the clean lines of monolithic hierarchy that we might see on a corporate table of organization" (Stein 1998:27). This fuzziness might also be expected to extend to the spatial dimensions of polities and political control: depending on the amount and nature of "conflict and contingency," centers which occupied the same position in a settlement (and therefore decision-making) hierarchy would have territories and lines of interaction which were different in size, intensity, and density, and did not necessarily conform to the kind of regular, continuous patterning predicted by modern spatial models such as Thiessen polygons.

In addition to these criticisms of the decision-making model as originally defined, we should also note that the relationship between the scale (as defined by the use of demographic variables such as maximal community size, regional populations, and territorial size) and nature of a political system is now seen to be more complex. Variation is recognized in the population size of archaic states, from as low as 2,000–3,000 to as high as 14 million people, and there is no consensus on any kind of "threshold" between what are called chiefdom and state societies (Feinman 1998). "The ways in which ancient states were integrated and interconnected often varied markedly over space, and differences in organization and integration have profound implications on state size" (Feinman 1998:132). Estimates of population size in the Vera basin (an area of some 375 km²) of southeast Spain in the Argaric range from ca. 1,700–3,400, that is at the bottom end of Feinman's range, while the full extent of the Argaric over nearly 50,000 km² is over three times the size of Renfrew's (1975) Early State Module. We should be wary of simply equating cultural areas with political systems, but the range in the scale and organization of known early states removes the focus solely on the high-density, urban, bureaucratic states of areas such as the Near East, China, and Mesoamerica.

Alternative Reactions: Abandon the State

A third reaction would be to say "a plague on all your houses" and follow Smith (2003) in rejecting the use of the state as an analytical concept. He notes the problems in defining the state, and criticizes what he sees as the focus on its definition and recognition, on typological classification, and ultimately the "reification" of the concept as a "real historical phenomenon" (Smith 2003:81). The concentration on identification and classification (i.e., what is a state as opposed to a complex chiefdom?) has been at the expense of "studies that investigate the active construction of political authority" (Smith 2003:80). The outcome of such studies would be political histories in all their variability through time, rather than what Smith sees as the use of the concept of the state as a "back-story for the modern" (Smith 2003:80). If I understand him correctly, this last criticism echoes that of Rowlands (1989), who argues that the focus by archaeologists on the state, cities, bureaucracy, writing, social stratification, and long-distance trade (the last five being essential criteria for the identification of the state as civilization, as proposed by Flannery 1972) is determined by a wider need to trace the origins of the key features of European modernity and the West.

Given this line of criticism, Smith argues that we should discard the concept of the "archaic state," as used by archaeologists, and replace it with "early complex polities": the word "complex" here refers to the relative extent, heterogeneity, and differentiation in social formations, as seen in such features as inequalities in access to resources, variation in social roles, and the permanence of institutions (Smith 2003:103–104). Political relationships at different scales within and between polities constitute the objects of analysis and, Smith argues, the removal of debates over attribution of past societies to the categories of the chiefdom or the state helps us, as archaeologists, to focus on such relationships and what he calls "the constitution of authority" (Smith 2003:105). "The central question for the study of early complex polities is thus not the origin and evolution of an essentialized totality that we call the State but an inquiry into how an authoritative political apparatus came to gain varying degrees of ascendancy over all other social relations" (Smith 2003:108). In a significant addition, he writes that "what we should mean when we refer to states, if the concept is to have any utility … (is) those polities where a public apparatus holds the legitimate power to intercede in other asymmetric relationships in order to mark itself as the authority of last resort" (Smith 2003:108).

Smith's criticisms of the state and his analyses of different political relationships are detailed and illustrated by case studies from areas such as Mesoamerica, Mesopotamia, and the southern Caucasus. The implications for the subject of this paper are that the definitional debate would be removed and case studies of "early complex polities" from different regions, such as southeast Spain, would become of comparative importance in the analysis of the "constitution of authority." There is much to commend in Smith's critique of the study of the early state, its focus on definition and classification, and the need to undertake a more historical analysis of political relationships, their structures, and fluidity through time and space. This finds a congruence with the Marxist views of the early state cited earlier in this paper (e.g., Patterson 2003). Smith's discussion of the political landscape of the Classic period Maya lowlands (Smith 2003:122–135), in which he constructs a powerful argument against the assumption that "early complex polities" here lived in a set, geometric landscape, with continuous territories, rather than a fluid pattern of political domination and resistance, alliance and warfare, ties in well with earlier criticisms of the emphasis on decision-making hierarchies and centralization (e.g., Stein 1994 "fuzzy model", see above).

At the same time, I am not convinced by Smith's conclusion, that we should abandon the state in favor of the "early complex polity" as an analytical concept. He himself clearly has a concept of "what we should mean when we refer to states" (Smith 2003:108), so it is perhaps surprising that he does not decide to follow that meaning. His alternative, the early complex polity, would avoid definitional arguments, like that between chiefdom and state, thereby, I assume, expanding the range of societies that would be included under its umbrella. Given that the argument proposed earlier in this paper has the implication of expanding the range of societies known as early states beyond the early civilizations, then there is a similar outcome. The definition of the early state that has been applied in southeast Spain would surely permit the kinds of comparative analyses of political relationships advocated by Smith, while reducing the emphasis on a search for the origins of the West in the first cities, writing and bureaucracy? To be fair, Smith (personal communication) argues that his main concern was to realign a political archaeology from its focus on the evolution of the state, with what he calls "a shopping list of civilizational criteria," to one which is concerned with "the constitution of authority," rather than to replace the state with the "early complex polity." This was not clear to me in my reading of his text, and there is insufficient space to debate this issue further here.

Alternative States: In Their Own Right?

A fourth reaction would be to try and evaluate the "alternative state" model in its own terms: how clearly is it defined (if it is defined at all), what are the key analytical concepts and how are they defined and put to work in studying archaeological data, how coherent is the theoretical argument, and how successful is research in using multiple lines of evidence? We would not expect that, simply because an interpretive structure was labeled "Marxist" or "historical materialist," there would be readily agreed definitions of key concepts, but we would expect there to be debate about such definitions, followed by a clear statement about how higher-level theoretical arguments are linked to the analysis of empirical data. Given that concepts of state and class are now being applied increasingly to archaeological data from the second and even third millennia BC across southern Spain, how far are these expectations being met?

As we have seen, Lull and Risch (1995) propose an argument on Bronze Age society in southeast Spain, especially the Vera Basin, which centers on key concepts such as state, class, property, exploitation, surplus, production, and consumption. The theoretical basis of this proposal lies in classical Marxism. One line of critique might be that adopted by Jessop, who argues that "nowhere in the Marxist classics do we find a well-formulated, coherent and sustained theoretical analysis of the state" (Jessop 1990:29) and that Marx's reflections and observations on the state were of lesser scope and rigor than his analysis of capital (Jessop 1990:25). Jessop identifies six different approaches to the state in the classic texts of Marx, Engels, Lenin, Trotsky, and Gramsci: among these are not only positions which associate the state with economic exploitation and class rule, but also observations of historical cases in which the economically dominant class was not politically dominant, in other words there have been varying degrees of relationship between the state and the dominant class (Jessop 1990:26–29).

The next point to note is the structural coherence in the way in which research in the Vera Basin has been developed: higher-level theoretical arguments on the production of social life (including the relationships of production and consumption, the meaning and generation of surplus, property, and exploitation) are related through lower-level theories of social practices (how and where production occurs within the course of everyday activities), archaeological objects (how social production is linked to such material), and units of analysis in the archaeological record (how they are related to the kinds of historical knowledge we are seeking) (e.g., Castro et al. 1999b:14–33). This procedure and its outcomes effectively counter claims that concepts such as "exploitation" cannot be operationalized (Wenke 1981). Also we have seen how the arguments about class and state are based on multiple lines of evidence, both domestic and funerary, within and between sites.

Other claims for the early state or for class society in the Bronze Age of southern Spain, especially on the west of the Argaric area, do not have the same theoretical coherence and can be terminologically vague. For example, Cámara (2001) adopts an allegedly Marxist approach to propose that class relations were not only present in the second millennium BC, but emerged in a "theocratic" society in the third millennium BC. His focus is on dominant modes of production and the development of successive types of society, from "communal" societies in the Neolithic to "theocratic class" societies in the Copper Age and "simple aristocratic" societies for much of the Bronze Age. But not only is there no detailed discussion and definition of key concepts (state, property, exploitation, surplus, etc.) within the wider sphere of Marxist thought, but Cámara also omits any reference to Lull and Risch (1995) or Risch (1998), thereby failing to situate his own interpretive work within an immediate, local context. Thus he moves from higher-level theory to interpretation of empirical data, seemingly without the kinds of linkages that make for theoretical coherence. Much of his argument for Bronze Age class society depends upon the evidence from the settlement of Peñalosa in the upper Guadalquivir valley (Fig. 10.1), where three classes are distinguished on the basis of wealth items deposited with (a small sample of) burials, but such spatial differences in the disposal of the dead cannot be clearly related to differences in production and consumption. The latter relationship is critical to the state model and the use of multiple lines of evidence, as was seen at Fuente Álamo in the Vera Basin (see above).

I am not arguing that the proposal of a Bronze Age class system, and by inference an early state, in Granada is necessarily wrong. There are clearly wealth differences between burials, as well as concentrations of grain storage and horse bones (inferred as being consumed in feasting) in upper or central fortified areas in sites like Peñalosa and Cerro de la Encina, which may relate to social asymmetries both within these settlements and between them and other, tributary settlements (as can also be seen in the concentration of metalworking at Peñalosa). While such empirical evidence is suggestive, there is still a need for a more coherent theoretical argument and clearer definition of key concepts and how they can be studied empirically.

Learning from Alternatives

What can we learn from this debate over the early state? One response would be to reject the hypothesis of the state in Bronze Age southeast Spain because it fails to match the prevailing definition in archaeology of the early/archaic state, which stems from information theory and cultural ecology and uses material "markers" which equate it with a restricted number of early "civilizations" in the Old and New Worlds. Without these "markers," there can be no state, only at best chiefdoms or stratified societies (using analogy from the ethnographic record and a cross-cultural comparison of the archaeological records of settlement hierarchies, population scale, centralization, monument construction, regional, and inter-regional trade, etc.). Such a rejection confuses the structure of a state with its materialization. Also, it fails to engage with the critiques of the early state as a decision-making hierarchy and the adoption of a contested and heterogeneous rather than centralized model of political and economic organization.

Another response would be to reject what Kohl (1984:128) has called "tiresome disquisitions" on whether to attribute a specific society to a specific evolutionary type. One outcome, whether intended or not, of Smith's (2003) replacement of the state with "early complex polity" is that such "disquisitions" on the chiefdom versus the state are eliminated at a stroke. While this may seem attractive, it still leaves another "disquisition," for those who are that way inclined, on what are, or are not, "early complex polities." The view taken here is that the concepts and definitions we use determine and initiate our ability to engage in comparative analyses (Chapman 2003:88). The state is a concept with which to think and learn about past societies and, as such, must have defining criteria and structural linkages that enable us to relate these criteria to their material forms. The very definition of a concept like the state is not theory neutral, it embodies assumptions and it stems from specific theoretical contexts and arguments. A good example of an assumption is whether the state is regarded as good or bad, benevolent or malevolent, and in the interests of its members or not. The Marxist conception of the state, whether early or not, has its roots in opposition to the state. But this does not impede analyses of the relations between different interest groups, between rules and ruled. Indeed the development of concepts such as "exploitation" and "property" (the latter rarely given major treatment in Anglo-American archaeology, e.g., Earle 2000; Hunt & Gilman 1998) gives us tools with which to analyze political, economic, and social relations between different interest groups. This is not a typological exercise: the state as defined here has the concepts with which to engage in comparative analyses of class-divided societies.

The intellectual tradition from which this "alternative" state model stems is both broad and deep. Lull and Risch (1995) are not alone in proposing a Marxist-based definition of the state, or what are sometimes called "initial class societies," especially in Spain and in Latin America (e.g., Bate 1998; Lumbreras 1994). Their work ties in with both open and closeted use of Marxist ideas in Anglo-American, Latin American, and Mediterranean archaeology. This use cuts across regional traditions and varies according to local contexts, but it has been an essential part of this history of archaeology and Western thought, whether focused on the state or other problems (McGuire 1992). The Spanish case study presented in this paper is not simply an isolated example from a separate regional tradition, but one that contributes to a wider challenge of the prevailing model of the early state in the Anglo-American world.

Rather than reject the "alternative" state, or perhaps simply not engage with it because it stems from another tradition (whether Marxist or non-Anglo-American), we should take the opportunity for self-criticism (What problems are raised for the definition and study of the state? What advantages does the alternative approach have?) and examine carefully how the model is constructed and applied in specific contexts. In the case of southeast Spain, I have argued that the model of Lull and Risch (1995), and its development in the analytical and theoretical work of the Gatas project, makes a clear distinction between the structural characteristics and material forms of early states, it develops a coherent theoretical argument linking higher-level concepts to the study of empirical material, and it uses multiple lines of evidence in proposing the hypothesis that there was a state society in the southeast during the early second millennium BC. As I have tried to indicate above, the development of a coherent theoretical argument, including definitional clarity and robust inferences, is not equally represented in all claims for early state, or initial class, societies in other parts of southern Spain: each case has to be examined on its merits.

In conclusion, I take the value of the alternative state model to be the challenges posed by a different theoretical tradition for what is the dominant mode of thought about early states in the Anglo-American world. In addition to the challenges posed by this change of view as mentioned above, I am also led to ask three questions. First, why is there not more theoretical debate within Anglo-American archaeology about the nature of the state, given the focus on this within political theory and sociology during the last two decades (e.g., Jessop 1990; Hoffman 1995)? Secondly, what difference would it make to our understanding of prehistory in areas like Mesopotamia if we coupled class and state, rather than making the former precede the latter by centuries? Thirdly, is it now the time to de-couple the concepts of state and civilization, and consider more openly the possibility of states as political units that were not necessarily identical with, and did not necessarily evolve into, the cultural areas known as civilizations? It is all very well to follow current practice, cite Yoffee's Rule ("if you can argue whether a society is a state or isn't, then it isn't" – Yoffee 2005:41), and restrict the use of the term initially to the regions of the early civilizations, but that assumes that we agree on what constitutes early state society.

Acknowledgments I would like to thank the editors for inviting me to participate in the symposium on which this volume is based at the Society for American Archaeology meetings in Montreal, as well as for their patience while I revised the paper for publication. Thanks are also due to the British Academy and the University of Reading for the grants that made possible attendance at the meetings. Adam Smith, Randy McGuire, and Roberto Risch have offered valuable criticism on an earlier draft of this chapter and I am grateful to all of them. As always the final version is my own responsibility. I thank Vicente Lull and Roberto Risch for the challenge of the alternative state and hope that I have grasped the nettle! Finally, I thank all members of the Gatas project for the stimulating experience of an intellectual engagement between different traditions.

References

Arteaga, O. (1992). Tribalización, jerarquización y estado en el territorio de El Argar. *SPAL,* 1, 179–208.

Arteaga, O. (2000). El proceso histórico en el territorio argárico de Fuente Álamo. La ruptura del paradigma del Sudeste desde la perspective atlántica-mediterránea del Extremo Occidente. In H. Schubart, V. Pingel, & O. Arteaga (Eds.), *Fuente Álamo: Las excavaciones arqueológicas 1977–1991 en el poblado de la Edad del Bronce* (pp. 117–143). Seville: Junta de Andalucía.

Arteaga, O. (2001). La sociedad clasista inicial y el origin del estado en el territorio de El Argar. *Revista Atlántica-Mediterránea de Arqueología Social,* 3, 121–219.

Barker, G., & Rasmussen, T. (1998). *The Etruscans.* Oxford: Blackwell Publishers.

Bate, L. F. (1984). Hipótesis sobre la sociedad clasista inicial. *Boletín de Antropología Americana,* 9, 47–86.

Bate, L. F. (1998). *El Proceso de Investigación en Arqueología.* Barcelona: Crítica.

Blanton, R. E. (1998). Beyond centralization: steps towards egalitarian behaviour in archaic states. In G. M. Feinman & J. Marcus (Eds.), *Archaic States* (pp. 135–172). Santa Fe: School of American Research Press.

Cámara, J. A. (2001). *El ritual funerario en la Prehistoria Reciente en el Sur de la Península Ibérica.* Oxford: British Archaeological Reports, International Series 913.

Cámara, J. A., Contreras, F., Pérez, C., & Lizcano, R. (1996). Enterramientos y diferenciación social II. La problemática del Alto Guadalquivir durante la Edad del Bronce. *Trabajos de Prehistoria,* 53(1), 91–108.

Castro, P. V., Chapman, R. W., Gili, S., Lull, V., Micó, R., Rihuete, C., Risch, R., & Sanahuja, Ma. E. (1993–1994). Tiempos sociales de los contextos funerarios argáricos. *Anales de Prehistoria de la Universidad de Murcia,* 9–10, 77–107.

Castro, P. V., Gili, S., Lull, V., Micó, R., Rihuete, C., Risch, R., & Sanahuja Yll, Ma. E. (1998). Teoría de la producción de la vida social. Mecanismos de explotación en el sudeste ibérico. *Boletín de Antropología Americana,* 33, 25–77.

Castro, P. V., Chapman, R. W., Gili, S., Lull, V., Micó, R., Rihuete, C., Risch, R., & Sanahuja, Ma. E. (1999a). Agricultural production and social change in the Bronze Age of southeast Spain: the Gatas Project. *Antiquity* 73, 846–856.

Castro, P. V., Chapman, R. W., Gili, S., Lull, V., Micó, R., Rihuete, C., Risch, R., & Sanahuja, Ma. E. (1999b). *Proyecto Gatas 2. La Dinámica Arqueoecológica de la Ocupación Prehistórica.* Seville: Junta de Andalucía.

Castro, P.V., Chapman, R. W., Gili, S., Lull, V., Micó, R., Rihuete, C., Risch, R., & Sanahuja Yll, Ma. E. (2002). La Sociedad Argárica. In M. Ruiz-Gálvez Priego (Eds.), *La Edad del Bronce, Primera Edad de Oro de España? Sociedad, Economía e Ideología* (pp. 181–216). Barcelona: Crítica.

Chapman, R. (1990). *Emerging Complexity.* Cambridge: Cambridge University Press.

Chapman, R. (2003). *Archaeologies of Complexity.* London: Routledge.

Clark, J. E. (1993). Una reevaluación de la entidad política olmeca: Imperio, estado o Cacicazgo. *Segundo y Tercer Foro de Arqueología de Chiapas* (pp. 159–169). Chiapas: Instituto Chiapaneco de Cultura.

Clark, J. E. (1997). The arts of government in early Mesoamerica. *Annual Review of Anthropology,* 26, 211–234.

Clemente, I., Gibaja, J. F. and Vila, A. (1999). Análisis funcional de la industria lítica tallada procedente de los sondeos de Gatas. In P. V. Castro et al. (Eds.), *Proyecto Gatas 2. La Dinámica Arqueoecológica de la Ocupación Prehistórica* (pp. 341–47). Seville: Junta de Andalucía.

Cordy, R. H. (1981). *A Study of Prehistoric Social Change: The Development of Complex Societies in the Hawaiian Islands.* New York: Academic Press.

Crumley, C. L. (1979). Three locational models: an epistemological assessment for anthropology and archaeology. In M. B. Schiffer (Ed.), *Advances in Archaeological Method and Theory* 2, 141–173.

Cruz-Auñon, R., & Arteaga, O. (1995). Acerca de un campo de silos y un foso de cierre prehistóricos ubicados en "La Estacada Larga" (Valencina de la Concepción, Sevilla). Excavación de urgencia de 1995. *Anuario Arqueológico de Andalucía,* 600–607.

Earle, T. (2000). Archaeology, property and prehistory. *Annual Review of Anthropology,* 29, 39–60.

Eiroa, J. J. (2004). La Edad del Bronce en la region de Murcia. In L. Hernández Alcaraz & M. S. Hernández Pérez (Eds.), *La Edad del Bronce en Tierras Valencianas y Zonas Limítrofes* (pp. 399–427). Villena: Ayuntamiento de Villena.

Emerson, T. E. (1997). *Cahokia and the Archaeology of Power.* Tuscaloosa: University of Alabama Press.

Engels, F. (1972). *The Origins of the Family, Private Property and the State.* London: Lawrence and Wishart.

Feinman, G. M. (1998). Scale and social organization: perspectives on the Archaic State. In G. M. Feinman & J. Marcus (Eds.), *Archaic States* (pp. 95–133). Santa Fe: School of American Research Press.

Flannery, K. V. (1972). The cultural evolution of civilizations. *Annual Review of Ecology and Systematics,* 3, 339–426.

Flannery, K. V., & Marcus, J. (2000). Formative Mexican chiefdoms and the myth of the "Mother Culture." *Journal of Anthropological Archaeology,* 19, 1–37.

Fried, M. H. (1967). *The Evolution of Political Society.* New York: Random House.

Gailey, C. W. & Patterson, T. C. (1987). Power relations and state formation. In T. C. Patterson & C. W. Gailey (Eds.), *Power Relations and State Formation* (pp. 1–26). Washington D.C.: American Anthropological Association.

Gailey, C. W., & Patterson, T. C. (1988). State formation and uneven development. In J. Gledhill, B. Bender, & M. T. Larsen (Eds.), *State and Society: The Emergence and Development of Social Hierarchy and Political Centralisation* (pp. 77–90). London: Unwin & Hyman.

Gibaja, J. F. (2002). Análisis del material lítico tallado de Fuente Álamo. In R. Risch (Ed.), *Recursos naturales, medios de producción y explotación social: Un análisis económico de la industria lítica de Fuente Álamo (Almería), 2250–1400 antes de nuestra era* (pp. 163–77). Mainz am Rhein: Philipp von Zabern.

Gilman, A. (1991). Trajectories towards social complexity in the later prehistory of the Mediterranean. In T. Earle (Ed.), *Chiefdoms: Power, Economy and Ideology* (pp. 146–168). Cambridge: Cambridge University Press.

Gilman, A. (2001). Assessing political development in Copper and Bronze Age Southeast Spain. In J. Haas (Ed.), *From Leaders to Rulers* (pp. 59–81). New York: Kluwer Academic/Plenum.

Grove, D. C. (1997). Olmec archaeology: a half century of research and its accomplishments. *Journal of World Prehistory,* 11, 51–101.

Hodder, I. (1982). *Symbols in Action.* Cambridge: Cambridge University Press.

Hodder, I, (Ed.). (1991). *Archaeological Theory in Europe.* London: Routledge.

Hodder, I. (1999). *The Archaeological Process.* Oxford: Blackwell.

Hoffman, J. (1995). *Beyond the State.* Cambridge: Polity Press.

Holtorf, C., & Karlsson, H. (2000). Changing configurations of archaeological theory: an introduction. In C. Holtorf & H. Karlsson (Eds.), *Philosophy and Archaeological Practice: Perspectives for the 21st Century* (pp. 1–11). Göteborg: Bricoleur Press.

Hunt, R. C., & Gilman, A. (Eds.). (1998). *Property in Economic Context*. Lanham: University Press of America.

Jessop, B. (1990). *State Theory: Putting the Capitalist State in its Place*. Cambridge: Polity Press.

Johnson, G. A. (1978). Information sources and the development of decision-making organizations. In C. Redman et al. (Eds.), *Social Archaeology: Beyond Subsistence and Dating* (pp. 87–112). New York: Academic Press.

Johnson, G. A. (1982). Organizational structure and scalar stress. In C. Renfrew, M. J. Rowlands & B. A. Segraves (Eds.), *Theory and Explanation in Archaeology* (pp. 389–421). New York: Academic Press.

Jover, J., & López Padilla, J. A. (2004). 2100–1200 BC: Aportaciones al proceso histórico en la cuenca del río Vinalopó. In L. Hernández Alcaraz & M. S. Hernández Pérez (Eds.), *La Edad del Bronce en Tierras Valencianas y Zonas Limítrofes* (pp. 285–302). Villena: Ayuntamiento de Villena.

Knappett, C. (1999). Assessing a polity in Protopalatial Crete: the Malia-Lasithi state. *American Journal of Archaeology*, 103, 615–639.

Kohl, P. (1984). Force, history and the evolutionist paradigm. In M. Spriggs (Ed.), *Marxist Perspectives in Archaeology* (pp. 127–134). Cambridge: Cambridge University Press.

Kristiansen, K. (1991). Chiefdoms, states and systems of social evolution. In T. Earle (Ed.), *Chiefdoms: Power, Economy and Ideology* (pp. 16–43). Cambridge: Cambridge University Press.

Kristiansen, K. (1998). *Europe before History*. Cambridge: Cambridge University Press.

Lenin, V. I. (1969). *The State and Revolution*. London: Central Books Ltd.

Lull, V. (2000). Argaric society: death at home. *Antiquity*, 74, 581–590.

Lull, V., & Estévez, J. (1986). Propuesta metodológica para el estudio de las necrópolis argáricas. In *Homenaje a Luis Siret 1934–84* (pp. 441–452). Seville: Junta de Andalucía.

Lull, V., & Risch, R. (1995). El estado argárico. *Verdolay*, 7, 97–109.

Lull, V., Micó, R., Rihuete, C., & Risch, R. (2005). Property relations in the Bronze Age of southwestern Europe: an approach based on infant burials from El Argar (Almería, Spain). *Proceedings of the Prehistoric Society*, 71, 247–268.

Lumbreras, L. G. (1994). Acerca de la aparición del estado. *Boletín de Antropología Americana*, 29, 5–33.

Manning, S. (1994). The emergence of divergence: development and decline on Bronze Age Crete and the Cyclades. In C. Mathers & S. Stoddart (Eds.), *Development and Decline in the Mediterranean Bronze Age* (pp. 221–270). Sheffield: J. R. Collis Publications.

Mathers, C., & Stoddart, S. (1994). Introduction. In C. Mathers & S. Stoddart (Eds.), *Development and Decline in the Mediterranean Bronze Age* (pp. 13–20). Sheffield: J. R. Collis Publications.

McGuire, R. (1992). *A Marxist Archaeology*. New York: Academic Press.

Montero, I. (1999). Sureste. In G. Delibes & I. Montero (Eds.), *Las Primeras Etapas Metalúrgicas en la Península Ibérica II: Estudios Regionales* (pp. 333–357). Madrid: Instituto Universitario Ortega y Gasset.

Nocete, F. (1989). *El espacio de la coercion: La transición al Estado en las Campiñas del Alto Guadalquivir (España)*. Oxford: British Archaeological Reports, International Series 492.

Nocete, F. (1994). Space as coercion: the transition to the state in the social formations of La Campiña, Upper Guadalquivir valley, Spain c. 1900–1600 B.C. *Journal of Anthropological Archaeology*, 13, 171–200.

Nocete, F. (2001). *Tercer milenio antes de nuestra era: Relaciones y contradicciones centro/periféria en el Valle del Guadalquivir*. Barcelona: Bellaterra.

Olivier, L. (1999). The origins of French archaeology. *Antiquity*, 73, 176–183.

Olsen, B. J. (1991). Metropolises and satellites in archaeology: on power and asymmetry in global archaeological discourse. In R. W. Preucel (Ed.), *Processual and Postprocessual*

Archaeologies: Multiple Ways of Knowing the Past (pp. 211–224). Carbondale: Southern Illinois University.

Patterson, T. C. (1991). *The Inca Empire: The Formation and Disintegration of a Pre-Capitalist State*. Oxford/New York: Berg.

Patterson, T. C. (2003). *Marx's Ghost: Conversations with Archaeologists*. Oxford/New York: Berg.

Politis, G. G. (2003). The theoretical landscape and the methodological development of archaeology in Latin America. *American Antiquity*, 68(2), 245–272.

Potter, D. R., & King, E. M. (1995). A heterarchical approach to lowland Maya Socioeconomics. In R. M. Ehrenreich, C. L. Crumley, & J. E. Levy (Eds.), *Heterarchy and the Analysis of Complex Societies* (pp. 17–32). Archaeological Papers of the American Anthropological Association, No. 6.

Renfrew, C. (1973). *Before Civilization: The Radiocarbon Revolution and Prehistoric Europe*. London: Jonathan Cape.

Renfrew, C. (1975). Trade as action at a distance: questions of integration and communication. In J. A. Sabloff & C. C. Lamberg-Karlovsky (Eds.), *Ancient Civilization and Trade* (pp. 3–59). Albuquerque: School of American Research Press.

Risch, R. (1998). Análisis paleoeconómico y medios de producción líticos: el caso de Fuente Álamo. In G. Delibes de Castro (Ed.), *Minerales y Metales en la Prehistoria Reciente: Algunos Testimonios de su Explotación y Laboreo en la Península Ibérica* (pp. 105–154). Valladolid: Universidad de Valladolid.

Risch, R. (2002). *Recursos naturales, medios de producción y explotación social: Un análisis económico de la industria lítica de Fuente Álamo (Almería), 2250–1400 antes de nuestra era*. Mainz am Rhein: Philipp von Zabern.

Rowlands, M. J. (1989). A question of complexity. In D. Miller, M. Rowlands, & C. Tilley (Eds.), *Domination and Resistance* (pp. 29–40). London: Allen & Unwin.

Sanz, J. L., & Morales, A. (2000). Los restos faunísticos. In F. Contreras (Ed.), *Análisis Histórico de las Comunidades de la Edad del Bronce del piedemonte meridional de Sierra Morena y Depresión Linares-Bailen: Proyecto Peñalosa* (pp. 223–235). Seville: Junta de Andalucía.

Schoep, I. (2002). Social and political organisation on Crete in the Proto-Palatial period: the case of Middle Minoan II Malia. *Journal of Mediterranean Archaeology*, 15(1), 101–132.

Schubart, H., & Arteaga, O. (1986). Fundamentos arqueológicos para el estudio socio-económico y cultural del area de El Argar. In *Homenaje a Luis Siret 1934–84* (pp. 298–307). Seville: Junta de Andalucía.

Service, E. R. (1962). *Primitive Social Organization: An Evolutionary Perspective*. New York: Random House.

Shelmerdine, C. (2001). The palatial Bronze Age of the southern and central Greek mainland. In T. Cullen (Ed.), *Aegean Prehistory: A Review* (pp. 329–381). Boston: Archaeological Institute of America.

Smith, A. T. (2003). *The Political Landscape: Constellations of Authority in Early Complex Polities*. Berkeley: University of California Press.

Stein, G. J. (1994). The organizational dynamics of complexity in Greater Mesopotamia. In G. Stein & M. S. Rothman (Eds.), *Chiefdoms and Early States in the Near East. The Organizational Dynamics of Complexity* (pp. 11–22). Madison, Wisconsin: Prehistory Press.

Stein, G. J. (1998). Heterogeneity, power and political economy: some current research issues in the archaeology of Old World complex societies. *Journal of Archaeological Research*, 6, 1–44.

Stos-Gale, S. (2000). Trade in metals in the Bronze Age Mediterranean: an overview of lead isotope data for provenance studies. In C. F. E. Pare (Ed.), *Metals Make the World Go Round. The Supply and Circulation of Metals in Bronze Age Europe* (pp. 56–69). Oxford: Oxbow Books.

Trigger, B. G. (1993). Marxism in contemporary western archaeology. *Archaeological Method and Theory*, 5, 159–200.

Trigger, B. G., & Glover, I. (1981). Editorial. *World Archaeology*, 13(2), 133–137.

Ucko, P. J. (Ed.) (1995). *Theory in Archaeology: A World Perspective*. London: Routledge.

Vázquez Varela, J. M., & Risch, R. 1991. Theory in Spanish archaeology since 1960. In I. Hodder (Ed.), *Archaeological Theory in Europe* (pp. 25–51). London: Routledge.

Wailes, B. (1995). A case study of heterarchy in complex societies: early medieval Ireland and its archaeological implications. In R. M. Ehrenreich, C. L. Crumley, & J. E. Levy (Eds.), *Heterarchy and the Analysis of Complex Societies* (pp. 55–69). Archaeological Papers of the American Anthropological Association, No. 6.

Wenke, R. J. (1981). Explaining the evolution of cultural complexity: a review. *Advances in Archaeological Method and Theory, 4,* 79–127.

White, J. C. (1995). Incorporating heterarchy into theory on socio-political development: the case for Southeast Asia. In R. M. Ehrenreich, C. L. Crumley, & J. E. Levy (Eds.), *Heterarchy and the Analysis of Complex Societies* (pp. 101–123). Archaeological Papers of the American Anthropological Association, No. 6.

Wright, H. T. (1977). Recent research on the origins of the state. *Annual Review of Anthropology, 6,* 379–397.

Wright, H. T. (1984). Prestate political formations. In T. Earle (Ed.), *On the Evolution of Complex Societies: Essays in Honor of Harry Hoijer 1982* (pp. 41–77). Malibu: Undena Publications.

Wright, H. T. (1986). The evolution of civilizations. In D. J. Meltzer, D. D. Fowler, & J. A. Sabloff (Eds.), *American Archaeology Past and Future: A Celebration of the Society for American Archaeology 1935–85* (pp. 323–365). Washington D.C.: Smithsonian Institution Press.

Wright, H. T., & Johnson, G. A. (1975). Population, exchange and early state formation in southwestern Iran. *American Anthropologist, 77,* 267–289.

Yoffee, N. (2005). *Myths of the Archaic State: Evolution of the Earliest Cities, States and Civilizations.* Cambridge: Cambridge University Press.

Chapter 11
Irish Archaeology and the Recognition of Ethnic Difference in Viking Dublin

Patrick F. Wallace

Introduction

Ireland, an island of rare natural beauty, has a rich, well-preserved archaeological heritage. The waterlogged conditions of the country's peat bogs and some of its early towns, most notably Dublin, preserve the most delicate of organic remains (Waddell 1998). The historical nondestructive accidents of the prevalence of pastoral farming, and the relative absence of an industrial revolution, furthermore, have left Ireland with a unique surviving archaeological heritage that includes extensive stretches of prehistoric landscape and ancient estuarine remains.

Only now, with the country's recent economic advances, is this archaeologically happy situation being seriously challenged for the first time. Economic progress has brought problems. For instance, as the country installs much needed infrastructure, building development and road construction on an unprecedented scale have led to much developer-led, contract archaeology. While some of such contract work is of a high standard, it has resulted in problems ranging from an insufficiency of Irish-trained or even of English-speaking archaeologists to the lack of a coordinated plan for the preparation of adequate excavation reports. In addition, we still lack a national program for the synthesis of the new information and dating evidence now coming to light.

My aims of this chapter are threefold. First, my chapter shows how the political history of Ireland, which suffered from a series of conquests, fostered a sociopolitical milieu of Irish archaeology with an emphasis on past glories of indigenous cultures. In this context, prehistoric archaeology, particularly the study of the ancient Celtic culture, was highly valued, while medieval historical archaeology, including the study of the Viking Age and Anglo-Norman invasions, was nonexistent until the 1960s. Second, using the excavation results of early medieval Dublin as a case study, my chapter suggests that, despite its late start, medieval archaeology is critical in understanding the Irish past. This case study also demonstrates that, by examining some of the key issues in contemporary archaeology, including identity and material culture, ethnicity, and culture contact, Irish medieval archaeology can contribute significantly to world archaeology. Finally, the epilogue of my chapter touches upon the rapidly changing social, political, and economic contexts of contemporary

J. Habu, C. Fawcett, and J. M. Matsunaga (eds.), *Evaluating Multiple Narratives: Beyond Nationalist, Colonialist, Imperialist Archaeologies.*
© Springer 2008

Irish archaeology in relation to media coverage, museum and popular exhibitions, tourism, and the waves of new immigrants.

Overview of the Population of Ireland

Ireland has only been populated since the last Ice Age, about 9,000 years ago. It lacks, therefore, evidence of Paleolithic habitation, but has excellent archaeological remains from the Mesolithic onward (Herity & Eogan 1977:16–56; O' Kelly 1989:1–33). The island is particularly well endowed with megalithic monuments of the Neolithic, notably Passage Tombs (Herity 1974), several of which exhibit the most extensive runs of megalithic art in Atlantic Europe (Shee Twohig 1981). The central repository of the island's portable heritage, the National Museum of Ireland, has the finest collection of Bronze Age gold ornaments, made of native gold, in northern or western Europe. These artifacts bear witness to a rich Bronze Age characterized by sheet gold ornaments, bronze weapons, implements, and pottery in the earlier phase, and by sheet bronzework, cast weapons, and a variety of sumptuous gold ornaments in the later (Cahill 2002:86–124).

Not being subjected to conquest by the Romans, though in receipt of Roman artistic, technological and economic influences from Britain, the island's Celtic society persisted long after its disappearance in other parts of western Europe. Even after it became Christianized in the fifth century, Ireland's rurally based, cattle-centered society and economy, with its archaic social and regal structures, persisted. It did so, however, within the context of Christianity that was based on a monastic rather than an Episcopal model. The Golden Age of Irish Early Christianity, centered on places of great learning, was characterized by manuscript illumination, sacred metalwork production, sculpture, and architecture. Irish monks evangelized great parts of northern Britain and continental Europe from the seventh century onward (Bieler 1963; Bullough 1982; Richter 1988).

The Vikings, who began to come to Ireland from Scandinavia in the late eighth century, were apparently attracted initially by the wealth of the monasteries and their potential as centers for slave collection and sacred metalwork that could be converted to jewellery. This changed through time, however, and the Scandinavians began to bring large quantities of silver with them. This silver was utilized by native Irish silversmiths to produce exquisite jewellery. A silver weight economy also developed, which gave way to a coin-using one by the end of the tenth century (Gerriets 1985; Graham-Campbell 1976; Wallace 1987).

The first towns in Ireland were established by the Vikings in the mid-ninth century. Initially slave exporting emporia, these towns gradually developed into centers of trade and manufacture (Wallace 1985a; Heckett 2003). The towns received internationally derived, long-distance trade items (e.g., oriental silks, possibly from Bagdad, have been found in Dublin excavations (Wallace 1985a)), exported cloth and manufactured goods, and serviced passing ships. In addition, inhabitants of Dublin hired out their fleet for mercenary use at a time when the Irish Sea had virtually become a Viking Dublin lake.[1] Despite stubborn survivals of Scandinavian influence, Viking traditions merged with indigenous traditions to produce a rich culture in the eleventh and earlier twelfth centuries (see, for example, Bradley 1988; Henry 1962, 1967).

In 1169, almost a century after their conquest of England, the Normans (or as they were by then the Anglo or Cambro [Welsh] Normans) came to Ireland. In contrast with the Vikings before them, the Anglo-Normans came in much greater numbers. Consequently, they had a huge impact on population and settlement patterns over a large part of the island. Their impact on society, buildings, settlement forms, art, and government may still be seen in the towns, buildings, sculpture, and devotional remains of the Middle Ages which survive in Ireland.

Despite their large number, the Normans too became "more Irish than the Irish themselves" and, by the time of the Elizabethan English conquest of the late sixteenth century, they were an assimilated part of the overall Irish scene. After the enforced exile of the last of the native aristocrats in 1607, the Elizabethan's deliberate population plantations and more extensive plantations undertaken in Ulster, the northern province, resulted in a new order in English-dominated Ireland.

The culmination of the English conquest of Ireland was the Act of Union of the Parliaments, and the creation of what was termed the United Kingdom in 1800. The new political order resulted in the political, social, and economic marginalization, if not exclusion, of the majority of the indigenous population, who were Roman Catholic rather than Protestant. The Irish people and their leaders linked their struggle for repeal of the Union, and later their fight for national independence, with ideas of cultural revival. Beginning in the 1840s, Irish people struggling for political, social, and economic autonomy consciously used antiquity, and the archaeological remains which they believed reflected a glorious past to express the legitimacy and lineage of their cause and to develop a sense of Irish culture. From this background national independence eventually emerged in 1922 (Comerford 2003).

The Social and Political Context of Dublin Archaeology

The direction and emphasis of archaeology and archaeological research often reflects contemporary interests and obsessions. This is true of the development of Irish archaeology over the past 80 or so years. The establishment of Irish independence, in 1922, ended centuries of colonial dominance of the small island by England. The postindependence era witnessed the growth of Irish nationalism, the surfacing of Gaelic culture, a literary revival, and the emergence of a sizable Roman Catholic middle class. These trends were mirrored, after the establishment of the Free State in the 1920s, by the foundation of Chairs of archaeology. The first generation of Irish born and educated archaeologists in the postcolonial period were people of their time, strongly nationalist (Cooney 1996; Waddell 2005; Woodman 1995) and, consciously or not, anti-British in their evaluation of the external influences on ancient Ireland. Who could blame them for their Irish nationalism when the Free

State government recruited the first two postindependence Keepers of Irish Antiquities (archaeologists in charge of the National Museum collection) from Germany and Austria, respectively (Herity & Eogan 1977:4–15; McEwan 2003; Wallace 2004a)? If help or advice was needed, it must not be seen to come from the land of the old colonial master.

Not surprisingly given this background, the teaching of archaeology in the three colleges of the National University of Ireland (Dublin, Cork, and Galway) and the practice of the subject in the two State services (artifacts and the portable heritage at the National Museum and monuments, and built heritage and licensing of excavations at the National Monuments branch of the Office of Public Works) focused on antiquity rather than on Medieval and later times. Researchers concentrated on the perceived greatness of ancient Ireland with its megaliths, its gold ornaments and the distinctiveness of the "Celtic" Iron Age. Their main concern was to understand the origins of the newly independent indigenous population.

Archaeology was a justification, even a celebration, of indigenous Irish culture rather than an objective and dispassionate study of the island's past. This meant that, in contrast to historical studies, archaeological research on the Viking Age and particularly of the Anglo-Norman and later medieval periods were shortchanged. Popular association of the Vikings with the destruction of the great monasteries hindered the broad acceptance of the period and its material remains as subjects for either museum display or scholarly research. Even the arguably greatest contribution of the Vikings to Ireland, the foundation of enduring Irish towns such as Dublin, failed to gain much attention from a community which, until recently, was rurally based, conservative, and suspicious of things urban. The archaeological remains of the Anglo-Normans, who arrived in Ireland in the later twelfth century and were seen as the earliest representatives of eighth centuries of English presence in Ireland, were in even less favor among Irish archaeologists than those of the Vikings.[2] Although Anglo-Norman abbeys and castles were maintained by the National Monuments Branch, until the 1970s, university courses largely eschewed this period.

Knowledge of the archaeological remains of Ireland was also influenced by how Irish towns and cities were excavated during the twentieth century, particularly after the Second World War. The most extensive information about the buildings, layout, economy, and waterfront of any European transalpine town of the Early Middle Ages is that now available for Dublin. This information was generated during more than four decades of archaeological excavation by the National Museum of Ireland and other teams. The foundation remains of several hundred buildings have been found, many in almost intact condition in the waterlogged conditions which provide excellent preservation for wood and other organic materials (Wallace 1992a).

Except for an apparent mistake at Dublin's North Strand, the towns of neutral Ireland were not bombed during the Second World War. The postwar redevelopment of English and continental towns gave rise to urban archaeological excavation in the 1950s and early 1960s, but this was not matched in Ireland with the exception of the area around the heart of the old city of Dublin. Here, in 1961, a small-scale excavation by Marcus Ó hEochaidhe at Dublin Castle and later, in 1962, by Breandán Ó Ríordáin at High Street showed the amazing quality of the preservation of urban deposits (National Museum of Ireland 1973; Ó Ríordáin 1971, 1973). Following up on this, Ó Ríordáin worked on Christchurch Place and Winetavern Street before, in 1974, the writer began to excavate at Wood Quay-Fishamble Street, where Dublin Corporation (now City Council) planned to use an extensive 4-acre site to house their Civic Office Complex.

The necessarily hurried nature of the work on the thirteenth-century waterfront site at Wood Quay (Wallace 1985b) and threat of destruction to as yet unexcavated tenth- and eleventh-century defensive embankments led to a "Save Viking Dublin" campaign by the voluntary preservation group, the Friends of Medieval Dublin and their charismatic leader, the medieval historian Professor Rev. F. X. Martin osa. He led a number of protest marches and a site occupation and brought Dublin Corporation to the High Court where, while the conservation case was lost, sufficient time was gained for the Museum's archaeological team to complete the excavations often in the glare of national political and international media attention (see several of the articles in Bradley 1984; Heffernan 1988).

Before Fr Martin and the Friends of Medieval Dublin began their campaign, few scholars had appreciated the potential of archaeology to shed light on Irish urbanism and the origins of Dublin. G. F. Mitchell and Liam de Paor were two scholars who did realize that archaeology could shed light on Dublin's past. After studying references in the diary/notebooks of nineteenth-century antiquarian Thomas Ray to a "bog" containing artifacts, G. F. Mitchell (1987) had suspected that Dublin might have excellent conditions for the preservation of archaeological remains. Liam de Paor (1967) was also an early believer in the value of the excavations. He and his wife Maire de Paor (1958) had contacts in Scandinavia, who introduced them to urban archaeological developments that might relate to finds made in Dublin.

While Breandán Ó Ríordáin, the archaeologist on the ground, knew that the results of his and Patrick Healy's careful excavation program were important, Ó Ríordáin's boss, the then Director of the National Museum, A. T. Lucas, felt that, by 1974, after more than a decade of work, enough had been excavated to allow for full publication. He called for the Museum's exit from the old Dublin excavation. Joseph Raftery, Ó Ríordáin's immediate senior administrator, and later Director of the National Museum, was even less sympathetic to the excavation. He was unable to admit to the importance of the Wood Quay or earlier Viking Age urban discoveries. An avowed nationalist and a Celtic archaeologist of distinction, Raftery saw Viking influences as "foreign." He agreed with the then received orthodoxy that early Irish society was familial, rural, and hierarchical, a world in which towns had no place (Binchy 1962).

As documented above, a postcolonial mindset impeded the thorough exploration of the origins of the Irish people and their beginnings as a nation. Various scholars have used archaeology to justify Irish beliefs about who they thought they were. This reluctance to face the reality of non-Celtic, that is, Viking, Anglo-Norman, and English facets in Irish archaeology and history has only been addressed recently with the establishment of a national folk museum at Castlebar, County Mayo in 2001 (Wallace 2002), and the military history exhibition "Soldiers and Chiefs:

The Irish at War at Home and Abroad" in 2006. The latter was the first recognition that thousands of Irishmen died in uniforms of other countries, most notably British.

Disentangling Ethnicity: Archaeology of Early Medieval Dublin

The previous section sketched the complex political milieu in which archaeology in Ireland developed during the early decades of Independence, and touched upon the background to the Dublin excavations. My next aim is to discuss the archaeological assemblage from these excavations. My analysis suggests that, although three main strands of ethnicity could be identified within the assemblage, the validity of the traditional ethnical approach needs to be evaluated with caution.

The Irish monk annalist, who in the late tenth century referred to the language of Dublin as "gioch gach" or gibberish, was not just parading the snobbery of the scholar commentator: he was also deploring the pidgin of mixed Irish, Norse, and possibly some English that was spoken in Dublin, the international port harbor built at the tidal estuarine mouth of the river Liffey on the east coast of Ireland and the west side of the Irish Sea. The annalist had no doubt about the Scandinavian origins of Dublin's dominant ethnicity. Equally, the indigenous population regarded Dublin as a place apart even a century and a half after its establishment. Dubliners, despite their alliances with various native kings and chieftains, despite their probable reliance on local supplies of building materials, foodstuffs, farm produce and animals, despite their local wives and workforce and despite their increasing Hibernization over the decades, still did not see themselves as part of the island and appear to have remained in contact with Scandinavia until the early twelfth century, almost three centuries after their arrival (Bradley 1988).

Proof of the Dubliner's sense of their own separateness is shown implicitly in their close friendship with the Anglo-Saxon Godwinsson dynasty in the middle of the eleventh century (Hudson 1979). Even before this, they had their bishops consecrated not at Kildare or Armagh in Ireland but at Canterbury in England (Richter 1988; Forte et al. 2005:226). Archaeological support for this sense of separateness from Ireland is also demonstrated by the runic inscriptions found in the Dublin excavations. Many of these runes are in later eleventh-century contexts when one would expect the Norse language and its script, after two centuries, would have been in decline. Such an expectation would be especially reasonable in Ireland which was then consciously embarking on a powerful literary, artistic, sculptural, and religious phase of reformation in the Celtic church. Perhaps the runes, even a solitary Thor's hammer and some "pagan Viking" figurines and snake pendants, should be seen as some kind of reaffirmation of origins against the all-conquering cultural and religious tide which must have besieged the Viking town after its inception in the mid-ninth century. There is probably even a case to be made for the greater inevitability of the cultural and religious, rather than the military, conquest of the Norse by the Irish.

The Dubliners were not alone in seeing themselves as a separate part of the Irish polity. They were so regarded by the native Irish and by the English in the eleventh century, and also by the Anglo-Normans especially after *their* conquest of Dublin in 1170. The native annalists refer to the Vikings, who first settled in Dublin, as the Genti or Gentiles (i.e., non-Christians) or the Lochlannai (possibly from Rogoland in present southwest Norway) (Ó Corráin 1997). The Anglo-Normans called them the Ostmanni or Ostmen (the "East Men") (Curtis 1908). The German commentator Saxo Grammaticus referred to Dublin as filled with "the wealth of Barbarians" (Smyth 1975, 1979). In contrast with other parts of Europe, Ireland during the early middle ages is an historical era, so language and terminology provide insights into ethnicity and hybridity. The Irish, for example, seem to have found the concept of an urban entity comprised of multiple plots of individual properties so novel that, when they first described the plots in the earlier tenth century, all they saw were the fences (*airbeada*) which divided the properties. As they became more familiar with the plots and their potential to be levied individually for cesses or ransoms ("an ounce of gold for every plot, etc.") they borrowed a word (*garrda*) from Old Norse to describe them (Wallace 2000).

According to Ireland's relatively rich early medieval historical sources, Dublin was established by the Vikings in 841 (Forte et al. 2005:81–117, 217–240). Forty years of archaeological excavation of Dublin's well-preserved layers have yielded the most extensive evidence for urban buildings, defenses, and layout for later ninth-, tenth- and eleventh-century Western Europe. In addition, thousands of artifacts relating to crafts, decoration, commerce, and everyday life have been unearthed as has the largest assemblage of animal bones of any period, not to mention other countless samples from which the environment and economy can be reconstructed (Wallace 1987).

Among the most interesting contacts in early Medieval Europe is that of the Scandinavians with the Gaels or Celts of the West. From the late eighth century, the Scandinavians raided Ireland with its then rich monastic culture (Henry 1967). Neither the Gaelic nor the Norse areas had been officially dominated by the Romans, although both were to be strongly influenced by that culture. The Roman influence was particularly evident in Ireland where the material culture, especially art, decorative jewellery, and bronze horse trappings, betrays considerable Romano-British and Gaulish contact (M. de Paor & L. de Paor 1958). Roman influence is less evident among the Scandinavians, whose aristocracy's response in the post Roman era partly resulted in a pagan Germanic revival. After a raiding phase, the Norse poured into the Irish Sea, eventually setting up permanent bases by the mid-ninth century. One of these bases survived to become Dublin, the main Norse urban center in the West and the principal Viking port town in insular Europe after the recovery of York by the English in the 930s (Smyth 1979).

One of the biggest challenges a scholar faces when examining Dublin's artifact assemblage is distinguishing which artifact types and production methods or techniques can be regarded as ethnically Scandinavian (Norse/Viking) and which can be seen as indigenous. Furthermore, the scholar must determine what elements may be the mutations or overlaps of Scandinavian and indigenous influence while also identifying, in the assemblages and in the built environment items and traits, which originated from a third source, i.e., undoubtedly England.

Excavation results suggest that five building types were represented in the three hundred or more buildings remains excavated at Dublin. Among these, the three-aisled house type was dominant. Comparative work on the overall evidence for the layout and buildings suggests that the three-aisled house type had already been worked out elsewhere in the northern world before it was introduced to Ireland (Wallace 1992a,b). It is also known that Ireland had primarily been a round house province until the advent of the Scandinavians. Although the concept for this three-aisled house type came from the broader Norse Atlantic area, the building methods employed and the materials used were of local inspiration and derivation.

The division of the town into plots or tenements represented something new and radically different in Irish urbanization, since, until the ninth century, the Christian monastery was the principal urban expression.[3] The idea of the town was brought from England to Ireland by the Norse. The Norse, while having witnessed earlier attempts at urbanization in southern Scandinavia, seem to have used mainly their urban experience in England as the model for their slaving emporium at Dublin which quickly developed into a harbor town (Wallace 1985a, 1992a,b).

Going on the perceived cultural influences that lay behind the artifact assemblage, the Dublin evidence divides into three different areas of origin – Scandinavia, England, and indigenous Irish. The difficulty of interpreting these materials is appreciated when it is realized that Dublin's Viking Age population was probably derived from a blending of the Scandinavians with the local population from the outset. We do not know whether the Dublin's residents desired to maintain the biological and cultural "purity" of the population. It is unlikely that there would have been sufficient numbers of Scandinavian women to maintain the "purity" of the population. Historical documents also indicate that even linguistically the homogeneity of Scandinavia was slowly breaking down. In any case, it is likely that the settled and relatively racially pure colonial farming populations on the Northern Isles of Scotland and the Isle of Man would have continued to supply some of Dublin's population, especially spouses for the higher orders of society.

The English Contribution

Dublin's contacts with England were stronger than is often imagined. This is especially true when, as the Viking Age wore into the eleventh century, England became the inspiration for Dublin's (and Ireland's) first currency and the main hirer of its war fleet at a time when Dublin's kings had political contact with England (Wallace 1986). Dublin's first bishops were consecrated in England rather than in Ireland. It was to northern England that the Dublin leaders and their warriors fled when they were banished for about 15 years at the beginning of the tenth century. For some decades in the late ninth and early tenth centuries, the senior branch of the relevant Scandinavian dynasty ruled at York while its cadet was in charge in Dublin.

Chester was the main English port in contact with Dublin in the ninth and tenth centuries with Bristol becoming more prominent as the eleventh century wore on.

By far, the smallest and the easiest of the three ethnic components in the Dublin assemblage to distinguish is the English. Leaving aside the historical references to political and ecclesiastical contact and at least one of the buildings which has English elements,[4] the most important archaeological evidence of English influence on Dublin is found in the enclosing defensive embankments which, to date, find their closest parallels at York and are built to the scale and demands of English (and Irish) warfare (Wallace 1981, 1992b). It is probable, furthermore, that the idea or concept of the town as it took form in Dublin (as well as at the other Hiberno-Norse towns) was brought by the Scandinavians from England (Wallace 2000). It is, therefore, worth combing through the artifact assemblage for items of English origin.

The most obvious artifacts of English origin are the Anglo-Saxon pennies which were to influence Dublin's (and Ireland's) first coinage struck beginning in 997. The excavations at Castle Street and Werburgh Street produced three *hoards* of Anglo Saxon pennies, while some of the other sites, most notably Fishamble Street, yielded a series of individual pennies (Wallace 1986). Also found were leather knife sheaths (one with an Anglo-Saxon inscription: *Edric me fecit*) (Okasha 1981) and a leather scrap with the first letters of the alphabet in Anglo-Saxon script (Bradley 1979). Other English artifacts include carved ivory and bone plaques, a Wallingford bridge sword pommel type, and a series of (probably London originating) base metal disc brooches, a type of which was also found at York.

Unlike England and the Western Isles of Scotland, Dublin and Ireland appear to have been aceramic until the twelfth century. Despite this, numerous Anglo-Saxon and, later, Saxo-Norman glazed and, more commonly, unglazed potsherds have turned up in the Dublin excavations. Some smaller copper alloy ornament types, including garter hooks and a wider squatter strap tag of Anglo Saxon type, have also been found.

The Scandinavian Contribution

The Scandinavian contribution to early medieval Dublin is enormous. In the overall Irish experience, the Scandinavian input is arguably disproportionate to the numbers of people who came to the island and it remained influential for a long time. The population size of Dublin at the height of its Scandinavian phase at *circa* 1000, while difficult to measure, was probably between 2000 and 5000, possibly even slightly more. The actual numbers of the population of direct Scandinavian or Norse colonial origin, while obviously high, are impossible to accurately measure, as is the scale of their intermixture with the indigenous and other populations. There is historical and family name evidence of much intermixing between the native and Scandinavian populations for several decades before 1000.

The merging of the Norse and Gaelic populations in the Western Isles shows that the two populations were not inimical. This merging resulted in the emergence of the Gall Gael, who are ancestral to the Gallowglasses (the later medieval warrior mercenaries).

The original Viking beliefs probably continued on even after the official conversion to Christianity of the king and presumably his ruling class at around 1000. Only the warriors', women's, and merchants' burials at the beginning of the settlement, the runic inscriptions, and possible other Viking cult objects later on indicate the existence of non-Christian beliefs in Dublin. An Irish wooden high cross boss, some Anglo-Saxon book cover ivories, and slivers of green and red porphyry, which were brought probably by Dublin pilgrims from altar shrines in Rome, suggest possible Dublin contacts with Christianity (Lynn 1985). The slivers may portend the zeal of the converted.

The vibrancy of the decorative metalwork craft workers of Dublin is demonstrated in the huge numbers of trial- or motif-pieces that have been recovered in the excavations as well as in the other evidence for metalworking (National Museum of Ireland 1973; O'Meadhra 1979, 1987). An examination of this metalwork suggests that some of Ireland's eleventh and even early twelfth-century metal reliquaries may have been made in Dublin by craftsmen at best recently converted and at worst still adhering to the beliefs of their pagan fathers. Others possibly continued to have it both ways as the decoration on the curious stone grave slabs owned by the Hiberno-Norse in the farming hinterland south of Dublin implies (Ó hÉailidhe 1957). It is not coincidental that some of the first crozier shrines and other ornaments of the period are covered in the Hiberno-Norse *Ringerike* style, which finds its greatest expression among the wood carvers of Dublin, and that the early twelfth-century *Urnes* style has such strong Nordic connections. If metalwork masterpieces like the Lismore crozier were not made in Dublin, they were probably made by someone who was at least trained in the workshops of the eleventh-century town.

Aside from clarifying the possible remote origins of the town itself, the plots and the Norse Atlantic origins of the main house type, the archaeological assemblage can only throw limited light on language. It can also give us little help understanding belief and religion. The same holds for the introduction of new life style practices and technologies. We know, for example, that the Irish borrowed their word for "beer" from Old Norse. They also used Old Norse words for ships and ship fittings and, significantly, they even took the word for "market" from Old Norse. There can be little doubt that the Scandinavians contributed to an increased awareness of trade and commerce in Dublin. Silver ornaments, ingots, and hack silver, found both in hoards and as single items, as well as the discovery of weighing scales and hundreds of lead weights targeted on what has been established as a unit of 26.6 g, provide evidence for Dubliners' interest in trade and commerce[5] (Wallace 1987).

Finished products and raw materials from the Scandinavian homelands and colonial areas are easier to identify in Dublin's archaeological record. These include oval and other brooches, whalebone (caulking?) bats, plaques, and clamps, walrus ivory, and amber, the latter being imported in bulk. Lignite or canal coal was also imported in bulk to be worked in Dublin itself. Other imports include soapstone bowls, whetstones, bone skates, a piece of *Mammen*-style ornament, and a pair of ring pins of Danish origin. Ships' planks and other main timbers as well as the ubiquitous clenched nails, while undeniably of Scandinavian conceptual origin, must be analyzed before we can be sure they were brought from Scandinavia or, more likely, made in Dublin under Scandinavian influence to Dublin, Irish, English, or

Viking order (McGrail 1993). The dendrochronological ascription of the Skuldelev warship to the port of Dublin in the early 1040s (and its repair to the same port some 20 years later) urges caution about assuming that all products of Scandinavian type were imported.

Apart from shipbuilding, the next greatest Scandinavian contribution to Dublin's (and probably Ireland's) artifact stock and technical knowledge centers on iron. Comparisons between the Dublin artifact assemblage and that of the rest of Ireland in the period preceding the advent of Scandinavian influence suggest that, apart from advances in the use of carburized steel in the edges of iron implements like swords and knives, the range of weapons and implements increased after the arrival of the Scandinavians, and that the edges and overall durability of the iron used also improved. Additional iron items include horse and animal harnesses, spurs, stirrups, bells and harness swivels, saws, half-moon blades, and pronged implements for bone and leatherworking, respectively, possibly spoon bits (the precursors of augers), spokeshaves, draw-knifes, and winged chisels for woodworking as well as harpoons and the conical ferrules or butts known in Ireland as "dibblers." The range of hammers extended. Also found are axe heads produced in a variety of sizes with the peaked cheeks characteristic of Scandinavian axes. Plough shares, coulters and sickles as well as keys and box/door straps were also apparently improved. Beyond increasing the variety of iron implements available in Ireland, it is in the range and quality of weapons of war and hunting that the new iron technology mostly makes its presence felt. Swords were imported and probably copied in Dublin. So were the so-called slave collars (*recte* fetters or hobbles). Some shield bosses were of indigenous manufacture as inevitably must have been some, if not most, of the wide range of spearheads and arrowheads (Wallace 1998).

The Scandinavian composite comb replaced the single-piece indigenous type, although the composite combs found in the Dublin excavations had the unique local trait of using red deer antler pins rather than the metal rivets found in other parts of the Viking world. The virtual exclusive use in Dublin of red deer antler for the combs and comb cases is noteworthy (Dunleavy 1988). A very few horn combs and one wooden specimen also survive. Lead working is also common in Dublin. The town also saw the introduction of shoes with separate soles and uppers. Also new to Ireland is the idea of craftsmen producing of imported raw material rings, pendants, bracelets, and beads in amber and lignite and, in the same craft context, the manufacture of beads and gaming pieces in walrus ivory.

Unlike other aspects of material culture, glass was not introduced into Dublin by the Scandinavians. In fact, the quality and size of glass beads and bracelets in Ireland before the Vikings were superior to anything that was introduced afterward. However, after the arrival of the Scandinavians, the variety of the glass products did increase, with a greater focus on necklaces of segmented beads and larger beads. In addition, glass culet, an obvious novelty, was introduced, some of which were seemingly from rediscovered late Roman sources.

Other possible introductions from Scandinavia include spoons which were made in copper alloy, iron, and wood, stone loom weights and grinding stones, small single-piece wooden boxes with sliding lids, weavers' swords, and wooden bladed objects of unknown function. It is unlikely the Scandinavians impacted on the range of indigenous wooden objects, except chairs.

In addition to ships' timbers, ships' nails and the range and quality of ironwork, the other principal contribution of the Scandinavians to Dublin's artifact range seems to have been in dress, accessory, and personal toilet items. It seems possible that the wearing of trousers was mediated through Dublin and that silks, gold braids, worsteds, and other quality cloths and decorated leathers were brought in through the Viking port towns. So also may have been fashions for having buns tied behind the head (for men) and long tresses (for women) and so very definitely were the fashions for having imported silk bonnets and head bands, many of which have been unearthed (Heckett 2003). Even copper-alloy toilet sets have been found. Accessories included polished bone pins (some with sinuous birds' heads, others with exotic beasts) and a whole range of wooden charms, like coiled snakes, worn as pendants. Related to these were the apparently very un-Irish practices of carving, in wood, subjects like wolf-like figures playing with a ball, bears' heads at the ends of trays and two-dimensional caricatures of human heads (Lang 1988).

The Indigenous Contribution

The Irish or indigenous contribution to the artifact assemblage of Dublin is the most difficult to pinpoint with confidence. The main reason for this is that what appears to be indigenous in origin or tradition could well belong to a common post-Roman, pan-European experience of related craft, construction, and technological approaches rather than belonging exclusively to one of the islands of the northwest European archipelago. The Dublin archaeological assemblage does not tell us much about the composition of the population, the degree to which society interacted with the hinterland, particularly in regard to the procurement of spouses, the acceptance or otherwise of Christianity and of Irish language, customs, beliefs, and traditions. Nor does it tell us about literacy, literary forms, and the communication and retention of folklore. The importance of the hinterland goes without saying for the supply of building materials like timber, wattles and stone, straw and rushes for roofing, mosses for cleaning, bracken fern for insulation, plants and herbs for cooking and healing as well as cattle and sheep for cooking, and red deer antler/bone for comb working and related manufactures. The ethic of not wasting was probably shared with the surrounding population and is best manifested in the multiple uses to which slaughtered cattle were put: meat, leather for shoemaking, scabbards, sheaths or whole hides for possible export, horns for comb-working, bones for pins, combs, handles, gaming pieces, and possibly hooves for glue and gut for fishing line. Even rib bones could be scavenged for use as trial-or motif-pieces. Pigs were probably raised around the immediate town area while dogs and cats would undoubtedly have been the first species to have interbred with the new comers. Despite the identification of new forms of lead fishing line weights, it seems likely that the newcomers would have adopted local ways of scavenging, collecting and fishing persisting with tried and trusted hooks, floats, and sinkers. More settled subsistence practices and the milling of flour continued in the hinterland where the use of the indigenous quernstone persisted. It is also likely that Dublin, like the rest of Ireland, remained loyal to a flat bread tradition despite possible early attempts to change as noted in the discovery of an oven at Essex Street West.

The most obvious indigenous practices evident in the physical record are the acceptance by the Dubliners of local building methods, which, like the building materials, came from the hinterland. The scale of the defenses of these buildings too, if not English inspired, look as if they were constructed to the demands of local warfare and the potential of local arrow range.

The Dubliners were attached to the Irish ringed pin and its later relative, the plain stick pin, as the main form of dress fastening. This was so much so that the fashion for copper-alloy ringed pins transmitted through the Nordic world even as far as L'Anse aux Meadows in Newfoundland (Fanning 1994; Vésteinsson 2000:172). It would seem that Irish inspired copper-alloy technology quickly became one of the main craft pursuits in Dublin, where strap tags of a Dublin-Irish Sea type as well as kite brooches were locally produced as were toilet sets and probably weighing scales (Wallace, in press). Although not actually found in the Dublin assemblage itself, silver brooches of Irish type, including bossed pennanulars, kites and thistles, were widely coveted by the Scandinavians, who supplied the silver in various forms for their production in indigenous schools. It seems that the crucibles, moulds, ingot types, trial- or motif-pieces and heating trays involved in nonferrous metalwork were of local derivation. Weaving and cloth production seems to be another area where indigenous traditions held sway, at least to go by the total lack of clay loom weights of doughnut type which are so characteristic of the southern Scandinavian area of influence: stone weights continued to be used in Dublin as in the rest of Ireland.

The principal indigenous iron object types that seem to have impressed themselves on the Scandinavians were L-shaped door hangers or *bocáin* and iron shears, although occasionally hinges, barred padlock keys and iron straps, and strike-a-lights, as well as the very rare shield boss, appear to relate more to local inspiration than to the outside. Wood turned products such as plates, platters, bowls, and dishes also seem to be of indigenous origin as does the simple rectilinear ornament with which the taller container specimens and bowls among them often feature. This is somewhat in contrast with the evidence for coopering for which there was a long local tradition before the advent of the Scandinavians. Obviously, there are also actual items which originated locally like the *circa* twelfth century souterrain ware, the (mainly) blue glass brackets and beads and the wooden high cross boss already noted. These were brought in from the hinterland and should not be seen as large-scale craft influences (Wallace 1987).

Hybridity

A copper-alloy sheet-plated, lead-alloy star-shaped brooch seems to represent one of the best examples of multiculturalism and hybridity among the finds from Dublin. It is a brooch produced in the lead-alloy tradition of the Anglo-Saxons, but approaching the kite shape beloved of the Irish and provided with bright plates to make it look expensive. It was produced in Hiberno-Norse Dublin because the star mould from which it was issued also turned up in the excavations. There are other examples which consciously cross over like this but few with the graphic hybridity implicit in this brooch.

Discussion and Conclusions

Visits to contemporary early medieval collections, especially from town excavations such as those at Szczechin and Gdansk in Poland, Stare Ladoga, Gorodice, and especially Novgorod in Russia, Sigtuna in Sweden, Oslo and Trondheim in Norway, York, London, and Lincoln in England, and Waterford, Limerick, Wexford, and Cork (e.g., Hurley et al. 1997) in Ireland, caution against the wholesale ascription of ethnicity to much of what we have been looking at in Dublin. It is possible that, with the exception of high art styles, dress, and accessory fashions, many of the items, found throughout Europe, are regional craft responses. These would have been made using locally available raw materials within the context of regional geography and climate. They would have been limited by local standards and the available wealth. As such, they belong more to a common post-Roman transalpine material culture than to one that can be determined only by ethnicity.

The statement above was borne home to me most clearly after a recent review of the published assemblages from contemporary Irish rural sites prepared for a comparison between the Dublin assemblage and the finds from the early medieval royal village on the prehistoric mound at Knowth, Co. Meath (Eogan 1977). This comparison was extended to include other sites, which showed that many of the surviving artifact types from such sites, particularly the smaller finds in copper-alloy and iron find, parallel in the ranges represented at Dublin. Because the Scandinavians could not possibly have influenced the related crafts early enough and extensively enough over the whole island, we must conclude that, with notable exceptions (viz. shipbuilding and iron technology), both the indigenous and Scandinavian ranges belong to wider shared transalpine craft traditions and approaches.

Epilogue

This conclusion, which was based largely on the Wood Quay/Fishamble Street excavations in 1981, was followed by the setting up of a joint committee of the National Museum of Ireland and the Royal Irish Academy to research and publish the results of the Dublin excavations. More than eight volumes have appeared, the process is ongoing and from 2007 the publication program will be under the National Museum's own banner. Television and radio documentaries have been made in 1969, 1973, and 1988, and large exhibitions of the results of the excavations have been mounted at the National Museum in 1973, 1995, and 2000.

Artifacts from the sites have been sent abroad to various Irish, British, Scandinavian and Council of Europe exhibitions.

At a popular level, Dublin decided to celebrate its Millennium birthday in 1988 (the town was actually 1147 years old that year) in a big way. An Irish insurance corporation funded a reconstruction of a tenth century street scene populated with live actors operating with free scripts to engage with the public in the first person. This "Viking Adventure" was inspired by a combination of the experiences at Jorvik (York) and Brighton Pier (Lancashire), and was conceived and designed by the writer. The characters, their dress, and particularly their environment and their information drew heavily on, and were inspired by, discoveries made during the excavations. "Dublinia," a second more enduring and research-based exhibition, inspired more by the excavation results from the thirteenth and later centuries, followed. In this exhibition, the information is presented in a contextualized way rather than in the more interactive style of the child-orientated "Viking Adventure." With these events, we could say that the Vikings had finally found acceptance in Ireland, especially in the capital they had founded. Of course, they were also good for business.

The success of the "Viking Adventure," unfortunately, led to a rash of heritage experiences in Ireland, many of which failed. The importance of heritage to tourism, while long recognized, was underlined by the success of the short-lived "Viking Adventure." Its success to some extent can be blamed for an overuse of the fake and the ersatz rather than the real thing as in other tourist-oriented, archaeologically-based events. Despite the high profile of the "Viking Adventure," the popularity of Viking Splash Tours and the general awareness of the Viking origins of Dublin, the capital still lacks a museum dedicated to its own story.

History tells us that the Irish Free State (1922) gradually became a more confident Republic (1949), which took its place at the United Nations (1957), joined the European Economic Community, now the European Union, (1972), stemmed the tide of emigration, and, over the last decade, developed the highest level of economic growth in Europe to earn the nickname "Celtic Tiger." At the same time, Ireland has witnessed the erosion of conservative moral positions, which means people are now more tolerant as well as more outgoing, inclusive and confident. After three decades of turmoil, the north of Ireland is at relative peace and Anglo-Irish relations have never been as good. Not only is the material culture of the Medieval Anglo-Normans taught and celebrated, the material remains of the Anglo-Irish (the successors of more recent waves of influence from Britain in the post-Medieval period) are also now accepted in an inclusive and less xenophobic Ireland, which welcomes workers from dozens of countries to its shores. This is in complete contrast to the Ireland of just 20 years ago, when local people were still emigrating abroad rather than welcoming immigrants from around the world.

The recent census (2006) shows population levels at their highest since 1861. Dublin's maternity hospitals last year saw the births of children whose parents came from more than one hundred countries. To write about ethnicity in the Dublin of a thousand years ago is difficult, but nothing to the challenge that early twenty first century Ireland will pose to a parallel future commentator.

Notes

[1] A Dublin-built warship has turned up in the Danish fjord of Roskilde; its replica is expected to sail back to its home port in 2007.

[2] As recently as 1969, attempts to have a postage stamp commemorating what is popularly called the 1169 Norman "Invasion" of Ireland generated such controversy that it was not proceeded with.

[3] With the exception of the other Scandinavian founded settlements at Limerick, Waterford, and Wexford and the Scandinavian influenced settlement at Cork, the Christian monastery remained the model of urbanism in Ireland for long afterward.

[4] This building had a plan conforming to the main Atlantic Scandinavian derived building type but also had a seemingly English truss roof support system.

[5] This unit of 26.6 g is found in one of the contemporary ornament types, the Hiberno-Norse arm ring which was obviously made for the easy transport of silver bullion that could be hacked as the need arose.

References

Bieler, L. (1963). *Ireland Harbinger of the Middle Ages*. London: Oxford University Press.

Binchy, D. A. (1962). The passing of the old order. In B.Ó Cuív (Ed.), *The Impact of the Scandinavian Invasions on the Celtic Speaking Peoples c.800–1100 A.D.* (pp. 119–132). Dublin: Institute of Advanced Studies.

Bradley, J. (1979). An inscribed axehead from Gorteen, Co. Clare. *North Munster Antiquarian Journal*, 21, 11–14.

Bradley, J. (Ed.). (1984). *Viking Dublin Exposed: The Wood Quay Saga*. Dublin: O'Brien Press.

Bradley, J. (1988). The interpretation of Scandinavian settlement in Ireland. In J. Bradley (Ed.), *Settlement and Society in Medieval Ireland* (pp. 49–78). Kilkenny: Boethius Press.

Bullough, D. A. (1982). The mission to the English and Picts and their heritage (to c. 800). In H. Löwe (Ed.), *Die Iren und Europa im Früheren Mittelalter* (pp. 80–98). Stuttgart: Klett-Cotta.

Cahill, M. (2002). Before the Celts: Treasures in gold and bronze. In P. F. Wallace & R. Ó Floinn (Eds.), *Treasures of the National Museum of Ireland – Irish Antiquities* (pp. 86–124). Dublin: Gill and Macmillan.

Comerford, R. V. (2003). *Ireland (Inventing the Nation)*. London: Hodder Arnold.

Cooney, G. (1996). Building the future on the past: Archaeology and the construction of national identity in Ireland. In M. Díaz-Andreu & T. Champion (Eds.), *Nationalism and Archaeology in Europe* (pp. 146–163). London: UCL Press.

Curtis, E. (1908). English and Ostmen in Medieval Ireland. *English Historical Review*, 23, 209.

de Paor, L. (1967). Age of the Viking wars. In T. W. Moody & F. X. Martin (Eds.), *The Course of Irish History* (pp. 91–106). Cork: Mercier Press.

de Paor, M., & de Paor, L. (1958). *Early Christian Ireland*. London: Thames and Hudson.

Dunleavy, M. (1988). A classification of early Irish combs. *Proceedings of the Royal Irish Academy*, 88c, 341–422.

Eogan, G. (1977). The Iron Age – Early Christian settlement at Knowth. In V. Markotic (Ed.), *Ancient Europe and the Mediterranean* (pp. 69–76). Warminster: Aris and Phillips.

Fanning, T. (1994). *Viking Age Ringed Pins from Dublin*. Series B, Volume 4. Dublin: Royal Irish Academy for National Museum of Ireland and Royal Irish Academy.

Forte, A., Oram, R., & Pedersen, F. (2005). *Viking Empires*. Cambridge: Cambridge University Press.
Gerriets, M. (1985). Money among the Irish: Coins hoards in Viking Age Ireland. *Journal of the Royal Society of Antiquaries of Ireland*, 115, 121–139.
Graham-Campbell, J. (1976). The Viking-Age silver hoards of Ireland. In B. Almqvist & D. Greene (Eds.), *Proceedings of the Seventh Viking Congress* (pp. 39–74). Dundalk: Dundalgan Press.
Heckett, E. W. (2003). *Viking Age Headcoverings from Dublin*. Series B, Volume 6. Dublin: Royal Irish Academy for National Museum of Ireland and Royal Irish Academy.
Heffernan, T. F. (1988). *Wood Quay: The Clash over Dublin's Viking Past*. Austin: University of Texas Press.
Henry, F. (1962). The effects of the Viking invasions on Irish art. In B. Ó Cuív (Ed.), *The Impact of the Scandinavian Invasions on the Celtic-Speaking Peoples c. 800–1100 A.D.* (pp. 61–72). Dublin: Institute of Advanced Studies.
Henry, F. (1967). *Irish Art During the Viking Invasions*. London: Methuen and Co., Ltd.
Herity, M. (1974). *Irish Passage Graves*. Dublin: Irish University Press.
Herity, M., & Eogan, G. (1977). *Ireland in Prehistory*. London: Routledge and Kegan Paul.
Hudson, B. (1979). The family of Harold Godwinsson and the Irish Sea Province. *Journal of the Royal Society of Antiquities of Ireland*, 109, 92–100.
Hurley, M., Scully, O. M. B., & McCutcheon, S. W. J. (1997). *Late Viking Age and Medieval Waterford Excavations 1986–92*. Waterford: Waterford Corporation.
Lang, J. T. (1988). *Viking Age Decorated Wood*. Series B, Volume 1. Dublin: Royal Irish Academy for National Museum of Ireland and Royal Irish Academy.
Lynn, C. (1985). Some fragments of exotic porphyry found in Ireland. *Journal of Irish Archaeology*, 2, 25–31.
McEwan, J. M. (2003). *Archaeology and Ideology in Nineteenth Century Ireland: Nationalism or Neutrality?* BAR British Series 354. Oxford: John and Erica Hedges Ltd.
Mc Grail, S. (1993). *Medieval Boat and Ship Timbers from Dublin*. Series B, Volume 1. Dublin: Royal Irish Academy for National Museum of Ireland and Royal Irish Academy.
Mitchell, G. F. (1987). *Archaeology and Environment in Early Dublin*. Series C, Volume 1. Dublin: Medieval Dublin Excavations 1962–81, Royal Irish Academy for National Museum of Ireland and Royal Irish Academy.
National Museum of Ireland. (1973). *Viking and Medieval Dublin*. (National Museum Excavations 1962–73), Catalogue of Exhibition. Dublin: National Museum of Ireland.
ÓCorráin, D. (1997). Ireland, Wales, Man and the Hebrides. In P. Sawyer (Ed.), *The Oxford Illustrated History of the Vikings* (pp. 83–109). Oxford: Oxford University Press.
ÓhÉailidhe, P. (1957). The Rathdown slabs. *Royal Society of Antiquaries of Ireland Journal*, 87, 75–88.
Okasha, E. (1981). Three inscribed objects from Christchurch Place, Dublin. In H. Bekker-Nielsen, P. Foote, & O. Olsen (Eds.), *Proceedings of the Eighth Viking Congress* (pp. 45–51). Odense: Odense University Press.
O'Kelly, M. J. (1989). *Early Ireland*. Cambridge: Cambridge University Press.
O'Meadhra, U. (1979, 1987). *Early Christian, Viking and Romanesque Art Motif-Pieces from Ireland*. 2 parts. Stockholm: Almqvist and Wiksell International.
ÓRíordáin, A. B. (1971). Excavations at High Street and Winetavern Street, Dublin. *Medieval Archaeology*, 15, 73–85.
ÓRíordáin, A. B. (1973). Life Within the Walls. In E. Gillespie (Ed.) *The Liberties of Dublin* (pp. 10–15). Dublin: O'Brien Press.
Richter, M. (1988). *Medieval Ireland: The Enduring Tradition*. Houndsmill: Macmillan Education Ltd.
Shee Twohig, E. (1981). *The Megalithic Art of Western Europe*. Oxford: Oxford University Press.
Smyth, A. P. (1975, 1979). *Scandinavian York and Dublin*. I and II. Dublin: Temple Kieran Press.
Vésteinsson, O. (2000). The archaeology of *Landnám*. In W. Fitzhugh & E. I. Ward (Eds.), *Vikings: The North Atlantic Saga* (pp. 164–174). Washington, D.C.: Smithsonian Institution Press.
Waddell, J. (1998). *The Prehistoric Archaeology of Ireland*. Galway: Galway University Press.
Waddell, J. (2005). *Foundation Myths: The Beginning of Irish Archaeology*. Dublin: Wordwell.

Wallace, P. F. (1981). Dublin's waterfront at Wood Quay. In G. Milne & B. Hobley (Eds.), *Waterfront Archaeology in Britain and Northern Europe* (pp. 109–118). CBA Research Report No. 41. London: Council for British Archaeology.

Wallace, P.F. (1985a). The archaeology of Viking Dublin. In H. B. Clarke & A. Simms (Eds.), *The Comparative History of Urban Origins in non-Roman Europe* (pp. 103–145). B.A.R. International Series 255 (1). Oxford: British Archaeological Reports.

Wallace, P. F. (1985b). The archaeology of Anglo-Norman Dublin. In H. B. Clarke & A. Simms (Eds.), *The Comparative History of Urban Origins in Non-Roman Europe* (pp. 103–145). B.A.R. International Series 255 (2). Oxford: British Archaeological Reports.

Wallace, P. F. (1986). The English presence in Viking Dublin. In M. A. S. Blackburn (Ed.), *Anglo-Saxon Monetary History Essays in Memory of Michael Dolley* (pp. 201–221). Leicester: Leicester University Press.

Wallace P. F. (1987). The economy and commerce of Viking Age Dublin. In K. Düwel et al. (Eds.), *Untersuchungen zu Handel und Verkehr der vor- und frühgeschichtlichen Zeit in Mittel- und Nordeuropa, 4, Der Handel der Karilonger- und Wikingerzeit* (pp. 200–245). Göttingen: Vandenhoeck und Ruprecht.

Wallace, P. F. (1992a). *The Viking Age Buildings of Dublin*. 2 volumes, Series A, Volume 1, Dublin: Royal Irish Academy for National Museum of Ireland and Royal Irish Academy.

Wallace, P. F. (1992b). The archaeological identity of the Hiberno-Norse town. *Journal of the Royal Society of Antiquaries of Ireland*, 122, 35–66.

Wallace, P. F. (1998). The use of iron in Viking Dublin. In M. Ryan (Ed.) *Irish Antiquities Essays in Memory of Joseph Raftery* (pp. 201–222). Dublin: Wordwell.

Wallace, P. F. (2000). *Garrda* and *Airbeada*: The plot thickens in Viking Dublin. In A. P. Smyth (Ed.), *Seanchas: Essays in Early and Medieval Irish Archaeology, History and Literature in Honour of F.J. Byrne* (pp. 261–274). Dublin: Four Courts Press.

Wallace, P. F. (2002). Viking Age Ireland, AD 850–1150. In P. F. Wallace & R. Ó Floinn (Eds.), *Treasures of the National Museum of Ireland -Irish Antiquities* (pp. 213–256). Dublin: Gill and Macmillan.

Wallace, P. F. (2004a). Adolf Mahr and the Making of Seán P. Ó Ríordáin. In H. Roche, E. Grogan, J. Bradley, J. Coles, & B. Raftery (Eds.), *From Megaliths to Metals: Essays in Honour of George Eogan* (pp. 254–326). Oxford: Oxbow Books.

Wallace, P.F. (in press). *Weights, Scales and Leadworking in Viking Age Dublin* (Medieval Dublin Excavations 1962–81. Series B). Dublin: National Museum of Ireland.

Woodman, P. (1995). Who possesses Tara? Politics in archaeology in Ireland. In P. J. Ucko (Ed.), *Theory in Archaeology: A World Perspective* (pp. 278–297). London: Routledge.

PART III
DISCUSSION

Chapter 12
"Alternative Archaeologies" in Historical Perspective[1]

Bruce G. Trigger

In 1984, I never imagined that 20 years later I would be participating in an SAA seminar that would select "Alternative Archaeologies: Nationalist, Colonialist, Imperialist" as a point of departure for discussing subsequent developments in archaeology. Since that time, classifications of archaeologies have proliferated. French archaeologists have distinguished "national archaeologies" from "nationalist" ones (Fleury-Ilett 1996) and the term "continental archaeology" has been invented to recognize the deep interest that many European archaeologists share in the prehistory of their continent (Morris 1994:11). "Third World archaeology" has been defined as a type of archaeology that develops in postcolonial nations (Chakrabarti 2001:1191–1193). It has also been observed that countries such as Spain have produced "regional" in addition to, or perhaps instead of, nationalist archaeologies (Díaz-Andreu 1996:86), while David Kojan and Dante Angelo (2005)[2] present a powerful regionalist challenge to the official, centralizing narrative of prehistory that grounds Bolivia as a nation state. Matthew Spriggs (1992) writes about "micronational" as well as "regional" and "national" prehistories. Recent studies of Israeli archaeology reveal not one but a growing number of competing archaeologies, each promoting a rival concept of Israeli nationhood (Abu El-Haj 2001; Finkelstein & Silberman 2001).

Moving away from concepts directly related to nation states, Neil Silberman (1995:261) has coined the terms "touristic archaeology" and "archaeology of protest"; "community archaeology" has been used to designate the participation of community members in the design and execution of archaeological research (Marshall 2002; Moser 1995); Sandra Scham (2001) writes about the "archaeology of the disenfranchised" and the "archaeology of cultural identity"; and First Nations archaeologists seek to delineate "indigenous" (Atalay, this volume) or "internalist" (Yellowhorn 2002) archaeologies. The most transformative and influential standpoint archaeology of all, gender archaeology, differs from those listed above as a result of its successful incorporation into all forms of archaeological interpretation, a position now theoretically validated by third-wave feminism (Meskell 2002). Gender archaeology is therefore not simply a type of archaeology characterized by a particular standpoint but has become a necessary and integral part of all archaeological practice.

I have no problem with this proliferation. On the contrary, I welcome it. My original three types – nationalist, colonialist, and imperialist archaeology – were

J. Habu, C. Fawcett, and J. M. Matsunaga (eds.), *Evaluating Multiple Narratives:*
Beyond Nationalist, Colonialist, Imperialist Archaeologies.
© Springer 2008

intended to explore only one axis of variability in archaeology, that associated with the position of countries in the world-system. While I continue to regard this as a significant class of variation, it was never intended to account for all existing variability in archaeological interpretation, or variability for all time. Variability, of course, includes that produced by the unique personalities and life experiences of individual archaeologists. I also observed in 1984 that my three types were often not clearly distinguished from one another and that in single countries different approaches often characterized the study of different periods. My primary goal was to challenge positivist assumptions about how archaeological data should be interpreted by exposing readers to epistemological relativist alternatives.

The idea that interpretations of archaeological data are influenced by the beliefs of archaeologists, and those in turn by the particular sociocultural milieus in which archaeologists operate, is currently associated with postprocessual archaeology, but did not begin with it. Such ideas were eloquently expounded by the British classical archaeologist R. G. Collingwood (1939, 1946) in the 1930s, and influenced British culture-historical archaeologists such as Glyn Daniel (1950), Christopher Hawkes (1954), and Stuart Piggott (1950). Epistemological relativism was widespread in the 1950s. I remember, as an undergraduate at the University of Toronto in the late 1950s, long before I knew anything specific about Marxism, attending a staff-student seminar that was discussing how archaeological findings concerning indigenous people might be introduced into elementary and high school history curricula. I remarked that, since the purpose of teaching history was to indoctrinate students rather than to teach them to think, anything we suggested would be of little consequence unless we could also critique the goals of the history curriculum, which seemed to me most unlikely given the mandate of our discussion. My comment was followed, as I expected, by an abrupt change of subject. Yet it was clear that no one present failed to understand what I was saying. To my surprise, after the seminar Professor William Dunning, a social anthropologist who was very conservative in his outward demeanor, said that he agreed with me completely. He was soon after to publish a trailblazing exposé of hypocrisy and self-interest among the Euro-Canadian officials who staffed the Department of Indian Affairs (Dunning 1959).

My systematic understanding of epistemological relativism was subsequently shaped by my reading of the later writings of Gordon Childe (1949, 1956) and his Marxist sources concerning matters such as true and false consciousness. This understanding structured a paper titled "Engels on the Part Played by Labour in the Transition from Ape to Man" published in *The Canadian Review of Sociology and Anthropology* in 1967, a time when the scars of McCarthyism were still raw enough to ensure its rejection by an American anthropological journal that had already published my work. In that paper I examined the role that materialist and idealist orientations played in constructing theories of human evolution during the nineteenth and early twentieth centuries. I concluded that the role of beliefs became less important as the amount of factual data increased.

The detailed research that I carried out in the 1960s and 1970s for *The Children of Aataentsic* (1976), an ethnohistorical study of the Wendat (Huron) people of southern Ontario from about AD 900 until their dispersal in the 1640s, led me to realize the extent to which historical, anthropological, and archaeological interpretations of aboriginal peoples had been distorted by the popular negative stereotypes that European colonists had created in the course of their projects to dominate indigenous peoples and appropriate their resources. At first, I was mainly concerned with the way these stereotypes interfered with an objective understanding of the past and how these distortions might be corrected, but as I tried to cope with these problems I also grew concerned with the negative impacts that such stereotypes had on indigenous peoples and how they were treated (Trigger 2001). In 1980, in "Archaeology and the Image of the American Indian" I documented the changing ways in which stereotypes about native people had influenced Americanist archaeology over the course of its development, not only in terms of the questions archaeologists asked but also with respect to the answers that they deemed acceptable. While most processual archaeologists were prepared to accept that the questions archaeologists ask might be influenced by the society in which they lived, they generally assumed that, provided enough data were available and correct scientific procedures were employed, objective answers could be provided for any reasonable question. I concluded that objective knowledge of this sort was unattainable. Yet I was able to demonstrate that over time the accumulation of unexpected data forced archaeologists to formulate, however unwillingly and incompletely, interpretations that called into question their negative stereotypes about indigenous people. This provided the basis for the moderate relativism that I have advocated ever since.

"Alternative Archaeologies," which was prepared for a lecture tour of Australia in 1983, sought to counter processual claims that a unified scientific archaeology was everywhere replacing the theoretically diverse, "prescientific" schools that had prevailed hitherto. My arguments were based mainly on papers prepared for two issues of *World Archaeology* edited by Ian Glover and myself (Trigger & Glover 1981/1982). The conclusions of that paper were generally the same as those of "Archaeology and the Image of the American Indian" and the substance of both papers was incorporated into *A History of Archaeological Thought* published in 1989. All this work now seems to be remembered more for its advocacy of epistemological relativism than for its defense of a limited objectivity.

More recent research has led me to qualify my claims about nationalist archaeology. As Minkoo Kim has shown for Korea, nationalist archaeology continues to play an important role in many countries, and in parts of Eastern Europe and the former Soviet Union it resurged dramatically during the 1990s. Yet, while nationalism has been the European middle class's very successful weapon of choice for containing class conflict and opposing communism for over 150 years, nationalist archaeology seems to have gained prominence most often in times of social and political crises and when new regimes are trying to legitimate themselves. Case studies reveal that European archaeologists have often failed to elicit desired levels of state support in countries not in a state of crisis or transition or where textual data are deemed sufficient to support the social order.

My concern with bias in "Alternative Archaeologies" can rightly be construed as an advocacy of the desirability of multivocality within archaeology. Yet I was and remain far more concerned with revealing how bias has resulted in erroneous interpretations of archaeological data. I have never subscribed to the Marxist fantasy that the production of knowledge by (or for) the proletariat would automatically replace false consciousness with true consciousness. Nor have I warmed to the now largely discredited idea of some postprocessual archaeologists that there is no hope of ever overcoming bias and hence the only functions archaeologists can perform are to discredit hegemonic views in archaeology and use archaeological data to support their own preferred political agendas. I was and remain committed to the idea that it is the archaeologist's responsibility to seek an objective understanding of archaeological data by revealing biases in archaeological interpretation and by the systematic testing of interpretations against a broader data base, a view that not withstanding our differences in nomenclature I believe I share with Rosemary Joyce's and Michael Blakey's papers in this volume.

As for multivocality, I believe that the more questions that are asked and the more narratives of the past that are formulated the better. Because of that, I oppose the idea that any specific group should be accorded an exclusive right to control the interpretation of their own past. I also reject, however, the suggestion that all narratives are of equal historical value. Multivocality enhances rather than relieves the need for archaeologists to weed out erroneous assumptions and interpretations and to synthesize divergent viewpoints to produce more holistic explanations of the past. To be acceptable, archaeological interpretations must be grounded in archaeological facts, and the more solidly grounded they are the better. Events, such as those that have resulted in the demolition of the Babri Mosque at Ayodhya (Ratnagar 2004), indicate the need for deliberate falsification of archaeological data for political purposes to be legally classified as a criminal offense at the national and international levels. This is one form of multivocality that must be resolutely suppressed.

It is, however, time for archaeologists once again to heed David Clarke's (1968:30–31) warning that archaeological interpretation has to be based on something other than the narrative fantasies of prehistorians, as he argued was too often the case in the late phase of culture-historical archaeology. Where multiple interpretations of the past have been proposed, the primary duty of archaeologists is to determine to what extent these can be combined to produce a more comprehensive understanding of the past. This has profitably been done with the findings of feminist archaeologists, despite their understandable deprecation of an "add-and-stir" approach. Where explanations are mutually exclusive, there is need for a more detailed examination of the data to try to discover which interpretation accords best with the facts or whether a better alternative can be devised. While multivocality has many roles to play in interpreting the past outside of archaeology, I view it within the discipline mainly as a source of alternative interpretations to be tested through what has long been called the method of multiple working hypotheses (Chamberlin 1944).

The idea that we must evidentially ground ideas in archaeological data and test them means, among other things, that archaeologists must critically assess the alternative explanations offered by processual, postprocessual, Darwinian, and other theoretical approaches. Only in this way is it possible to establish empirically the strengths, weaknesses, and specific applications of each approach (Trigger 2003b).

In the evaluation of interpretations, not only the iron laws derived by middle-range theory but also Hodder's contextual approach (in which information derived from various classes of data is brought to bear on a single problem) have an important role to play. I take this to be the point of the papers by Michael Blakey, Bob Chapman, and Patrick Wallace. The ultimate in contextualism is addressing historical questions by comparing the findings of linguistic and bioanthropological as well as archaeological data. I agree with Tim Murray (1999:879) that "as our interests in 'the past' grow and diversify, and if archaeology is not to collapse into a welter of disabling relativism relying upon coercion, trickery, ignorance, or cultural prejudice to underwrite the plausibility of archaeological interpretations, then an acceptance of the power of the empirical to constrain interpretation is inevitable." At the same time, I believe that prejudices influence understanding and that no scientific method can totally eliminate the influences of such prejudices.

Finally, in her book *Facts on the Ground*, Nadia Abu El-Haj (2001:281) has questioned the usefulness of categories such as "colonialist archaeology." She argues that the various archaeologies ascribed to this category have played a different role and had a different importance. There is therefore a need to study specific local practices in order to determine how colonialist discourses were transformed by local realities and such transformations in turn altered metropolitan ideas and the social order (Anderson 1983; Cohn 1996). I agree completely with her analysis and acknowledge that such studies are essential. Yet I view her approach as enhancing rather than eliminating the usefulness of generic concepts such as "colonialist archaeology."

It is unfortunate that archaeologists have not yet freed themselves from the cyclical privileging of rationalism and evolutionism on the one hand and of romanticism and historical particularism on the other, which has bedeviled Western thinking since at least the eighteenth century. Accepting this dichotomy ignores the reality that convergent similarities and cross-cultural differences are equally characteristic features of human behavior and material culture (Trigger 2003a). Ironically, postmodernism, which is the reigning expression of romanticism, has become the prevailing elite culture of a world dominated by a transnational economy and a neoconservative ideology. Many view postmodernism as a progressive movement that challenges the prevailing order and empowers the resistance of many different human groups. It can also be argued, however, that postmodernism is a highly sophisticated modern equivalent of the ancient Roman policy of *divide et impera* (divide and rule) (Herzfeld 2004). Transnational capitalists clearly view their economic and political agenda as a universal one and repeatedly show themselves capable of cooperating to ruthlessly subvert any local, political, economic, or cultural arrangements that stand in the way of their increasing corporate profits. By reifying diversity and striving to discredit generic categories, postmodernists at the very least may help to undermine the ability of the victims and critics of transnational capitalism to identify and coordinate forces that might oppose transnationalism on a global basis. Still worse, they may succeed in encouraging such groups to oppose one another. Hence postmodernism may function to promote transnational exploitation, even though most of its advocates believe themselves to be on the other side. Comparative studies not only reveal the broader processes that are at work in the world but also assist people facing similar, but not identical, problems, to recognize their shared interests and forge alliances that permit them to defend these interests more effectively.

I do not wish, however, to suggest that the complementarity of rationalist and romantic views is merely a strategic one. On the contrary, I believe that their strategic effectiveness reflects deeper and more inherent complementarities. The greatest achievement of enlightenment morality is the Universal Declaration of Human Rights adopted by the United Nations in 1948. This document not only reaffirmed familiar rights, such as those to life, liberty, and security; to freedom from arbitrary arrest, detention, and exile; to a fair and public hearing by an independent judiciary; to freedom of thought, conscience, and religion; and to freedom of peaceful assembly and association, but also established far-reaching new rights to social security, work, education, participation in the cultural life of the community, enjoyment of the arts, and sharing in scientific advancement and its benefits. This document outlines a set of aspirations that no signatory has ever fully succeeded in living up to and which condemns the actions of the governments of many rich and poor nations. It was my privilege to know slightly John Humphrey, the lawyer who actually drafted this declaration. He taught at McGill University and all his life remained passionately concerned with defending human rights.

The Universal Declaration of Human Rights is a product of enlightenment philosophy and Western culture and in that sense it is ethnocentric. Some East Asian governments have denounced its emphasis on the rights of individuals as offensive to the family- and community-based ethics of their cultures. Yet, in these societies growing numbers of individuals face incarceration, or worse, because of their demands that individual rights be respected. Legally protected individual rights have not always been a feature of Western society and no one has the right to forbid change in the name of protecting a culture. At the very least the declaration today constitutes a formal legal curb (albeit an almost totally ignored one) on the freedom of tyrannical governments or amoral transnational corporations to abuse human beings. I would further argue that its provisions provide the very conditions that are needed for multiple cultures and value systems to coexist in harmony and cooperation. It has long been observed that in the absence of foreign domination economic prosperity leads to cultural florescence (Salisbury 1962; Trigger 1976). With its defense of the legal, economic, and cultural rights of each individual, this is the direction in which the Universal Declaration of Human Rights leads all human beings. It provides the framework within which cultural pluralism can flourish (Hall 2003:128–130) provided that each culture respects the rights of the individual. In their battles against racism and ethnocentrism, Boasian anthropologists sought to promote respect for the rights both of individuals and collectivities. Today the challenge is how to overcome an outdated opposition between rationalism and romanticism in order to create better understandings of human behavior and a better world. As the world becomes more complex and integrated, the only basis on which an overall system of justice can be built is the individual. If it is to truly serve the individual, however, it cannot be a system that ignores the varied attachments of family, friendship, community, religion, language, and culture that make life meaningful and enjoyable for each human being.

Enlightenment philosophy, together with its classifying and generalizing tendencies, can be blamed for many things, but it is far from being exhausted as a progressive force. In recent years, some archaeologists are again advocating the importance of looking for communalities (Hassan 1998:202) and the liberating power of universals (Coudart 1998). By working together, universalist and particularist analyses can complement one another and more effectively challenge the hegemonic aspirations of transnationalism.

Notes

[1] This chapter is a revised version of Trigger's commentary for a session titled "Beyond Nationalist, Colonialist, Imperialist Archaeologies: Evaluating Multiple Narratives" at the 69th Annual Meeting of the Society for American Archaeology in Montreal, 2004 (hereafter the 2004 SAA session). Since Bruce Trigger e-mailed this manuscript to the editors on June 16, 2005, before the other contributions were finalized, his comments are based on earlier drafts of each paper. In finalizing this manuscript, the editors made the following editorial changes: (1) typographic errors were corrected and several commas were added; (2) citations in the text and references were formatted according to the Springer style guidelines; (3) words in the British spelling were changed to the American spelling unless they are proper names or in quotes; (4) single quotation marks were changed to double quotation marks unless they are in quotes; (5) references to two 2004 SAA session papers by John M. Matsunaga & Nenad Tasić (Multiscalar approaches to multivocality: a case study from Serbia) and Nadia Abu El-Haj (From Biblical archaeology to genetic anthropology: the search for Jewish history), who chose not to contribute to this volume, were deleted.

[2] In Trigger's original manuscript, this sentence refers to a 2004 SAA session paper presented by David Kojan and Dante Angelo. This paper is not included in this volume but was published in the *Journal of Social Archaeology* (Kojan & Angelo 2005). After this publication, Kojan wrote a new piece for this volume as a single-authored chapter.

References

Abu El-Haj, N. (2001). *Facts on the Ground: Practice and Territorial Self-Fashioning in Israeli Society*. Chicago: University of Chicago Press.

Anderson, B. R. (1983). *Imagined Communities: Reflections on the Origin and Spread of Nationalism*. London: Verso.

Chakrabarti, D. (2001). South Asia. In T. Murray (Ed.), *Encyclopedia of Archaeology: History and Discoveries*, Vol. 3 (pp. 1183–1194). Santa Barbara, CA: ABC-Clio.

Chamberlin, T. C. (1944). The method of multiple working hypotheses. *Scientific Monthly*, 59, 357–362.

Childe, V. G. (1949). *Social Worlds of Knowledge*. London: Oxford University Press.

Childe, V. G. (1956). *Society and Knowledge: The Growth of Human Traditions*. New York: Harper.

Clarke, D. L. (1968). *Analytical Archaeology*. London: Methuen.

Cohn, B. S. (1996). *Colonialism and its Forms of Knowledge: The British in India*. Princeton: Princeton University Press.

Collingwood, R. G. (1939). *An Autobiography*. Oxford: Oxford University Press.

Collingwood, R. G. (1946). *The Idea of History*. Oxford: Oxford University Press.

Coudart, A. (1998). Archaeology of French women and French women in archaeology. In M. Díaz-Andreu & M. L. Stig Sørensen (Eds.), *Excavating Women: A History of Women in European Archaeology* (pp. 61–85). London: Routledge.

Daniel, G. E. (1950). *A Hundred Years of Archaeology*. London: Duckworth.

Díaz-Andreu, M. (1996). Islamic archaeology and the origin of the Spanish nation. In M. Díaz-Andreu & T. Champion (Eds.), *Nationalism and Archaeology in Europe* (pp. 68–89). London: UCL Press.

Dunning, R. W. (1959). Ethnic relations and the marginal man in Canada. *Human Organization*, 18, 117–122.

Finkelstein, I. & Silberman, N. A. (2001). *The Bible Unearthed: Archaeology's New Vision of Ancient Israel and the Origin of Its Sacred Texts*. New York: The Free Press.

Fleury-Ilett, B. (1996). The identity of France: Archetypes in Iron Age studies. In P. Graves-Brown, S. Jones, & C. Gamble (Eds.), *Cultural Identity and Archaeology: The Construction of European Communities* (pp. 196–208). New York: Routledge.

Hall, A. J. (2003). *The American Empire and the Fourth World*. Montreal: McGill-Queen's University Press.

Hassan, F. A. (1998). Memorabilia: Archaeological materiality and national identity in Egypt. In L. Meskell (Ed.), *Archaeology Under Fire: Nationalism, Politics and Heritage in the Eastern Mediterranean and the Middle East* (pp. 200–216). London: Routledge.

Hawkes, C. F. (1954). Archaeological theory and method: Some suggestions from the Old World. *American Anthropologist*, 56, 155–168.

Herzfeld, M. (2004). Comment. *Current Anthropology* 45, 254–255.

Kojan, D., & Angelo, D. (2005). Dominant narratives, social violence and the practice of Bolivian archaeology. *Journal of Social Archaeology*, 5(3), 383–408.

Marshall, Y. (Ed.). (2002). Community Archaeology. *World Archaeology*, 34 (2).

Meskell, L. (2002). The intersections of identity and politics in archaeology. *Annual Review of Anthropology*, 31, 279–301.

Morris, I. (1994). Archaeologies of Greece. In I. Morris (Ed.), *Classical Greece: Ancient Histories and Modern Archaeologies* (pp. 8–47). Cambridge: Cambridge University Press.

Moser, S. (1995). The 'aboriginalization' of Australian archaeology: The contribution of the Australian Institute of Aboriginal Studies to the indigenous transformation of the discipline. In P. J. Ucko (Ed.), *Theory and Archaeology: A World Perspective* (pp. 150–177). London: Routledge.

Murray, T. (1999). Epilogue: The art of archaeological biography. In T. Murray (Ed.), *Encyclopedia of Archaeology: The Great Archaeologists*, Vol. 2 (pp. 869–883). Santa Barbara, CA: ABC-Clio.

Piggott, S. (1950). *William Stukeley: An Eighteenth-Century Antiquary*. Oxford: Oxford University Press.

Ratnagar, S. (2004). Archaeology at the heart of a political confrontation: The case of Ayodhya. *Current Anthropology*, 45, 239–59.

Salisbury, R. F. (1962). *From Stone to Steel*. Victoria: Melbourne University Press.

Scham, S. A. (2001). The archaeology of the disenfranchised. *Journal of Archaeological Method and Theory*, 8, 183–213.

Silberman, N. A. (1995). Promised land and chosen peoples: The politics and poetics of archaeological narrative. In P. L. Kohl & C. Fawcett (Eds.), *Nationalism, Politics and the Practice of Archaeology* (pp. 249–262). Cambridge: Cambridge University Press.

Spriggs, M. (1992). Alternative prehistories for Bougainville: Regional, national, or micronational. *The Contemporary Pacific*, 4, 269–298.

Trigger, B. G. (1967). Engels on the part played by labour in the transition from ape to man: An anticipation of contemporary archaeological theory. *Canadian Review of Sociology and Anthropology*, 4, 165–176.

Trigger, B. G. (1976). *The Children of Aataentsic: A History of the Huron People to 1660*. Montreal: McGill-Queen's University Press.

Trigger, B. G. (1980). Archaeology and the image of the American Indian. *American Antiquity*, 45, 662–676.
Trigger, B. G. (1989). *A History of Archaeological Thought*. Cambridge: Cambridge University Press.
Trigger, B. G. (2001). The liberation of Wendake. *Ontario Archaeology*, 72, 3–14.
Trigger, B. G. (2003a). *Understanding Early Civilizations: A Comparative Study*. New York: Cambridge University Press.
Trigger, B. G. (2003b). *Archaeological Theory: The Big Picture*. Grace Elizabeth Shallit Memorial Lecture Series. Provo: Department of Anthropology, Brigham Young University.
Trigger, B. G., & Glover, I. (Eds.) (1981/1982). Regional Traditions of Archaeological Research, I, II. *World Archaeology*, 13(2); 13(3).
Yellowhorn, E. C. (2002). *Awakening Internalist Archaeology in the Aboriginal World*. Montreal: Doctoral dissertation, Department of Anthropology, McGill University.

Chapter 13
Multivocality and Social Archaeology

Ian Hodder

Multivocality remains for me a key component of archaeological practice, and it remains a core aspect of the methods we are using at Çatalhöyük. But I also recognize the dangers in the term and the idea, and I wish to respond here to those dangers.

In many ways, the dangers of multivocality parallel those associated with pluralism and multiculturalism. In all such cases, it appears as if the main intent is to allow the participation of more voices, more groups and more individuals without taking into account the fact that achieving the participation of marginalized groups involves a lot more than providing a stage on which they can speak. It involves changing practices and contexts so that disadvantaged groups have the opportunity to be heard and responded to. It involves trying to move away from the methods and principles that are attuned to the Western voice. It involves ethics and rights. This is why I have talked of moving "beyond dialogue" (Hodder 2004) and introducing reflexive methods (Hodder 2005) which involve doing archaeology differently – practicing it differently at all levels from the phase of research design to field methods to writing, publishing, and presenting the past. As I understand it, a reflexive approach is equivalent to what Atalay in this volume calls a deeper multivocality. As Joyce also shows, multivocality is not just the product of a theoretical argument, but is a result of sociopolitical and intellectual hybridity.

The opposite of a deep engagement with multiple voices is described by Silberman in his account of virtual archaeology and heritage. Silberman describes very well the differences between a socially engaged multivocality and the commercially conscious aim of including as many different voices (consumers) as possible. So just having new media at heritage sites and multiple perspectives may support a dominant and unified global narrative; here multivocality supports globalization and niche marketing. The new technologies of multivocality are therefore not enough to achieve a deeper multivocality or a reflexive archaeology. Archaeologists may, however, make use of the commercial interest in the past to engage in outreach, dialogue, engagement, and confrontation. I have certainly found in the Çatalhöyük project that the commercialization of the site allows all sorts of opportunities for strange alliances that can be used to enhance education and engagement in deeper ways. For example, international sponsorship can be used, as on many projects, to facilitate systematic educational programs at the local level. A lot of this "deeper"

J. Habu, C. Fawcett, and J. M. Matsunaga (eds.), *Evaluating Multiple Narratives:*
Beyond Nationalist, Colonialist, Imperialist Archaeologies.
© Springer 2008

work may happen outside the tourists' gaze, but there may also be opportunities for engaging archaeology in something parallel to eco-tourism or sustainable tourism where a deeper commitment can be reached.

There is a danger that multivocality is simply part of the imperialist archaeological tradition as defined by Trigger (1984). My own experience of opening up archaeological practice to multiple voices has been that marginalized or silenced groups have been relieved, excited, and engaged in the potential to explore their own heritage and identity. But of course, in many cases, there is also anger and suspicion resulting from past practices, and concerns that the reflexive process is no more than a ploy to achieve incorporation and agreement. Heritage is often seen as negative (Meskell 2002). To really listen to and incorporate other voices and to change what we do as archaeologists are difficult. Can the subaltern talk back (Spivak 1995)? In this volume, Kim notes the difficulty of transposing the practice of multivocality into the Korean context.

As Atalay shows, in order to achieve a deeper multivocality, shifts are needed in theoretical and methodological practices that begin at the planning stages of research and have an impact on long-term management of archaeological resources. She seeks real change in what archaeologists and heritage managers do, by combining Western and indigenous forms of knowledge. She does not just want to absorb Western mainstream approaches, but rather she is interested in producing hybrid methods, theories, ideas, and practice. She rightly describes this as a decolonizing impetus. The Ojibwe notion of multivocality has different nuances from the way the word is usually used in mainstream archaeologies. There seems more allowance of ambiguity and tension, with more acceptance of the notion that different stories can be true at the same time. Clearly the Western mainstream traditions have much to learn from this.

Many of the papers in this volume refer to the deeper shifts that are needed to make a socially responsible multivocality possible. For example, Blakey describes how his project at the New York African Burial ground presented a draft research design to African-Americans and others interested in the site in order to gain comment, criticism, and new ideas and questions. The aim was to involve the descendant community in a full way in the research design process. As with Atalay, the purpose was hybridity – a synthesis of scholarship and community interests.

In this volume, Habu and Fawcett suggest that it may be possible for previously decentered or subaltern subjects to effectively engage in dialogue. They give examples where multivocality and collaboration produce changed interpretations that challenge existing power structures. Kojan also argues for a deeper multivocality when he says that multivocality has to be seen as part of a wider political, social, and economic context. It is not enough just to allow different stories about the past to be heard. We have to engage with the realities behind the stories. Narratives about Tiwanaku are at the core of a story that reproduces other parts of Bolivia as "empty" or "marginal." This erasure of history helps the central elite to retain power (see also Kojan & Angelo 2005).

One of the key messages of this book then, is that multivocality needs to be allied with changes in archaeological practice which promote collaboration and which take into account the social positions of stakeholder groups. These groups are often divided into local and global categories. Use of the term multivocality often assumes an opposition between on the one hand, a global archaeological discourse of theoreticians, heritage managers, methods, laws, and codes of ethics, and on the other hand the local voice. The global is pitted against the local that has to act back against universalizing and homogenizing tendencies. Thus, it is difficult to imagine how to empower the multiple local voices against the dominant mainstream.

In practice, however, it often seems that this opposition is too simplistically drawn. In practice we often see complex alliances between local, regional, national, and international agencies and groups. We see complex alliances between governmental and nongovernmental groups, between archaeologists and nonarchaeologists. In this way, multivocality becomes cosmopolitan. I wish to use the term "cosmopolitan" to refer to the complex blending of the global and the particular in ways that do not replicate Western perspectives and which do not construct the local as a product of the global (Appiah 2006, xiii; Habermas 2000).

As an example of this cosmopolitanism, I have already mentioned the way that international companies sponsor local educational programs at Çatalhöyük that are run by local teachers, involving local and national government agencies. In this volume, Kim provides some examples of cosmopolitan alliances. In the case of the Sorori site in Korea, opposition mobilized an NGO, the National Trust of Korea, a group called the Citizen's Solidarity for Participation and Self-Government of Chungbuk, the Hosea Archaeological Society, the Korean Paleolithic Society, university professors, and the local government of Cheongwon. This alliance of NGO, governmental and scholarly groups involved local, regional, and national scales or organization. In the controversy over "the earliest rice," again strange alliances were created of marginal and dominant groups, including scholarly and international commercial interests, local, and nationalist groups.

It is often through these cosmopolitan alliances that local, marginal, or subaltern voices can be heard and can have an impact. If we think of heritage issues as involving only local versus global strategies, then it is difficult to see how local and indigenous groups can effectively be empowered. But in practice the proliferation of groups engaged in the past, both in terms of scale (international, national, regional, local) and in terms of type (governmental, non-governmental), allows opportunities for cross-cutting alliances and interdependencies that can be mobilized strategically. In practice, as Kim shows us, and as others in this volume exemplify, it is possible for subaltern groups to effect change in cultural heritage and archaeological practices, at least in some instances.

In the end, the problem is how to bring people to the cultural heritage table in such a way that they are all able to speak and influence the discussion. There are many difficult issues here. For example, should all those around the table have an equal voice? Or should those who have suffered more through the colonial process have a louder voice? Should those who have provided more funding have the most sway? Who "owns" the past – those associated most closely with it historically, or the world community, or those who found the site and can best preserve it, and so on?

In dealing with such ethical issues, there are often thought to be two main ways in which we can go. Either we refer to international codes and laws, derived from UNESCO, ICOMOS, the World Archaeological Congress, or other international bodies, or we say that all such issues need to be worked out locally and contingently. Both of these responses seem inadequate in the following ways.

I agree with Trigger's move in this volume to bridge rationalism (universalism) and romanticism (contextualism). I agree that in doing so there is a need to consider human rights, but there is a danger that any universal declaration of heritage rights would be just another dominating tool imposed by the West. For example, it is not clear that the focus on individual rights in Western law would be appropriate in all non-Western contexts. But equally, there is a danger in leaving heritage ethics to local negotiations. This is because, as Habu and Fawcett show in their chapter, previously marginal groups or indigenous groups are as capable as any other group of neo-nationalism. The "local" is not always right, and there may be need for intervention to protect local groups from destroying each other's heritage, to protect the interests of diasporic communities in their heritage, or to protect other global interests. I agree also with Joyce, that as professional archaeologists we have a duty to contest interpretations of the past that violate material data – this universal impulse has to develop in dialogue with interested groups and in dialogue with alternative interpretations, but it nevertheless implies a nonlocal component.

Thus neither reliance on universal principles nor strategic and contingent local engagement seem adequate to deal with the complex processes of heritage management and archaeological work. As interested parties sit round the heritage table, it is helpful to start with general codes of ethics, lists of best practice, legal guidelines, and so on. But in practice there are always special issues and specific claims that have to be evaluated in relation to the particular case. In practice the discussions around the table are impinged upon by what is beyond the table. There are always wider considerations regarding the historical context of the discussions, including the history of colonization. There are wider issues which are economic – the economic development that may or may not be associated with heritage projects. And there are questions of cultural and social context – whether groups feel empowered to speak and able to meet commitments made.

I doubt that it will be possible to define universal rights to cultural heritage. The underlying reason is that claims to heritage and origins have a tendency to be exclusive to some degree. They always involve saying "this is mine and not yours" to some extent. Whether such a claim to ownership is just or not has to be evaluated in relation to evidence of affiliation and descent, but it also has to be evaluated in relation to the questions outlined above (do those who have suffered loss of heritage under colonial rule have special rights, do those who can best protect the past have special rights, do those that fund conservation have special rights, and so on?). In the end it seems more likely to me that rather than defining universal rights to heritage it would be better to embed rights to cultural heritage within wider considerations of human rights. Then the question becomes, "do claims to cultural heritage enhance basic human rights – to life, liberty, economic welfare and so on?"

Evaluation of such a question would then always involve both universal consid-erations and local questions. It would involve hybrid syntheses. It would involve cosmopolitan alliances between various scales and types of group. Thus the search for a deeper multivocality takes us into uncharted territory, into new ways of embedding dialogue about the past in discussions of human rights, into closer collaboration with those that can contribute information about what is beyond the table. Discussion about empowering multiple voices involves necessary collaboration with sociologists, cultural economists (those that can evaluate the impact of heritage projects on regional economic development, for example), lawyers, and ethicists. Rights to cultural heritage need to be situated within specific historic circumstances, specific economies, relations of power, and cultural aesthetics.

References

Appiah, K. A. (2006). *Cosmopolitanism: Ethics in a World of Strangers*. New York: W.W. Norton & Company.

Habermas, J. (2000). *The Inclusion of the Other*. Cambridge, MA: The MIT Press.

Hodder, I. (2004). *Archaeology beyond Dialogue*. Salt Lake City: University of Utah Press.

Hodder, I. (2005). Reflexive methods. In H. D. G. Maschner & C. Chippindale (Eds.), *Handbook of Archaeological Methods* (pp. 643–669). New York: AltaMira Press.

Kojan, D., & Angelo, D. (2005). Dominant narratives, social violence and the practice of Bolivian archaeology. *Journal of Social Archaeology, 5*(3), 383–408.

Meskell, L. (2002). Negative heritage and past mastering in archaeology. *Anthropological Quarterly, 75*(3), 557–574.

Spivak, G. C. (1995). Can the subaltern speak? In B. Ashcroft, G. Griffiths, & H. Tiffin (Eds.), *The Post-Colonial Studies Reader* (pp. 24–28). London: Routledge.

Trigger, B. G. (1984). Alternative archaeologies: Nationalist, colonialist, imperialist. *Man, 19*, 355–370.

Chapter 14
The Integrity of Narratives: Deliberative Practice, Pluralism, and Multivocality

Alison Wylie

When Trigger argued, almost 25 years ago, that dominant archaeological narratives embody and transact nationalist, colonialist, and imperialist interests, he opened space for multivocality in two senses. In most general terms, he drew attention to the way in which all knowledge claims reflect and constitute the contexts of their production; in this he made the case for a "situated knowledge" thesis. At the same time he argued, more specifically, for a structural understanding of the relationship between archaeological narratives and the contexts in which they arise, a point that is particularly salient today. His thesis was that the distinct "orientations" embodied in archaeological narratives reflect, not just the idiosyncratic interests of individual narrators and local communities but, through them, the "roles that particular nation states play, economically, politically, and culturally, as interdependent parts of the modern world-system" (1984:356). Multivocality was called for specifically to counter the hegemonic power of these state formations; it was centrally and crucially, for Trigger, a form of oppositional practice.

The contributors to this volume both embrace and problematize this understanding of mulitvocality. On one hand they acknowledge, as more crucial now than ever, Trigger's central point about the need to understand the local dynamics shaping archaeological narratives in terms of large scale geopolitics. On the other hand, however, all are mindful that, in a globalizing political economy, transnational flows of capital, goods, and labor condition archaeological interests in complex ways that radically exceed the boundaries of nation-states and reconfigure the international dynamics through which colonizing and imperialist ambitions are enacted. This expands the terms of internal debate about the politics of archaeology in ways that anticipate Trigger's reference to world systems theory but that, at the same time, put considerable pressure on the categories of analysis invoked in the title of Trigger's pivotal 1984 paper. Whatever their other differences, each contributor offers examples and analyses that throw into relief the layered complexity of the interests that impinge upon (archaeological) narrations of the past. The choice of subjects, their representation, their use in the present are all structured by power dynamics that operate at multiple scales and through diverse mechanisms. It is a signal contribution of these papers that, collectively, they set a forward-looking

J. Habu, C. Fawcett, and J. M. Matsunaga (eds.), *Evaluating Multiple Narratives:*
Beyond Nationalist, Colonialist, Imperialist Archaeologies.
© Springer 2008

agenda on which the reworking of these categories is a critical challenge facing any who endorse multivocality as an oppositional practice in archaeology.

Hodder's (1986, 1999) brief for multivocality, the second catalyst and reference point for these discussions, can be read as a response to precisely this complex over-determination of local archaeological narratives; it is at once more expansive and more diffuse than Trigger's. Hodder presupposes a situated knowledge thesis that is more perspectival than structural, and he advocates multivocality on grounds of a jointly normative (moral, political) and epistemic argument for inclusive practices that promise to enrich our understanding of the past by ensuring the articulation and engagement of marginal perspectives. This is also an oppositional stance – Hodder (1997) urges the institution of deliberative processes that will decenter authoritative narratives – but it is not framed primarily in terms of opposition to large-scale state structures; it is more "momentary, fluid, and flexible." As Trigger argued, not long after he himself had made a particularly uncompromising case for a social (structural) constructionist view of knowledge (1989), an open-ended endorsement of proliferat-ing difference carries the risk of solipsism and an associated relativism, a conse-quence that he strenuously resisted; there must be grounds for a discerning appraisal of competing claims, he insisted[1]. To put this point in terms relevant to current debate about multivocality, a stance that validates a cacophony of self-warranting voices threatens to undermine precisely the forms of sustained deliberative engagement that holds the potential for (mutually) transformative insight – for Hodder the chief attrac-tion of practices that foster multivocality. In one way or another, explicitly or by example of their own practice, the contributors to this volume make it clear that they reject forms of multivocalilty that leave dissonant, competing narratives unaccounta-ble just as decisively as they reject the ideal of a single authoritative (true) narrative. Such a stance – a relativist pluralism – loses critical traction; not only is it disingenu-ous but also, as Kojan points out, it risks serving the interests of the powerful rather than empowering the disenfranchised. A second challenge therefore extends the first: if multivocality is to be sustained as an oppositional practice, one that has the potential to do critical, transformative work in archaeological contexts, it will be crucial to establish grounds on which to warrant (and contest) both the claims about the past that constitute archaeologically-based narratives, and reflexive claims about the con-temporary conditions – the situated interests – that structure the production of these narratives. The question is, then, what sorts of grounds and what sorts of reflexive critique are defensible, given commitment to a situated knowledge thesis?

As a first step toward answering these questions, consider some distinct kinds and sources of multivocality that are at issue in archaeological contexts, as engaged by the contributors to this volume. One is captured by an ontological thesis: that multivocality in various senses is a feature of the past itself, the puta-tive subject of inquiry and narration[2]. As Wallace describes Dublin in the ninth through twelfth centuries, it is a striking example of cacophonous and hybridized multivocality, a port town with Norse, Gaelic, Celtic, and English ties that was identified at the time as a place and people apart; it is an historical subject that, on critical reexamination, resists categorization in terms of the neatly distinct ethnic identities that Wallace finds the stock in trade for narratives of Irish heritage. Wallace's focal concern is with the ways in which this multivocality in the past is suppressed or selectively represented in contemporary narratives about the past. In this he draws attention to the conception of multivocality that is central to these discussions.

Multivocality in this latter sense is a present-day affair. It presupposes a diversity of situated interests and perspectives and is, at bottom, an epistemic thesis: that any representation of the cultural past is necessarily partial (to varying degrees, in various senses) in what it reconstructs and in how it narrates, interprets or explains the past that is its selective focus (however multi- or univocal this past may be). As an oppositional practice, multivocalilty further presupposes that this contemporary pluralism is differentially reflected in our understanding of the cultural past, depending on the power dynamics that determine whose interests shape collective understandings of the past: narratives of the past "track power" (Trouillot 1995:25). That said, this endorsement of epistemic pluralism does not lead inevitably to the kind of relativism according to which any account is justifiable, nor does it entail that all accounts are equally warranted, given a judicious selection of framing assumptions. This conclusion – the "hyperrelativism" that concerned Trigger (1989) – requires several additional premises: for example, that strict incommensurability holds between competing claims about the cultural past; that the principles invoked to justify these claims are self-warranting and provide no basis for comparative assessment; and that the content of specific historical/archaeological claims, including evidential claims is determined (wholly and comprehensively) by context-specific interests either directly or as a proxy for the social and material conditions of life that give rise to them. There are a number of positions located along the epistemic continuum opened up by a rejection of epistemic absolutism – the quest for a single true account of the past – that take seriously the possibility of a (contingent) plurality of credible alternative accounts, but stop short of endorsing this hyperrelativist extreme. These differ in the kinds and sources of pluralism they recognize.

Consider, for example, the epistemically conservative, but not inconsequential, thesis that archaeologists must necessarily choose a focus for inquiry, and when they take different questions as their point of departure for investigation of broadly the same past, they can be expected to generate historical, archaeological accounts that illuminate different aspects of this past. On the model of an integrative pluralism that presumes a commitment to ontological and epistemic unity (in the sense outlined by Mitchell 2002:55–57),[3] these fragments might all be expected to coalesce into a single coherent narrative, as pieces of a puzzle developed independently that should fit together if each is accurate of the elements of the past they claim to represent. At a superficial level the narratives inflected by nationalist interests described here might seem to reflect this kind of selective partiality. The preoccupation with particular formative events, cultural lineages and social institutions – the Celtic roots of an "indigenous" Irish culture, rather than its later Viking or Anglo-Norman elements (Wallace); Tiwanaku conceived as the seat of pre-conquest power in Bolivia (Kojan); the origins of rice production in Korea (Kim); the formation of distinctively Mayan proto-states exemplified by Copan (Joyce); the "making of the English village" (Johnson) – sets up question-specific historical and archaeological puzzles the resolution of which directs attention to particular aspects of the surviving record or forms of evidence. Kim and Joyce describe cases in which counter-hegemonic alternatives are structured by the same principles as those they contest; they are univocal, just with respect to a different selection of privileged cultural, historical reference points. On the reading suggested by an integrative pluralism, the chief failing of such accounts is that they are over-extended; the (incomplete) part is taken to stand for the whole. In principle, evidence of pasts not considered calls into question, not the credibility of the part, but the ambitions of those who invest it with exclusive significance; it throws into relief the need for inquiry animated by different questions, aimed at illuminating dimensions of this past not addressed by the dominant research tradition. But even when a past of many parts is represented in terms of a plurality of subject positions and stories, Silberman details the narrative and technical strategies by which a "mosaic of conflicting and contrasting voices" – rendered as sound bites and individualized messages – can be scripted as elements of an essentially unilinear narrative, subject to a corporate mandate to produce a marketable "heritage" experience: widely accessible, personally (affectively) engaging, and legible by the standards of a dominant culture. Integrative pluralism offers too simple a picture of the silences perpetuated by dominant narratives (Trouillot 1995:26–28).

More challenging forms of pluralism are never far from the surface, and it is these that are chiefly at issue in discussions of multivocality. As Johnson's analysis of the "English village" makes clear, the choice of question is rarely innocent in the sense presumed by an integrative pluralism of the kind described above. In the case that he discusses it reflects a distinctive set of post-war, nationalist (assimilationist) convictions that find articulation in the heritage construct of a "common English culture" and that deflect attention from features of context, chronological anomalies, mechanisms by which a particular social order was constructed that threaten to disrupt the dominant narrative of unity and continuity. Some of these incongruous elements disappear as a consequence of reliance on conceptual categories that render them unintelligible while others are assimilated (if uneasily) to the frame of the focal question; Johnson notes that the dominant tradition has undergone internal revision but the central tenets of the Hoskins construct survive intact. The broader significance of these anomalies as a challenge to assumptions about what is natural, ancestral in the English village – their potential as a resource for understanding the English landscape in different terms – depends, Johnson suggests, on asking an alternative set of questions that reflect the interests and perspectives of those who dissent from the nationalist ideals at the core of traditional narratives of English heritage. When he objects that the "lack of multivocality has led...to a tangibly poorer and impoverished account of the historic landscape" (Johnson, this volume), he is not just insisting that an error of over-generalization be reassessed or arguing for research that will fill in the gaps in an incomplete picture. The multivocality Johnson enlists is, rather, a matter of contemporary differences in standpoint on the past – specifically, standpoints characterized by critical dissociation from dominant assumptions about English heritage – that bring into focus aspects of this past that have the potential to resituate and reinterpret key elements of the dominant account, as well as to expand on it.

Dissonant pluralism can arise in a variety of ways, and subverts to varying degrees the ideals that underpin integrative pluralism, that is, the hope (or expectation) that divergent narratives should ultimately coalesce into a single true, coherent account of the past. It can arise from internal theoretical differences among archaeologists, as in the case Chapman describes where multiple ways of reckoning state-hood generate divergent accounts of Bronze Age social formations in southern Spain. When inquiry is framed by questions about when and how class divisions and exploitative relations of production took shape in prehistory, there is a premium on lines of evidence relevant for tracing the development of "new productive forces"; and when archaic state societies are presumed immanent, evidence of growing social hierarchy, complex divisions of labor, and the intensification of production in the second millennium BC is interpreted as support for the thesis that the Argaric was characterized by a regional, class-based state. Under these conditions the investigation of early state societies in Spain might seem to be self-sustaining, effectively insulated from critiques that originate in alternative conceptions of social complexity and cultural evolution. But Chapman makes it clear that, even when competing accounts seem incommensurable, they are not strictly self-warranting. He identifies a range of evidence and conceptual lacunae that count variously for and against the claims central to the arguments for treating Bronze Age social formations as class-divided states, rather than as complex polities, chiefdoms, ranked or stratified societies. Despite consequential differences in theoretical orientation – differences that may well continue to generate an irreducible pluralism of perspectives on the past – the advocates of these contending models share a great deal where epistemic standards are concerned, and they hold one another accountable to these standards even as they disagree about how they should be interpreted, applied, weighed against one another. By contrast, Kojan, Joyce, and Atalay, among others, describe forms of multivocality in which shared epistemic and methodological reference points of this kind cannot be assumed. What is contested is not just the content of dominant accounts of the past or the framework assumptions that underpin them, but the grounds on which these are authorized, the standards of cogency and credibility to which they are held accountable. As Joyce suggests, this depth of challenge typically arises, not within the discourse of (disciplinary) archaeology, but as a function of divergent theoretical commitments, when a "multivocality enforced by dialogue with others outside the discipline...reframes the terms of engagement" (Joyce, this volume).

In principle, at least, it is with these forms of epistemically dissonant pluralism that the threat of Trigger's hyperrelativism arises. In the extreme, under conditions that meet the requirements of the additional premises cited above, divergent understandings of the past that reflect structurally different social interests carry with them their own self-warranting standards of adequacy. When these are sufficiently discontinuous with one another (that is, literally incommensurable), there will be no bases for critical engagement across contending frameworks. But this conclusion is not endorsed even by those who consider multivocality in its most challenging forms. Despite acknowledging that no one understanding of the Honduran past is inherently privileged, Joyce argues that archaeologically grounded insights do have a claim on her diverse interlocutors. When Atalay makes the case for decolonizing archaeology – when she advocates Indigenous archaeologies on grounds that they have a capacity to decenter presumptions of disciplinary authority – she insists that this is not a matter of dismantling mainstream archaeological practice wholesale. Rather she urges that the distinctive tools of inquiry and insights afforded by Indigenous experience should be actively engaged by, and incorporated into, a form of archaeological practice that is itself multivocal; this is a pluralist principle she finds central to Indigenous archaeologies. Likewise when Blakey endorses a "respect for pluralism," and an ethical commitment to working with those most marginalized by conventional narratives, he envisions a democratized form of practice in which the tools of scientific inquiry are put to work in new ways, not displaced but tempered by accountability to communities that have very different stakes in the outcomes of historical, archaeological inquiry. What Kojan finds discredited by arguments for multivocality is not, it seems, the empirical and conceptual rigor that disciplinary research can bring to the investigation of a potent and contentious past, but the "ideology of objectivity" in terms of which the (univocal) authority of its results is so often asserted. He, like Blakey, rejects epistemic ideals that systematically obscure the contingencies, the situated interests and power dynamics, that give rise to the focal questions and interpretive frames in terms of which dominant histories are written and authorized.

What emerges as a common theme in these discussions is, then, a conviction that debilitating relativism is not the only alternative to an untenable faith in transcendent epistemic standards, capable of stabilizing debate across contexts and of ensuring the convergence of claims they authorize on a unified, and uniquely authoritative, "view from nowhere" (Nagel 1979). More specifically, what emerges is commitment to a set of procedural (rather than criterial) epistemic ideals; taken together these papers suggest a set of general guidelines for deliberative process – forms of accountability, both epistemic and normative (ethical/political) – that might constitute a (provisional) framework for democratizing practice. To use a phrase Blakey introduces, drawing inspiration from Douglass, these articulate orienting ideals of "integrity in scholarship" on several dimensions.

The first principle I draw out of these discussions is a commitment to empirical integrity, captured by Blakey's phrase, "standing on evidence": citing Douglass, he urges a principle of "simultaneously tak[ing] sides and be[ing] fair to the evidence." This need not presuppose a foundational conception of evidence – as a self-authorizing source or ground of knowledge, of transparent significance and uncontestable authority – but it does require responsiveness to evidence both as it bears on specific claims about the past and on the background assumptions that inform the choice of questions, categories of analysis, and the identification of (relevant) data. Consider, for example, the objections raised by Kim and by Joyce when the advocates of politically salient narratives ignore or reframe archaeologically derived dates – when these are pushed back to sustain origins claims, as in the debate about the assertion that rice from the Sorori site is "the oldest in the world," or pushed forward to establish colonial era significance, as when Cerro Palenque is declared to have been a sixteenth-century site of conflict with the Spanish rather than a late stage Mayan site of the tenth-century AD. And consider the evidential dimension of Chapman's response to the definitional framing of Argaric sites as components of a class-structured regional state; to sustain this account, he argues, Gilman must "rule out diverse lines of evidence" that counter key assumptions about the nature of the state and social complexity that underlie the model. In these cases the objection is not that the empirical evidence in question is uncontestable but that it has not been systematically engaged; it has been declared irrelevant, or ignored without argument. In a complementary argument, Johnson makes a case for the transformative potential of practices that make the most of the "empirical strengths" of archaeology. He is optimistic that close and sustained attention to "very simple, very direct…'bread-and-butter' evidence of the archaeological record" (Johnson, this volume) – in the case he considers, evidence for patterns of activity and material conditions of life – can put pressure on conventional wisdom about the lives of those who occupied the ancestral English village, suggesting not just where specific claims need revision, but where framing questions are flawed.

A further, more specific conception of empirical integrity that figures in a number of these discussions is one that puts particular emphasis on the importance of juxtaposing multiple lines of evidence. For Chapman this is the necessary ground for "robust inferences" and, more specifically, for countering the selective elision of lines of (archaeological) evidence that do not fit expectations (Chapman, this volume). Johnson adds to this an argument for deploying the resources of cross-disciplinary multivocality; to extend his concluding argument, it is in the interplay of historical, anthropological, and archaeological approaches that the limitations of interpretive assumptions drawn from any one discipline may become evident. In similar spirit Blakey puts particular emphasis on the importance of bringing together multiple data sets – biogenetic and molecular, sociocultural and historical – on the principle that "standards of plausibility are elevated by the accountability that the facts generated by each method have to one another" (Blakey, this volume).[4] By extension, the epistemic implication of multivocality in the broader sense advocated by Atalay and by Blakey is that when collaborative interaction extends beyond the boundaries of professional archaeology (or physical anthropology, or history) it has the potential to widen the scope of this triangulation in consequential ways; it brings into play empirical resources and forms of evidential reasoning that sometimes enrich, sometimes challenge, and almost inevitably sharpen appreciation of the distinctive aims and scope – the strengths and limitations – of conventional disciplinary practice. Atalay describes the interpretive power of an exhibit that combines archaeological information about the production of the Sanilac Petroglyphs with Ojibwe oral tradition and spiritual teachings and, as noted earlier, Joyce identifies "dialogue with others outside the discipline" as crucial for disrupting the settled conventions of archaeological practice. So understood, the principle of empirical integrity provides the rationale for a form of methodological multivocality that is extra-disciplinary, as well as both intra- and inter-disciplinary.

A second principle that is more often implicit than this first is a requirement of conceptual integrity captured by Kojan and Angelo's injunction against claims that "defy reason" (2005:393), and by Chapman's call for definitional precision in framing "higher level concepts" and for "structural coherence" in their use as part of an explanatory theory. Chapman's discussion is particularly interesting on this last point. He argues that if "the state" is to function as a useful concept "with which to think and learn about past societies," not only must the criteria defining what counts as a state be clear, but also "structural linkages" must be specified that "relate these criteria to their material forms." The point here is not just that orienting concepts should be operationalized in archaeological terms, but that the background assumptions mediating the archaeological application of such concepts should be made explicit; this transparency is crucial, Chapman suggests, if competing claims about the past are to be effectively compared and assessed. As with appeals to evidence, this demand for "coherent theoretical argument" need not be construed in foundational terms, as presupposing a fixed, context- and interest-transcendent set of ideals of rationality. What it requires is that standards of "good reason" be publicly articulated and consistently applied, and that when fundamental differences arise in what counts as "reasonable," or "cogent," these be directly engaged.

These principles of empirical and conceptual integrity presuppose what might be described as a meta-principle of epistemic provisionality: a second-order principle, constitutive of a commitment to pluralism, that specifies the status of these first-order principles (from Longino 1994:483; Wylie 2007). On standard lists of epistemic virtue cited by authors as diverse as Kuhn (1977:321–322), Longino (1990), and Dupré (1993:11), counterparts to the principles of empirical and conceptual integrity identified here – requirements of empirical adequacy, internal coherence, and consistency with well-established collateral and background knowledge – are typically understood to require interpretation in any context of application (Kuhn 1977:322–325; Longino 1994:479; discussion in Wylie 2003). What will count as empirical adequacy, for example, depends on the problem at hand, the history of research, and the technical resources available. In addition, rarely it is possible to maximize these virtues, variously interpreted; for example, empirical adequacy in the sense of reliable extension to a range of domains (generalizability) often requires a trade-off of empirical adequacy in the sense of fidelity to a particular subject domain (e.g., in the case of modeling in population biology; Levins 1966), or of internal coherence if the complexity of a domain requires multiple (dissonant) models (e.g., in the case of climate modeling; Parker 2006). The upshot is that the principles of epistemic integrity identified here are themselves underdetermined (Doppelt 1988, 1990). Consequently, they must be treated as negotiable, as requiring justification; they must be held open to revision in light of what archaeologists learn about them in the process of inquiry, and from critical engagement with epistemic communities that have evolved different standards of empirical and conceptual integrity.

The two (first-order) requirements of empirical and conceptual integrity, conceived as provisional in the sense described, also seem to presuppose a set of procedural guidelines similar to those identified by Longino when she sets out social norms for discursive interaction that foster "transformative criticism" in research practice (1990:76–81). In one way or another all the contributors to this volume endorse what might be described, following Longino, as a principle of "tempered equality of intellectual authority" (2002:131; see also 1990:78). Indeed, it would seem to be the cornerstone of a commitment to multivocality that the insights of diversely situated epistemic agents and communities should be taken seriously, not only as a source of additional lines of evidence or interpretive perspectives but also, as Atalay argues, "long before the interpretive [or, indeed, the investigative] process begins" (Atalay, this volume), in the formation of questions, in the design of research, and in the articulation of orienting ideals of empirical and conceptual integrity. Taken on its own, a commitment to recognize diverse forms of critical and constructive input is ineffectual unless embodied in additional community norms of practice. Longino outlines three that are relevant here. One is a requirement that standards for adjudicating claims of epistemic credibility and critical challenges to them should be publicly articulated (2002:130). The pernicious effects of an "ideology of objectivity," as described by Kojan, arise from the tacit acceptance of orienting epistemic ideals as framework assumptions that are obscure in themselves and that obscure the ways in which they structure the terms of engagement. To make these explicit is to demystify their authority, to open them to critical assessment and hold those who endorse them accountable for the ways they are interpreted and weighed against one another in practice. A second procedural guideline proposed by Longino is that there be "recognized avenues for criticism," public venues in which diverse perspectives can be brought to bear in assessing focal claims and the framework assumptions (theoretical commitments, orienting questions, methodological ideals) in terms of which they are warranted (1990:67; 2002:129). And the third is a requirement for "uptake of criticism": that there be mechanisms in place which ensure that the research community is responsive to the insights generated by its diverse (multivocal) interlocutors (1990:78; 2002:129–130). The justification Longino offers for these procedural guidelines captures a central motivation for advocating multivocality in archaeological contexts: that in fostering "effective critical interactions" these are conditions for adjudicating the (provisional) credibility of knowledge claims, not because they "canonize…one subjectivity over others" but because they ensure that "what is ratified as knowledge has survived criticism from multiple points of view" (2002:129; see also Lloyd 2005:246–255). Archaeological discussions of multivocality suggest one amendment: that what emerges from deliberative processes structured by these guidelines warrants provisional acceptance because it incorporates the wisdom of multiple points of view, including wisdom about how to interpret and apply requirements of empirical and conceptual integrity.[5]

I add to these procedural guidelines a final principle of grounded reflexivity: a commitment to deploying the insights of standpoint analysis in the design and practice of archaeological research, and in the adjudication of the explanatory, interpretive understanding it produces of the cultural past.[6] Kojan observes that, as situated historical agents, when we are confronted with an account of the past we ask: what kind of narrative is this?; who produced it and for what purposes? The standpoint principle I propose calls for the systematic engagement of these present-oriented questions with the aim of establishing grounds for an empirically informed (socio-historical) appraisal of the limitations of dominant narratives, in scope and in content, and of where relevant diversity lies that could productively reorient archaeological inquiry. Blakey suggests a more specific formulation of this principle: that archaeologists committed to democratizing inquiry should attend especially to the insights and concerns of those who "historiography puts at risk," those who are most dispossessed by dominant narratives and most likely to be negatively affected by archaeological inquiry. This is a jointly ethical and epistemic directive. In its epistemic aspect it is akin to the methodological principle central to feminist standpoint theory: that researchers should "start off inquiry from women's lives" (Harding 2006:84) or, more generally, from the lives of those who are, as Smith (1984) puts it, "eclipsed" in the accounts produced by social sciences that function as a form of "ruling practice" (Smith 1974:8). In its normative (ethical and political) aspect, it resonates with Kojan's insistence that archaeologists should counteract the impulse to treat oppressive contemporary "human realities as a mere backdrop to our archaeological research"; it is a directive to take responsibility for the implication of archaeology in contemporary political struggles and to make the "impact and implications" of this archaeological practice "an integral part of our research" (Kojan, this volume).

No doubt those whose work has inspired this list of principles and guidelines will find them wanting, certainly in need of finetuning and perhaps inimical to the spirit of the multivocality they embrace. I offer them provisionally in response to the challenges set out at the beginning of this commentary. My hope is that they capture, in a preliminary way, what I take to be the central insights articulated by contributors to this volume: that if the engagement of multiple voices is to be fruitful – if multivocality is to be sustained as an oppositional practice, capable of critically transforming archaeology – it must be embedded in a form of practice that exemplifies ideals of deliberative process; inquiry must be democratized.

Notes

[1] This analysis of Trigger's arguments against relativism is developed in more detail in Wylie (2006).

[2] I draw here on Trouillot's discussion of an ambiguity inherent in standard use of the term history, as a term that refers to "the facts of the matter and a narrative of those facts ... 'what happened' and 'that which is said to have happened ... the sociohistorical process...[and] our knowledge of that process" (1995:2).

[3] Mitchell distinguishes between competitive and compatible forms of pluralism (1992), and later considers what she calls integrative pluralism (2002:55–57). The latter is a form of pluralism that allows for idealized models of a complex system that cannot be integrated at a theoretical level but that are integrated, as partial accounts of components of the system, when applied to a concrete, particular case (2002:67). In such cases, she says, the diversity of theoretical models "does not issue in unrestrained pluralism"; pluralism characterizes "the models of potentially contributing causes [but] not their integrated application in specific, concrete explanation"

(2002:67). I use the term "dissonant" pluralism here to refer to the possibility, the central concern in discussions of multivocality, that archaeological and historical inquiry often seems to generate a plurality of interpretive, theoretical models of the cultural past that cannot be reconciled, as components of an explanatory account, when applied to specific cases.

⁴ More generically, it is through a process of triangulation that the limitations of distinct lines of evidence, and of the techniques and disciplines for handling them, becomes manifest (Wylie 2002:206–208).

⁵ On a procedural account, what it is for knowledge claims to be objective is that they have been produced, or ratified, through such a process.

⁶ I refer here to standpoint theory as conceptualized in Wylie (2003).

References

Doppelt, G. D. (1988). The philosophical requirements for an adequate conception of scientific rationality. *Philosophy of Science*, 55(1), 4–133.

Doppelt, G. D. (1990). The naturalist conception of methodological standards in science: A critique. *Philosophy of Science*, 57, 1–19.

Dupré, J. (1993). *The Disorder of Things: Metaphysical Foundations of the Disunity of Science*. Cambridge MA: Harvard University Press.

Harding, S. (2006). *Science and Social Inequality: Feminist and Postcolonial Issues*. Chicago: University of Illinois Press.

Hodder, I. (1986). *Reading the Past: Current Approaches to Interpretation in Archaeology*. Cambridge: Cambridge University Press.

Hodder, I. (1997). Always momentary, fluid and flexible: Towards a reflexive excavation methodology. *Antiquity*, 71(273), 691–700.

Hodder, I. (1999). *The Archaeological Process: An Introduction*. Oxford: Blackwell Publishers.

Kojan, D., & Angelo, D. (2005). Dominant narratives, social violence and the practice of Bolivian archaeology. *Journal of Social Archaeology*, 5(3), 383–408.

Kuhn, T. S. (1977). Objectivity, values, and theory choice. In T.S. Kuhn, *The Essential Tension* (pp. 320–339). Chicago: University of Chicago Press.

Levins, R. (1966). The strategy of model building in population biology. *American Scientist*, 54(4), 421–431.

Lloyd, E. A. (2005). *The Case of the Female Orgasm: Bias in the Science of Evolution*. Cambridge MA: Harvard University Press.

Longino, H. E. (1990). *Science as Social Knowledge: Values and Objectivity in Scientific Inquiry*. Princeton: Princeton University Press.

Longino, H. E. (1994). In search of feminist epistemology. *The Monist*, 77(4), 472–485.

Longino, H. E. (2002). *The Fate of Knowledge*. Princeton: Princeton University Press.

Mitchell, S. D. (1992). On pluralism and competition in evolutionary explanations. *American Zoologist*, 32, 135–144.

Mitchell, S. D. (2002). Integrative pluralism. *Biology and Philosophy*, 17, 55–70.

Nagel, T. (1979). Subjective and objective. In T. Nagel, *Mortal Questions* (pp. 196–213). Cambridge: Cambridge University Press.

Parker, W. (2006). Understanding pluralism in climate modeling. *Foundations of Science*, 11, 349–368.

Smith, D. (1974). Women's perspective as a radical critique of sociology. *Sociological Inquiry*, 44(1), 7–13.

Smith, D. (1984). A peculiar eclipsing. In *The Everyday World as Problematic: A Feminist Sociology* (pp. 17–44). Toronto: University of Toronto Press.

Trigger, B. (1984). Alternative archaeologies: Nationalist, colonialist, imperialist. *Man*, 19, 355–370.

Trigger, B. G. (1989). Hyperrelativism, responsibility, and the social sciences. *Canadian Review of Sociology and Anthropology*, 26(5), 776–797.

Trouillot, M.-R. (1995). *Silencing the Past: Power and the Production of History*. Boston: Beacon.

Wylie, A. (2002). *Thinking from Things: Essays in the Philosophy of Archaeology*. Berkeley: University of California Press.

Wylie, A. (2003). Why standpoint matters. In R. Figueroa & S. Harding (Eds.), *Science and Other Cultures: Issues in Philosophies of Science and Technology* (pp. 26–48). New York: Routledge.

Wylie, A. (2006). Moderate relativism/political objectivism. In R. F. Williamson & M. S. Bisson (Eds.), *The Archaeology of Bruce Trigger: Theoretical Empiricism* (pp. 25–35). Montreal: McGill-Queens University Press.

Wylie, A. (2007). "The feminism question in science: What does it mean to 'do social science as a feminist'?" In S. Hesse-Biber (Ed.), *Handbook of Feminist Research* (pp. 567–578). New York: Sage.

Index

Printed in the United States
97272LV00001B/94-105/A